Helene Druskowitz
A Manual for the Freest Spirits

Women Philosophers Heritage Collection

English Version and Introduction

Edited by
Ruth Edith Hagengruber

In Cooperation with
Antonio Calcagno and Priyanka Jha

Volume 4

Helene Druskowitz

A Manual for the Freest Spirits

On Free Will, Religion, Metaphysics, and Feminism

Edited, Translated, and with an Introduction by
Luka Boršić and Ivana Skuhala Karasman

DE GRUYTER

These works have originally been published in the German language:
Druskowitz, Helene. 1887. *Wie ist Verantwortung und Zurechnung ohne Annahme der Willensfreiheit möglich?* Heidelberg: Georg Weiß.
Druskowitz, Helene. 1886. *Moderne Versuche eines Religionsersatzes.* Heidelberg: George Weiß.
Druskowitz, Helene. 1888. *Zur neuen Lehre.* Heidelberg: Georg Weiß.
Druskowitz, Helene. [1905]. *Pessimistische Kardinalsätze. Ein Vademecum für die freiesten Geister.* Wittenberg: Herrosé Ziemsen.

ISBN 978-3-11-914865-8
ISSN 2510-9243

Library of Congress Control Number: 2025943929

Bibliographic information published by the Deutsche Nationalbibliothek
The Deutsche Nationalbibliothek lists this publication in the Deutsche Nationalbibliografie; detailed bibliographic data are available on the Internet at http://dnb.dnb.de.

© 2026 Walter de Gruyter GmbH, Berlin/Boston, Genthiner Straße 13, 10785 Berlin
Cover image: Ruth Edith Hagengruber

www.degruyterbrill.com
Questions about General Product Safety Regulation:
productsafety@degruyterbrill.com

Contents

Introduction —— 1

Translators' Notes —— 50

How Is Responsibility and Attribution Possible Without the Assumption of Free Will?
An Investigation by Dr H. Druskowitz —— 53

Modern Attempts at a Replacement for Religion.
A Philosophical Essay by Dr H. Druskowitz —— 73

Towards a New Doctrine.
Observations by Dr H. Druskowitz —— 126

Pessimistic Cardinal Propositions.
A Manual for the Freest Spirits by Erna (Dr Helene von Druskowitz) —— 152

Index of Names —— 173

Index of Subjects —— 175

Introduction

> There are several Helenes hidden within this one.
>
> —Marie von Ebner-Eschenbach, *Tagebücher*, 18 March 1885.

1 The Context

Helene Druskowitz's (1856–1918) *floruit* coincided with a fascinating period in the central European *Fin de siècle* culture. The *Fin de siècle* intellectual atmosphere in Central Europe (circa 1880–1914) was marked by philosophical innovation, cultural ferment, and societal tensions. Neo-Kantianism, represented by Hermann Cohen (1842–1918) and Wilhelm Windelband (1848–1915), addressed modern challenges in science and ethics, emphasising universal principles. At the same time, phenomenology, pioneered by Edmund Husserl (1859–1938), explored consciousness and intentionality, laying the groundwork for existentialism, structuralism, and personalism. Marxism thrived, with Rosa Luxemburg (1871–1919) and Karl Kautsky (1854–1938) addressing class struggle amid rapid industrialisation. Meanwhile, positivism, which emphasised empirical science and rejected metaphysics, found a powerful advocate in Ernst Mach (1838–1916), whose work influenced the nascent Vienna Circle. This group, formalised in the 1920s but rooted in earlier debates, sought to apply logical analysis to language and science, setting the stage for analytic philosophy.

Amid this intellectual ferment, nationalist movements in the Austro-Hungarian Empire sought autonomy, clashing with the dominant German and Hungarian elite. These tensions exacerbated rising antisemitism, prompting responses like Theodor Herzl's (1860–1904) political Zionism.

On the one hand, misogyny pervaded cultural and academic discourses, with figures like Cesare Lombroso (1835–1909), Richard von Krafft-Ebing (1840–1902),

---

Note: This book is the result of over a decade of research. During this period, we published several book chapters, journal articles, and one monograph in the Croatian language, addressing various aspects of Druskowitz's life and philosophy. With few exceptions, we have refrained from directly reproducing any of our previously published work. The research was conducted within the framework of the projects *New Topics in Croatian Philosophy from 1874 to 1945*, funded by the Croatian Science Foundation (IP-2022-10-5438), and *Croatian Women Philosophers*, funded through the NextGenerationEU initiative via the Ministry of Science, Education and Youth of the Republic of Croatia.

Paul Julius Möbius (1853–1907), and Otto Weininger (1880–1903) perpetuating harmful stereotypes about women through pseudoscientific and philosophical arguments. However, on the other hand, early feminist movements were key in challenging gender norms and advocating for women's rights. Influential figures included Clara Zetkin (1857–1933), a socialist feminist who promoted women's political and labour rights, and Bertha Pappenheim (1859–1936), a social reformer focused on women's education and their protection from exploitation. Bertha von Suttner (1843–1914), an Austrian pacifist and feminist, combined her advocacy for peace with the promotion of women's involvement in diplomacy and international relations. Her contributions were foundational in the peace movement, and she became the first woman to receive the Nobel Peace Prize in 1905. Another significant figure was Meta von Salis-Marschlins (1860–1939), who was an advocate for the education and empowerment of women, especially in Switzerland, and an early supporter of the suffrage movement. Her work helped establish connections between feminist ideas and social reform in the region.

Mysticism and occultism flourished as reactions to materialism. Helena Blavatsky (1831–1891) popularised Theosophy, promoting esoteric spirituality, while Rudolf Steiner (1861–1925) expanded these ideas into Anthroposophy, influencing education and the arts.

This complex intellectual landscape reflected the tensions of modernity, oscillating between a yearning for scientific rigour and the search for transcendent meaning. The interplay of progressive and reactionary forces in Central Europe profoundly shaped the philosophical and cultural currents of the twentieth century. All of these movements were reflected in Druskowitz's works.

1.1 The Question of Education

Before the second half of the nineteenth century, women's enrolment at universities was exceedingly rare, reserved only for exceptional—if not outright brilliant—women from the upper classes. This situation began to change in the latter half of the century. The integration of women in European universities unfolded against a backdrop of profound ideological tension. Institutions across the continent grappled with entrenched misogyny and rigid admission standards, often debating whether women, as biological beings, were even capable of higher intellectual pursuits. At the same time, most universities required prior secondary education for admission—a formal prerequisite that women, whose access to secondary schooling was still in its infancy, could seldom fulfil. Thus, the establishment of institutions offering preparatory education to women became a necessary precondition for their participation in university education.

These two issues—biological prejudice and formal barriers—were deeply intertwined, fuelling extensive contemporary debate and literature. The University of Zurich emerged as a beacon of progressivism, with its policies reflecting both the egalitarian ideals of the Enlightenment and the socio-cultural paradoxes of the era. For example, while some faculty members, such as the physiologist Ludimar Hermann, defended women's right to study medicine, they often did so with reservations, framing female enrolment as a precarious experiment that might threaten the very fabric of the university if women were ever to outnumber men.

Despite such ambivalence, Zurich's openness stood in contrast to more restrictive institutions, such as the University of Basel, which admitted women only on a trial basis and imposed additional requirements on foreign applicants. In Zurich, foreign women—especially from Central, Eastern and Southeastern Europe, where educational opportunities were even more limited—could enrol without proof of prior education, a policy that significantly broadened access.

Ultimately, the gradual admission of women to universities signalled both a response to changing social and economic realities and a challenge to longstanding epistemic hierarchies. The early female students were not only pioneers in academia but also pioneers in their field. However, they often became leading figures in the broader struggle for women's rights, embodying the philosophical and practical transformation of their age. Zurich's decision to admit women in 1864—formalised by the enrolment of Nadezhda Suslova (1843–1918), the first female medical student—represented a radical departure from European norms. Unlike contemporary institutions, which delayed women's admission and imposed restrictive local residency requirements, Zurich embraced a pragmatic openness. Its lack of stringent formal prerequisites for foreign students, particularly women from the Russian Empire, transformed it into a sanctuary for those excluded elsewhere. However, the early admission of women into academia did not occur without opposition and controversy.

The debate over women's education crystallised into two currents: the ethical pursuit of equality and the economic necessity of expanding professional opportunities. As legal scholar Hermann Rehm (1901) noted, the former drew from revolutionary ideals of universal rights, while the latter responded to shifting economic realities that left unmarried women of certain classes without viable livelihoods. Zurich's policies inadvertently linked these motives. By admitting foreign women—many of whom faced limited prospects in their homelands—the university became a site where intellectual aspiration intersected with pragmatic survival strategies. This duality underscored a broader tension: Could education serve as both a moral good and a tool for material independence?

The core of Helene Druskowitz's philosophy and literary oeuvre is her emphasis on women's education as a tool of emancipation—a rupture from the society that confined women to material and intellectual subjugation. For Druskowitz, education was neither a mere acquisition of knowledge nor a pragmatic tool for social mobility; it represented a transcendent act of self-creation, dismantling the Aristotelian binaries that equated biological sex with cognitive capacity. Her trajectory epitomised this struggle: when she sought entry into academia, the University of Zurich stood as the sole institution in Central Europe willing to enrol women as regular students. In 1878, she became the first German-speaking woman to earn a doctorate in philosophy through a regular procedure.

Druskowitz's intellectual project extended beyond personal ambition. The common thread throughout her opus—an educated woman—is the Archimedean point for dismantling what she termed the "male-dominated world"—a realm she associated with violence, exploitation, and spiritual degradation. In her last work, *Pessimistische Kardinalsätze* (*Pessimistic Cardinal Propositions*), she argued that true liberation required the radical reordering of society itself based on enlightened and educated women. Her vision of separatist utopias—women-only cities where intellectual and spiritual refinement could flourish—revealed a philosophical pessimism intertwined with revolutionary hope: if education could not reform existing structures, it must annihilate them.

By synthesising Schopenhauerian pessimism with proto-feminist radical critique, Druskowitz positioned education as both a weapon against epistemic injustice and a mirror reflecting society's unresolved contradictions. Her legacy lies not merely in advocating for women's enrolment but in demanding that education catalyse a metaphysical revolution—one where the "Over-Sphere" of intellectual and spiritual purity supersedes the material world's patriarchal decay.

2 Life

Helene Druskowitz's life is distinctive, bearing the qualities of an artwork imbued with an almost ancient tragic dimension—a narrative of a person unable to escape her destiny.

Helene Druskowitz was born Helena Maria Franziska Druschkovich in Hietzing near Vienna in 1856. Her father was Lorenz Druschkovich, whose origins most likely go back to the island of Korčula in Croatia. Her mother was born Magdalena Biber, and was a pianist with whom Helene had a close relationship throughout her life. After the premature death of Lorenz Druschkovich in 1859, Magdalena continued his business and remarried. Like her first husband, her second husband also achieved some business success, leaving the family financially secure, which provided Helene and her half-brothers with the opportunity to receive a good education.

In 1872, she completed her musical studies at the Vienna Conservatory, and a year later, in 1873, she passed her *matura* exam at the Piaristengymnasium in Vienna. Some of her talent is mirrored in her autobiographical drama *Unerwartet* (*Unexpected*), published in 1889, in which she wrote that she was seen as "ein Wunderkind" ("a child prodigy"), and "ein Gegenstand der Auszeichnung und Bewunderung" (an object of distinction and admiration" (Druskowitz 1889, 102).

Druskowitz moved to Zurich with her mother, where she studied from 1874 to 1876. The reason for her departure to Zurich was that she had tried to enrol at the University of Vienna but was refused admission, as the university did not accept female students at the time. In contrast, the University of Zurich was an institution where women were permitted to register as regular students and to receive degrees. According to the documents she submitted to the University of Zurich, she attended classes in comparative linguistics and Oriental languages, with an emphasis on Sanskrit, philosophy, classical philology, archaeology, and general history. She interrupted her studies after two years, and from 1876 until 1878, while still living in Zurich, dedicated her time to passionate private research until, as she testified, she "decided for philosophy". In 1878, at the age of twenty-two, she passed her doctoral examination. She received her doctoral title "mit Ehren" ("with honours") from the University of Zurich after defending her thesis, entitled *"Don Juan" by Lord Byron. Eine litterarisch-ästhetische Abhandlung* (*"Don Juan" by Lord Byron. A Literary-Aesthetic treatise*). Helene Druskowitz was the first German-speaking woman to earn a doctoral degree through a regular procedure.[1]

In 1880, Druskowitz returned to Vienna after spending time in Switzerland and Munich. In Vienna, she gave several public lectures, primarily on literary and cultural-historical topics, including Percy Shelley, Indian drama, and the Salon de Rambouillet, the last of which reflects Druskowitz's interest in women's emancipation. These lectures were successful and well-visited, and all of them received positive reviews in Viennese newspapers.

In 1881, via Ida von Fleischl-Marxow, a German-Austrian patron of arts and salonnière, Druskowitz became acquainted with the Austrian aristocrat and writer Marie von Ebner-Eschenbach (1830–1916), joining her intellectual circle. This association provided Druskowitz with opportunities to engage with other prominent intellectuals who frequented Ebner-Eschenbach's house or maintained close connections with her at the time. Among these figures were Betty Paoli (1814–

---

1 Sometimes Stefania Wolicka (1851–after 1895), a Polish historian, is mentioned as the first woman to earn a doctorate in philosophy at the University of Zurich in 1875 with a thesis entitled *Griechische Frauengestalten* (*Greek Female Figures*). However, due to political issues, she had to leave Zurich and was promoted *in absentia*, that is, without oral and written examinations (*Klausurarbeit*) in 1875.

1894), the renowned Austrian writer and journalist; Louise von François (1817–1893), the German author; and Conrad Ferdinand Meyer (1825–1898), the Swiss novelist, all of whom were influential intellectuals in the German-speaking regions.

Druskowitz was notably younger than the other members of the intellectual circle she joined. Fleischl von Marxow was 31 years older, Ebner-Eschenbach 26 years her senior, Paoli 42 years her senior, von François 39 years older, and Meyer 30 years older than she. At the time, Druskowitz was only 25 years old.

Druskowitz made a notable impression on the intellectuals around Marie von Ebner-Eschenbach. Testimonies from Ebner-Eschenbach's diaries reveal that Druskowitz was a frequent visitor to her home, sometimes meeting her several times a week and exchanging letters extensively.[2] This intense correspondence spanned from 1881 to 1885, after which their contact became less regular. As time progressed, the relationship became increasingly fraught with challenges. Druskowitz's volatile temperament and propensity for emotional outbursts strained their interactions, introducing an element of discord into their friendship. Despite these difficulties, Ebner-Eschenbach exhibited remarkable magnanimity, offering financial assistance during Druskowitz's internment in psychiatric institutions. This tension reveals the fragility of their connection, shaped by the interplay of personal pride and intellectual independence.

Ebner-Eschenbach's diary entries, though often laconic, provide insight into her perception of Druskowitz as a younger friend. These entries suggest a mix of admiration and tolerance for Druskowitz's intellectual fervour and volatile and nervous personality. From Ebner-Eschenbach's diaries, we learn that Druskowitz was quite proud, even arrogant, and distinct, paying little respect to the social norms of the time. Some people expressed dislike for Druskowitz (e.g., Marie's brother Moritz; cf. Ebner-Eschenbach 1993, 216). On the other hand, Druskowitz occasionally reacted harshly and brusquely—and later showed remorse.

From Ebner-Eschenbach's diaries, we also gain intriguing insights into some of Helene Druskowitz's works that remain otherwise untraceable. Among these are an essay on the Italian poet Leopardi (Ebner-Eschenbach 1993, 118), a treatise titled *"On Aesthetic Education"* (Ebner-Eschenbach 1993, 604), a play called *"Svante Sture"* (Ebner-Eschenbach 1993, 158), and an essay on the singer Therese Malten (Ebner-Eschenbach 1995, 38).

---

[2] Not many letters from their correspondence have been preserved. Most of Druskowitz's preserved letters are written in handwriting that is almost entirely illegible today, just as it was for her fervent correspondent Ebner-Eschenbach at the time. This is evidenced by Ebner-Eschenbach's diary entry from 11 August 1902: "[I sent a letter] to the poor Druskowitz, who had written me a completely illegible letter and an equally illegible postcard" (Ebner-Eschenbach 1996, 250).

However, there is another, more copious source about Druskowitz: the correspondence between Louise von François and Conrad Ferdinand Meyer, in which Druskowitz was quite often the topic of their discussions. Von François met Druskowitz through Ebner-Eschenbach in 1881. In the same year, while visiting Zurich, Druskowitz met Meyer, whom von François had recommended.

The correspondence between Louise von François and Conrad Ferdinand Meyer reveals the nature of their relationship with Helene Druskowitz. To a certain extent, it appears that Louise von François viewed the much younger Druskowitz as her protégée, a sentiment shared by Conrad Ferdinand Meyer. This is evident not only from the intensity and interest conveyed through numerous references to Druskowitz in their correspondence but also from their efforts to introduce her to prominent literary figures they knew. They attempted to guide her through her literary career and expressed regret over their inability to assist her with her psychological issues (François & Meyer 1920, 223, 225, 270, 272).

With many pages dedicated to Druskowitz in the von François–Meyer correspondence, we can learn a good deal about her character and behaviour.

Louise von François described her as "buoyant and vigorous in body and mind, upright to the core, happy as a child, determined of will. What she still needs to learn is that a certain acquired and all too positive positiveness can be discarded without compromising the truth and that it is possible to be capable, even scholarly perhaps, and remain a woman withal." Although Helene flaunted her erudition, Meyer was favourably impressed with his young visitor. There was something unusual about this "stately Germanic figure," this "stately Thusnelda," beside whom even the tall and slender Louise von François felt like a dwarf. Meyer, with his sharp eye for contrasts, could not fail to mark the exotic note on her face. [...] Helene was seemingly of Slavic extraction, at least in part [...]. It cannot be denied that Helene was talented and ambitious; as a result, friend and acquaintance alike were ready to overlook her idiosyncrasies. She had a positive manner and asserted her opinion freely and frankly. There is no doubt that she was well able to defend her contentions with the aid of a splendid intellect and a logically trained mind. Suggestions which were not to her liking she rejected without much ceremony. Thus, when Louise von François suggested that she try comedy writing, she rebuffed the idea as though the suggestion was an insult. Certain habits of hers, e.g., the swinging of her arms and her indistinct enunciation, were annoying. She found pleasure "in being rebuffed." She was "peculiar at times,"— "quite peculiar." Then again, she could be pleasant, friendly, even confidential. In some respects, she was quite innocent and naïve. Meyer writes to Louise von François on one occasion about his young dinner guest: "The doctor withdrew, and the good child remained behind." She was a splendid character, honourable, noble, and true. It was these qualities, coupled with her intellect that her friends admired. Needless to say, Helene scorned the idea of love and marriage since she aimed to be "merely a human being" and nothing else. It was, perhaps, her erraticism that separated her from kith and kin. Louise von François deplored the character of the relationship between mother and daughter. [...] A feeling for home was as alien to her as a feeling for fatherland, so we find her wandering about in Switzerland, Italy, Austria, and Germany, seeking stimulus and peace for her work, and hoping to forget in travel and exclusive society the non-realisation of her literary ambitions. Confusing talent with genius, Helene was deluded by the notion of her superiority. "The grain of intellectual pride, which she has in excess because she knows that she is an upright, noble, and forceful personality like few others, is spoiling her life," writes Louise von François. And Meyer answers: "Her trouble is her boundless ambition, with vague aims." Helene scorned teaching positions and journalistic work, yet she lacked the requisite self-discipline and readiness for compromises to perform a regular daily job. Overestimating her capabilities, she ventured into the fields of literature and philosophy, trying her hand at historical drama, comedy, and essays, as well as writing philosophical treatises.[3]

After 1890, Druskowitz divided her time between Vienna and its surrounding areas, as well as Zurich and its environs, including Kilchberg, where she frequently visited Meyer's residence. Before her mother died in 1889, Druskowitz relocated to Dresden. However, shortly after her mother's passing, she embarked on an extended journey to Rome, Capri, Sicily, and, possibly, Tunis, having inherited a sum of money (François & Meyer 1920, 240, 245, 248, 251). Thereafter, she returned to Dresden. Regarding her time in Dresden, we have a noteworthy account from Adolf Kohut, a prominent German-Jewish journalist, historian, translator, and trained philosopher who was also a resident of Dresden at that time. In an article titled "Two Lady Doctors," published on 1 June 1889, in "In Boudoir," a supplement to the progressive Viennese journal *Wiener Mode*, Kohut reports on two women intellectuals: Susanne Rubinstein and Helene Druskowitz, who shared a residence in Dresden.

Kohut introduced Druskowitz with those words:

> While Miss Dr. Susanne Rubinstein is primarily a psychologist, the philosophical domain of her colleague, Miss Dr. Helene Druskowitz, encompasses the comparative philosophy of religion and ethics—fields in which she has already produced outstanding contributions. The young lady exhibits a "boldness" and radicalism in her views, qualities rarely encountered in men, let alone women. The rigour of her methodology is most evident in the fact that her

---

3 This passage is a compilation from Dahme (1936, 363–378).

most ardent admirers reside in America, a nation known for its aversion to half-measures and its inclination to commit fully. (Kohut 1889, 21)[4]

After giving Druskowitz's short *curriculum vitae*, Kohut concluded:

> The mindset of the author [Druskowitz] is decidedly revolutionary and radical; she is not nourished by the "milk of pious thinking." She does not hesitate to confront existing views with remarkable boldness and does not fear contradiction or attacks from her opponents. She takes pride in being taken seriously by philosophical criticism and not being treated as a "lady." (Kohut 1889, 22)

During her years in Dresden, Druskowitz was remarkably productive, publishing six dramatic works and two philosophical books within a two-year period.[5] It is possible that she initiated—or intended to initiate—a romantic relationship with the renowned soprano Therese Malten (1855–1930); however, there is no evidence to confirm whether this was an actual or merely an intended affair. Furthermore, Druskowitz struggled with alcohol addiction and was a habitual smoker of both cigars and pipes, which was, at the time, perceived as a symbol of women's independence. During this period, Druskowitz became increasingly aware of her mental health issues. Evidence indicates that in 1889, she consulted a specialist in Berlin for a condition described in general terms as *Nervenleiden* (François & Meyer 1920, 252).

The loss of her mother and brothers, compounded by her near-total failure as a playwright—given that none of her plays were likely ever staged—led to a significant deterioration in her emotional stability. Her alcohol consumption escalated dramatically during this period, accompanied by frequent emotional outbursts. By 1891, her already fragile mental health worsened, culminating in an existential crisis. At the beginning of 1891, Druskowitz experienced a mental breakdown and was involuntarily committed to a mental health institution.[6] First, it was the

---

4 The reference to America's disdain for *Halbheiten* (half-measures) and its preference for *aufs Ganzen gehen* (committing fully) reflects nineteenth-century European perceptions of American industriousness and decisiveness. However, there is no evidence to suggest that any of Druskowitz's works received scholarly or artistic recognition in America by 1889. It is possible that Kohut conflated Druskowitz's admiration for the American philosopher William Mackintire Salter and her inclusion of several American characters in her plays (*International, Die Emancipations-Schwärmerin, Die Pädagogin*) with her alleged American reception.
5 Two of them were slightly modified reprints from the year before: *Zur Begründung einer überreligiösen Weltanschauung* and *Die Emanzipations-Schwärmerin*.
6 That happened most likely in Dresden. However, according to some other contemporary newspaper sources (e. g., *Kölnische Zeitung*, 17 October 1891; *Hamburger Fremdenblatt*, 17 October

Siechenhaus in Dresden, then the Niederösterreichische Landes-Irrenanstalt in Wien, then the *Irrenanstalt* in Ybbs, then, for a few months in 1902, Kaiser Franz Joseph-Landes-Heil- und Pflegeanstalt Mauer-Öhling, then again in Ybbs, and then, finally, from June 1903 till her death on 31 May 1918 in Mauer-Öhling, which was, at the time, one of the best and most progressive mental institution in Europe. Conrad Ferdinand Meyer, in a letter dated 19 November 1891, describes the circumstances:

> Furthermore, you also wanted to hear about the fate of the unfortunate Druscovich, and at the same time, you said, "Why dwell on such sadness?" Well then: I have shared in this sadness since last spring, [...] until the outbreak of her illness was finally announced by acquaintances—delusions of grandeur, in a despotic, almost raging manner. The cause of this was the unanimous—unfortunately justified!—rejection of her theatrical attempts, which she regarded as *masterpieces*. In my opinion, the reason lay even more in her complete lack of means. I did not fear *this*, but I always dreaded a dark outcome for her, given the unsympathetic nature of her disposition and her fate: without a sentiment of homeland and paternal home, without any connection of a feminine kind—even to her unfortunate mother—least of all to a religious cult, she is a follower of a heartless philosophy; with an intensely aristocratic character and a lofty spirit, capable of and ready for all introspection, but quite unskilled in rendering it—for knowledge is far from ability—too proud to earn a modest living, as a teacher or everyday publicist, for instance, too wilfully ungraceful to attract a man. What was to become of her since she lacked the means to find a substitute for her failed poetic endeavours in travel, the pleasures of art, exclusive society, etc.? Necessity would never have taught her to beg or even to ask. In the summer, she was transferred to an institution in her native Vienna, where the rageful, consuming madness suddenly turned into a happy one. Physically healthy, flourishing as never before, and condescendingly ruler-like in her behaviour, [...] she saw herself as the recognised regent of all emperors, kings, and rulers of the world through magnetic influences from a higher dimension. She alone guides everyone and everything. Her doctor, Vienna's first psychiatrist, N. N., considers these hallucinations—this incessant hearing of voices—to be the most alarming phenomenon of all. Friends bear the costs of her accommodation; I think I know who they are. "[...] An angel in human form" is what she calls Frau von Ebner, who takes excellent care of her. Her brother in Bolivia has promised a larger sum for next year. So things are bleak, hopeless—and yet a happy woman in delusion. For how long? (François & Meyer 1920, 270–271)

From 1891 onward, she spent the remaining twenty-seven years of her life in various psychiatric institutions without interruption. During her extended institutionalisation, she was financially supported by her sole surviving brother, as

---

1891), the incident that led to her confinement in the mental institution occurred during Druskowitz's visit to Vienna.

well as by multiple wealthy friends, including Marie von Ebner-Eschenbach, at least until 1905.

Druskowitz was diagnosed with "hallucinatory insanity", "primary insanity", and "paranoia" and was sedated most of the time.[7] She experienced auditory and visual hallucinations, continued consuming alcohol—with or without doctors' approval, and communicated "telepathically" with many people, mostly principal European nobility.[8] Her different states are described in detail in her *Krankenakte*,[9] In 1891, she was diagnosed in the following way:

> The patient presents her case with extraordinary vehemence through a torrent of words that is sometimes impossible to follow. She frequently loses her train of thought, visibly straining to regain the thread of her narrative. After the interview, she sits upright abruptly and demands to know whether the physician considers her mentally ill. Shortly thereafter, she initiates a telepathic exchange with the Empress of Austria (whom she describes as one of her closest confidantes). Leaning forward with intense concentration, she alternates between posing questions and offering responses, her voice oscillating between loud declarations and whispered utterances. [...] She engages minimally with her surroundings, vehemently insisting on her immediate release. At times, she clenches her fists in frustration or breaks into tears of rage when discussing what she deems her unlawful confinement. (*Krankenakte*, folio 54)

Three years later, in 1894, another medical doctor gave a different description of her condition:

> The patient expounds at length regarding the peculiar condition in which she finds herself. She reports experiencing copious hallucinations, which she claims to distinguish clearly from genuine sensory perceptions. Notably, the apparitions she describes possess an insubstantial quality—shadow-like forms through which she asserts she can discern underlying objects and individuals with perfect clarity. She maintains these manifestations constitute not symptoms of pathology but rather the hallmark of exceptional genius. All phenomena, she explains, derive from telepathy: when concentrating intensely on distant persons, she

---

7 Emil Kraepelin (1856–1926), the influential German psychiatrist widely regarded as the founder of modern scientific psychiatry, integrated "originäre Verrücktheit" into his developing taxonomy. In his 1883 textbook, he described it as a disorder of intellectual faculties marked by systematised delusions (Kraepelin 1883, 285–286). By 1899, this evolved into "dementia praecox" (modern schizophrenia) and "paranoia", cementing the distinction between psychotic and affective disorders.
8 As stated in her "Declaration" ("Erklärung"), written during her psychiatric internment—yet in an exceptionally clear and festive hand—she consistently held "occult" and "spiritistic" experiences in high esteem, feeling herself particularly receptive to and affected by them.
9 Druskowitz's medical records (*Krankenakte*) are preserved in Niederösterreichisches Landesarchiv St.Pölten in unedited form. They comprise 128 unorganised pages (folios). Most of the pages are numbered.

claims the ability to establish intellectual communion, visualising them vividly and engaging in dialogue. (*Krankenakte*, folio 35)

However, the most succinct description of her condition is given by Druskowitz herself in a letter from 1898: "[...] a remarkable amalgam of malaise, sorrow combined with mystical perceptiveness and heightened telepathic receptivity."[10]

It is difficult to assess the precise nature of Helene Druskowitz's psychological state during the twenty-seven years she spent in psychiatric institutions. Some scholars have suggested that her hallucinations might have been a consequence of her struggles with alcoholism, which was a prominent issue in her life. Additionally, it has been proposed that her institutionalisation may have been involuntary, possibly triggered by the scandal surrounding her alleged romantic involvement with the world-renowned primadonna Therese Malten (Gronewold 1992, 108, 111). This purported relationship, if true, could have jeopardised Malten's career.

Druskowitz's confinement raises broader questions about how unconventional women were treated in the late nineteenth century, particularly those whose behaviour or relationships challenged societal norms. Her case exemplifies the intersection of gender issues (particularly homosexuality), mental health, and societal expectations, suggesting that her institutionalisation may have been influenced as much by prejudice and social ostracism as by genuine medical concerns. During that time, she continued working on her literary endeavours: "She composes poems in praise of alcohol, writes illegible androphobic satires for women's newspapers, and feels she is at the peak of her literary creativity [....]" (*Krankenakte*, folio 20).

In 1907, she drafted her last will, in which she requested that all her letters, writings, and manuscripts be burned. This request likely accounts for the significant gaps in her body of work. Druskowitz passed away on May 31, 1918, at the Kaiser-Franz-Joseph-Landes-Heil- und Pflegeanstalt in Mauer-Öhling, succumbing to multiple very serious medical conditions.

Helene Druskowitz's life constitutes an idiosyncratic synthesis of intellectual audacity and existential turbulence, rendering it not merely a biographical curiosity but a conceptual artwork that mirrors her philosophical and artistic preoccupations. As the first (or second) German-speaking woman to earn a doctorate in philosophy and an unrelenting critic of patriarchal structures, her trajectory defied nineteenth-century norms through both deliberate transgression and tragic vulnerability. The arc from prodigious scholar to institutionalised patient confined for nearly three decades encapsulates a performative tension between rad-

---

10 Quoted in Merz 2011, 61.

ical self-determination and societal rejection. Her sustained literary output amid psychiatric confinement, including pseudonymous publications and the feminist manifesto, suggests a conscious shaping of identity as philosophical practice, where lived experience became a substrate for theorising gender, power, and mental alienation.

2.1 Druskowitz and Nietzsche

Friedrich Nietzsche became aware of Helene Druskowitz's existence as early as 1882. In a letter addressed to Franz Overbeck in Basel, Nietzsche requested the address of "Ms. Helene Truschkowitz" (Nietzsche 2000, 179).[11] This misspelling of her surname is understandable, considering that by 1882, Druskowitz had published only her doctoral dissertation, *On Lord Byron's "Don Juan"* (Druskowitz 1879), and one drama, *Sultan and Prince* (Druskowitz 1881). At the time, Nietzsche likely knew of her not through her writings but rather through their mutual acquaintances. Despite his evident interest in her, it took over two years for them to meet. Their first encounter took place on 21 October 1884, between 2 and 3 PM, as documented in a brief note from Druskowitz inviting Nietzsche to meet her at the Reading Room of the "Museumgesellschaft" in Zurich, where both were residing at the time (Druskowitz 1981, 469).

This initial meeting must have been amicable and intellectually stimulating for both parties. In a letter to his sister written shortly afterwards, Nietzsche enthusiastically described his encounter with Druskowitz:

> In the afternoon, I went for a long walk with my new friend Helena Druscowicz, who lives with her mother a few houses away from the Neptune guesthouse. Of all the women I met, she studied my books most seriously and not in vain. [...] I think she is a noble and fair creature who does not harm my "philosophy".[12]

---

[11] In the secondary literature, it is sometimes claimed that Helene Druskowitz became acquainted with Malwida von Meysenbug (1816–1903) and, through von Meysenbug, was introduced to Friedrich Nietzsche. However, this assertion appears to be unsubstantiated and unreliable, as there is no concrete evidence to support the notion that Druskowitz met von Meysenbug, who had been residing in Rome since 1874. The same goes for the claim that Druskowitz became acquainted with the significantly younger Lou Salomé (1861–1937). This chapter partially relies on Boršić 2018.

[12] Friedrich Nietzsche, Letter to Elisabeth Nietzsche of 22 October 1884. This is the letter nr. 549 in the *Digitale Kritische Gesamtausgabe. Werke und Briefe* (eKGWB).

Nietzsche also praised Druskowitz's scholarly work on Percy Bysshe Shelley (Druskowitz 1884) and her studies on English poetesses (Druskowitz 1885). Despite their brief interaction—spanning no more than a day—Nietzsche referred to Druskowitz as "my new friend (Freundin)" in this letter. This designation is noteworthy not only because of its potential amorous undertones but also because it contrasts sharply with Nietzsche's assertion in *Thus Spoke Zarathustra* (1883) that "woman is not yet capable of friendship: she knows only love" (Nietzsche 2006, 41). Nietzsche's admiration for Druskowitz was further evident in an October 1884 letter to Overbeck, where he mentioned that their mutual friend Johann Heinrich Köselitz (known as Peter Gast) was staying in the same building as the "excellent" Druskowitz and her mother (eKGWB/BVN-1884,551).

In a November 1884 letter to his sister, Nietzsche expressed his wish to part ways with his publisher, Ernst Schmeitzner, whose publishing house had published some of Nietzsche's most important works, including *Schopenhauer as Educator and Thus Spoke Zarathustra, Part III*. Nietzsche had been unhappy with Schmeitzner for some time: it was not only a pecuniary issue, but Nietzsche was also dissatisfied with Schmeitzner's promotion of his works, as well as with his open antisemitism (Brown 1987, 263; Janz 1978, 356). As an alternative to Schmeitzner, Nietzsche suggested giving his books to the publisher Robert Oppenheim in Berlin. In his letter to his mother and sister from November 1884, Nietzsche argued that Oppenheim had already published not only some works by the relatively famous historian and essayist Karl Hillebrand, who was responsible for Nietzsche's interests in French culture after his disappointment with Wagner and Schopenhauer (Montinari 2014) but also some of Druskowitz's books (eKGWB/BVN-1884, 552). Nietzsche had the above-mentioned *Percy Bysshe Shelley* and *Three English Poetesses* in mind.

While Nietzsche was fostering feelings of connection and respect toward Druskowitz, her feelings took a different turn. In a short letter to Conrad Ferdinand Meyer, probably written in late autumn or winter 1884, just a month or two after their meeting, she returned one of Nietzsche's books to Meyer and commented on "Nietzsche's latest work *Thus spoke Zarathustra*" ironically saying it belonged to "the series of the 'holy books', the Vedas, the Old Testament etc. Something of a spirit and rhapsodic enthusiasm of the old prophets lives in Nietzsche" (Druskowitz 1884a). In a letter also addressed to Meyer and dated 22 December 1884, Druskowitz gave her verdict on Nietzsche:

> My enthusiasm for Nietzsche's philosophy has only turned out to be a *passion du moment*, a poor flash in the pan. Nietzsche's prophetic expression now seems ridiculous to me. Who would deny this man a fullness of mind and an excellent talent for form? However, his enthusiasm is only enough to express himself subtly about this and that in the form of reflec-

tions, but not, as he believes, for the significant philosophical problems which he treats without real seriousness and very superficially. But enough of that. (Druskowitz 1884b)

Nietzsche may not have been immediately aware of Druskowitz's change of heart. In August of 1885, he wrote to Köselitz from Sils-Maria and asked him to send a copy of *Zarathustra* to Druskowitz in Vienna; in the letter, he also claimed that she had previously written to him "very politely" and "without a reason [...] which is rare" (eKGWB/BVN-1885, 618). Since Druskowitz's letter is lost, and we have no further data about the circumstances preceding Nietzsche's letter, it can only be left to the arbitrariness of our imagination to fill the gap. Did she have second thoughts about her disappointment with Nietzsche? Did Nietzsche misplace her coldness with politeness? In any case, Nietzsche decided to have a rare copy of the privately printed fourth part of *Zarathustra*, intended for the closest and most respected audience, sent to Druskowitz. However, as we learn from a preserved draft of Nietzsche's letter to Druskowitz, composed just a few weeks after the book had been sent to her, she intended to return the book to Nietzsche and wrote a now-lost but likely very harsh letter. Nietzsche's disappointment was profound: in the preserved draft of a letter to Druskowitz, he wrote that the one who did not appreciate "his Zarathustra [...] lacks everything, ear, reason, depth, education, taste and, generally, the nature of a chosen human'." (eKGWB/BVN-1885, 623).

Following this incident surrounding the fourth part of *Zarathustra*, there is no evidence of any direct contact between Nietzsche and Druskowitz. In 1886, Druskowitz published her book *Modern Attempts at a Replacement for Religion*, in which she criticised several of Nietzsche's works (99–106, 225–234), most sharply *Zarathustra*. Druskowitz perceives Nietzsche primarily not as a philosopher but as a soul aflame with artistic intensity—a poetic intellect whose prose shimmers with aesthetic brilliance. She sees in him a mind rare in its originality, steeped in learning, yet burdened by a paradox: the very gravitas of the questions he posed often eclipsed the philosophical depth of his answers. His writings, she suggested, oscillate between genuine flashes of metaphysical clarity and moments clouded by rhetorical excess, dazzling yet hollow ingenuity, and sophistry that veers dangerously close to illusion. Within Nietzsche's thought, profound truths and profound errors lie entwined—wisdom and confusion dancing together in a dialectic that never quite resolves. He appeared, to her, as a thinker in constant self-opposition, each insight shadowed by its negation. Nevertheless, even amidst this tumult, Druskowitz grants him an extraordinary talent: the rare ability to orchestrate philosophical ideas into powerful forms of expression, to give voice to chaos in ways that seduce the intellect.

Although there are no Druskowitz books in Nietzsche's library as it is preserved today, Nietzsche read some of them; he explicitly mentioned *Percy Bysshe Shelley* and *Three English Poetesses*. There is no direct evidence that Nietzsche also possessed or read the *Modern Attempts at a Replacement for Religion*; however, from a letter to his friend Malwida von Meysenbug from the end of February 1887, it is evident that Nietzsche was aware of Druskowitz's criticism: "A Miss Druscowicz is said to have recently sinned against my son Zarathustra through some precocious babble of literati: it seems that by some crime I have turned the female quills against my breast – and so it is right! For, as my friend Malvida says: 'I am even worse than Schopenhauer'" (eKGWB/BVN-1887, 809). In the same letter Nietzsche wrote to Meysenbug about "all the young and less young girls [...] all these crazy little animals, between you and me" and mentioned a "very worshipful" letter by Meta von Salis-Marschlins (who, despite everything, financially supported Nietzsche and his sister until the end of his life), long silence by Bertha Rohr and Resa von Schirnhofer, and, disrespectfully, "*a* Miss Druskowitz".

Nietzsche's last mention of Helene Druskowitz is found in Nietzsche's letter to Carl Spitteler, dated 17 September 1887. Answering Spitteler's presumed provocation in an unpreserved letter, in a *postscript*, Nietzsche stated: "The little literature-goose Druscowicz is anything but my 'pupil' [...]." How far it is from his statement three years before that Druskowitz was the one among "women" who understood his philosophy the best!

We also have a third-party testimony about how hurt Nietzsche was by this criticism. Meta von Salis-Marschlins, in her apologetic book *Philosopher and Nobleman. A Contribution to the Characteristics of Friedrich Nietzsche* commented on Druskowitz's criticism of Nietzsche: "This deeply offended his sensibilities as a negative manifestation of intellectual parasitism. This case occurred when Dr. Helene Druscovich, in her *Attempts at a Replacement for Religion*, attacked him just as superficially as ruthlessly [...]. He had been on friendly terms with that lady in Zurich and had spoken favourably of her treatment of English poets. The poor woman has long since succumbed to madness" (von Salis 1897, 40).

After 1887, there is no further evidence of Nietzsche mentioning Druskowitz. However, the opposite is not the case: in all her philosophical works, Druskowitz mentions Nietzsche. Besides the above-mentioned general criticism of Nietzsche in her *Modern Attempts at a Replacement for Religion*, Druskowitz also criticised Nietzsche's "cult of genius", which, according to Druskowitz, was not radical enough: a true genius cannot be a product of society but must either go against society or offer society an alternative which is radically different from the values accepted by the society (Druskowitz 1886, 49–53). She also criticised Nietzsche's *Zarathustra* for being a mere derivation of Darwinism and nothing but a substitute for Christianity rather than an attempt at its destruction (Druskowitz 1886, 53–59).

In her book *Towards a New Doctrine*, Druskowitz attacked Nietzsche's concept of "Übermensch". However, her criticism is contained in a single footnote and is rather laconic: similarly to her position in the *Modern Attempts at a Replacement for Religion*, she claimed that Nietzsche's "Übermensch" was too similar and close to humans, whereas the true ideal is a genius that must surpass anything human: the Nietzschean "Übermensch" was, for Druskowitz, just an upgraded human, whereas she wanted to have a sort of a genius that would be quantitatively different from and nothing like humans (143 fn. 13, 273 fn. 14).

In her book *Eugen Dühring*, with a tendentious subtitle "A Study to Appreciate Him", Druskowitz criticised Nietzsche's critical approach to Dühring. According to Druskowitz, Nietzsche was so obsessed with Dühring's antisemitism that he missed the main intentions of Dühring's concept of justice. However, Druskowitz dedicated only one, though quite long, footnote to this criticism, which, in the end, remains lacunary (Druskowitz 1889, 61–62).

In her last and philosophically most important book, the *Pessimistic Cardinal Propositions*, more particularly, in the fourth part entitled "Man as Logical and moral Impossibility and the Curse of the World", she let herself go in her attack against Nietzsche by calling him a "stupid and totally idiotic writer" (164, 295).

The relationship between Druskowitz and Nietzsche started in 1884. The beginning was marked by mutual admiration and enthusiasm. Their contact ended three years later, and mutual offences and hatred marked the end. Based on the preserved evidence, it is difficult to determine what happened. Were there some private, psychological and/or emotional reasons included, as Druskowitz's friends Louise François and Conrad Ferdinand Meyer suspected (François 1888/1920, 235)? Were Nietzsche's misogynistic outbursts, which were especially prominent around the time of the publication of *Zarathustra* (Young 2013), something that drove Druskowitz away?[13] Was her philosophical project—an overturn of traditional values and the creation of a "new human"—in some respect too close to Nietzsche's so that she had to fight a fight against him, to paraphrase Nietzsche's own words directed to Socrates?

---

13 Although Druskowitz's intellectual development increasingly aligned with radical feminism, it is notable that she did not explicitly address Nietzsche's supposed misogyny in her critiques, even when comparing him to the notoriously misogynistic Schopenhauer.

3 Druskowitz's Literary Scholarship

Besides her published doctoral dissertation on Lord Byron, which oscillates between literary criticism and philosophy, Helene Druskowitz's literary-critical work includes a monograph on Percy Bysshe Shelley (Druskowitz 1884) and a study of three English poetesses—Joanna Baillie, Elizabeth Barrett Browning, and George Eliot—published in Berlin under the title *Drei englische Dichterinnen* (*Three English Poetesses*, Druskowitz 1885). These works were generally well-received and garnered the attention of contemporary literary critics, with Friedrich Nietzsche himself recommending them to his sister.

Druskowitz's biography of Shelley is particularly significant as the first German account of the poet's life. It offers a sympathetic exploration of Shelley's emotional journey, including his relationships, his ideals of freedom, and his tragic demise. While the biography focuses primarily on Shelley's personal life, it notably lacks broader historical context and neglects to address key literary influences such as Coleridge and Goethe. Despite these omissions, the work is praised for its engaging narrative style and skilful use of source materials and played a pivotal role in introducing Shelley to German-speaking audiences. Similarly, her *Three English Poetesses* received accolades for its insightful analysis of the lives and works of Baillie, Browning, and Eliot, further establishing Druskowitz as a significant figure in literary criticism during the late nineteenth century.

These contributions reflect Druskowitz's commitment to elevating English literature within German intellectual circles while showcasing her ability to blend biographical detail with broader philosophical reflections. Her work not only expanded the literary canon in Germany but also demonstrated her capacity to engage deeply with themes of individuality, creativity, and intellectual freedom—concepts that would later permeate her philosophical writings.

In *Three English Poetesses*, Helene Druskowitz constructs a critical triad of Victorian literary figures, interrogating their artistic merits while implicitly mapping their struggles onto her feminism. The text operates as both a hermeneutic project and a feminist treatise, reflecting Druskowitz's conviction that women's intellectual labour must transcend patriarchal constraints to achieve ascetic purity—a theme central to her later works, among them *Pessimistic Cardinal Propositions*.

Druskowitz frames Joanna Baillie's biography as one of existential stasis, noting her life unfolded "without great storms, exhausting struggles, or the violent passions typically endured by gifted women against family and society" (Druskowitz 1885, 4). This absence of friction, however, becomes a philosophical indictment: Baillie's unrealised dramatic genius—attributed to a deficit in "rigorous artistic discipline and metaphysical depth"—epitomises the systemic erasure of women's creative agency. While praising her "chivalric spirit" and moral vigour, Druskowitz underscores the dissonance between Baillie's latent potential and her socially conditioned acquiescence to mediocrity—a critique mirroring her later denunciations of patriarchal complacency.

Barrett Browning emerges as a figure of tragic ambivalence. Though lauded for her "profound emotionality" and "verses of tender beauty," Druskowitz identifies a fatal disconnect between the poet's "fervent spirit" and her inability to transmute abstraction into dramatic action—a flaw she attributes to Barrett Browning's confinement within Victorian femininity's "sentimental ghetto." The poet's lyrical intensity, while "captivating," remains ensnared in personal effect, failing to ascend to the "higher creative power" that Druskowitz associates with intellectual transcendence. Yet, in her conclusion, Druskowitz tempers criticism with reverence, framing Barrett Browning as a union of poetic immediacy and cultivated refinement that embodies the unfulfilled promise of women's artistry under systemic repression. This theme resonates with Druskowitz's later calls for female separatism.

Elevating Eliot as the apotheosis of literary womanhood, Druskowitz extols her "comprehensive grasp of life's moral complexities" and rejection of Christian dogma in favour of Comtean humanism (Druskowitz 1885, 157)—a secular shift mirroring Druskowitz's preferences which she later developed. Eliot's novels, with their psychological realism and rejection of sensationalism, exemplify the intellectual asceticism Druskowitz deemed essential for women's liberation from materialist delusions. Particularly notable is Eliot's nuanced portrayal of clergymen—figures she neither sanctifies nor condemns but interrogates as vessels of ethical ambiguity. For Druskowitz, this ambivalence reflects Eliot's reverence for overcoming world views (Druskowitz 1885, 169), a dialectic process central to her feminist epistemology: only through critical engagement with inherited structures can women forge new positions for themselves.

Druskowitz's analysis oscillates between veneration and dissatisfaction, a dialectic that reflects the deeper currents of her philosophical project. In celebrating these writers' achievements, she simultaneously measures them against a horizon of the impossible—an unattainable ideal, the *übermenschliche Dichterin*, whose art would wholly transcend the contaminations of patriarchy. Druskowitz's feminist stance in her engagement with the three English poetesses has already been observed (Chambers 2011, 99). Yet her critiques—of Baillie's passivity, Barrett Browning's emotionalism, and even Eliot's lingering sentimentalism—betray proto-radical feminism: for Druskowitz, true artistic genius demands not merely talent but an existential rupture with societal paradigms. This rupture, a breaking open of the self and the world, gestures toward what she would later theorise as the *Endesende*—the ultimate, final end—of gender itself. In this light, Druskowitz's literary criticism can be understood as a metaphysical quest for the possibility of art unbound by the strictures of gendered beings.

Druskowitz's *Three English Poetesses* thus functions as a palimpsest—its surface-level literary criticism underpinned by the subterranean currents of her incipient feminist philosophy, where art becomes both a testament to women's suppressed potential and a call to dismantle the structures that bind it.

4 Druskowitz's Dramatic Production

Regarding Druskowitz's dramatic opus, the contours of her literary ambition become clear through a range of sources, including Ebner-Eschenbach's diaries, the epistolary exchanges between Louise von François and Conrad Ferdinand Meyer, as well as Druskowitz's letters. These reveal a woman who, despite her polymathic intellect, yearned above all to be acknowledged as a dramatist. Her creative gaze, it seems, was turned towards the theatre as the ultimate stage for recognition. However, not a single one of her plays graced the stage during her lifetime, and within her intellectual circle—those very people she most esteemed—her dramatic efforts were met with cool detachment.

In total, Druskowitz published nine dramatic works, though two—*Aspasia* (1889) and its reissue as *Die Emancipations-Schwärmerin* (*The Emancipation Enthusiast*, 1890)—are near textual twins. Her early plays appeared under a succession of masculine pseudonyms—"E. René," "Erich René," and "Adalbert Brunn"—perhaps as a strategic masquerade in a literary world inhospitable to female voices. However, from 1890 onward, a shift occurs: she steps forth under her actual name, asserting "Dr. Phil. Helene Druskowitz (Adalbert Brunn)" or simply "Dr Helene Druskowitz." It is as though her growing philosophical defiance demanded a corollary literary transparency.

Druskowitz's most compelling work is *The Emancipation Enthusiast*. In it, Druskowitz reveals herself not merely as a dramatist but as a social diagnostician—one who peers into the soul of her era with a blend of irony, lucidity, and quiet rage.

At the heart of the play stands Alwina Dissen, a woman who, alongside her children—Zelia and Percy—relocates from New York to a serene university town in Switzerland.[14] The journey is not merely geographical but existential, born of her husband's belief that she must extricate herself from the ideological

---

14 The play has received some scholarly attention. Cf. Nachbaur (1999), Colvin (2003, 37–43), Merz (2011, 65–78).

fervour that had overtaken her. Immersed in the heady world of East Coast feminism without the ballast of rigorous study or lived comprehension, Alwina had thrown herself into the women's movement with the zeal of the untempered idealist. In the parlours of Boston and New York, the wry label bestowed upon her by distinguished gentlemen—"Aspasia"—was both mockery and myth.

In Switzerland, the family is received by Mr Jordan and his wife, Luisa. Alwina enrols in university courses, insisting that the emancipation of women demands breadth of knowledge and constant civic engagement. However, her zeal encounters a different voice in Dora Hellmuth, Luisa's protégée—a bright, accomplished medical student. Dora's stance is not theoretical but empirical: let women prove themselves in the crucible of professional rigour. A woman who diagnoses a rare illness or performs life-saving surgery, she argues, does more for the cause than volumes of impassioned rhetoric. For Dora, individual excellence is the sharpest weapon against structural prejudice.

To Alwina, however, Dora is narrow in scope, blind to the spiritual and societal depths of the "woman question." Yet as the narrative unfolds—through duels fought in her name, fortunes lost, and humiliations suffered—Alwina begins to awaken. She comes to recognise that talent, like reason, knows no gender. However, more crucially, she confronts herself: her role as a dreamer, lost in the mist of idealism, detached from the often-prosaic contours of reality. Moreover, towards the end of the play, Emil Dissen returns to save the situation.

The lesson is sobering. Passion is not in itself a principle. The path to truth does not always lie in struggle but sometimes in stillness, in recognising that the pursuit of imagined futures may blind one to the radiance of present joy. In this quiet epiphany, the construct of Aspasia dissolves, and the woman Alwina reemerges—not defeated, but transformed.

The play bears significant importance for Druskowitz, as it is indicated in the preface to *Aspasia* (and omitted in *The Emancipation Enthusiast*): "There can be little doubt, from the reader's perspective, as to the author's position on the subject of the play. – Owing to the author's own active and personal involvement in the great struggle for women's rights, he was compelled to depict, in a manner at once satirical and humorous, the category of *emancipation enthusiasts* and their misguided conduct" (Druskowitz 1889, 3).

The play presents at least three distinct approaches to feminism. Alwine embodies the first: her naïve feminist enthusiasm is portrayed as both absurd and ultimately dangerous—not only for the feminist cause, which her behaviour discredits and turns into a subject of ridicule, but also for her neglected family, which narrowly escapes disaster.

Dora Hellmuth represents the second, Druskowitz's evident *alter ego*. In Dora, Druskowitz offers a model of pragmatic, grounded feminism—an emancipated woman whose strength lies not in posturing but in competence and integrity. Dora stands in sharp contrast to Alwine's chaotic idealism: she is composed, intellectually disciplined, and quietly radical. Her vision of women's liberation is not built on rhetorical proclamations but on demonstrable achievements. Dora maintains that only through the visible proof of individual talent—through accomplishments that demand recognition in traditionally male domains—can societal perceptions of women's capabilities be elevated. Her feminism is meritocratic: the advancement of women as a whole depends on the public success of the few who can exemplify their worth in professional arenas.

The third approach is that of Luise Jordan. On the surface, she ironically identifies herself as an anti-feminist. However, in practice, she is far from an opponent of emancipation; instead, she represents a form of political pragmatism—if not opportunism. She rejects feminist activism only so long as her autonomy is respected in equal measure. Should that balance be disrupted, she intimates, she would not hesitate to join the movement. Luise is less a conservative figure than a realist—a reflective foil to Alwine's idealism, in whom we see the subtle logic of self-preservation masked as conformity.

Similarly, Druskowitz used her plays *Die Pädagogin* (*The Woman Pedagogue*) and *Unerwartet* (*Unexpected*) to launch a bold critique of the patriarchal systems that marginalise women's intellectual and artistic labour. Central to Druskowitz's feminist philosophy is the idea that societal structures systematically undermine women's autonomy and legitimacy, not through overt oppression alone, but by distorting the conditions under which women are allowed to think, teach, and create.

The Woman Pedagogue functions as a sharp satire of patriarchal pretensions toward education and social advancement. The play critiques a society in which intellectual development is less a genuine pursuit than a façade maintained for social respectability or acquiring a desired marital partner. Education becomes a site of farce, where those claiming authority are revealed as frauds, and those receiving instruction are instrumentalised for ulterior motives. The narrative exposes how intellectual and moral emptiness often masquerades as cultural sophistication, particularly when mediated by gendered expectations. Female ambition is often shown to be constrained and redirected toward romantic or social gain, frequently at the expense of solidarity and self-respect. Male authority, meanwhile, is uncritically revered, even when it lacks substance, reinforcing a hierarchy in which knowledge is conflated with performance and power.

Rather than offering a redemptive resolution, the play deliberately avoids a clear moral alternative. Even the conventional comedic ending—centred on love and marriage—is stripped of depth, exposing the hollowness of societal ideals. In doing so, the work serves as a broader philosophical critique of patriarchy, where education, desire, and legitimacy are intertwined in a web of appearances and where truth is often subordinated to social performance.

Druskowitz's dramatic works focus on interrogating how societal structures limit women's intellectual and creative agency. Through plays like *The Emancipation Enthusiast*, she dissects the tensions between idealism and pragmatism, exposing the pitfalls of performative feminism and education. Her characters—Alwina's naïve fervour, Dora's meritocratic rigour, and Luise's strategic conformity—embody competing responses to gendered oppression, reflecting Druskowitz's scepticism of simple solutions. Central to her philosophy, as represented in her plays, is the paradox of recognition: women must navigate systems that demand both conformity to societal norms and the erasure of their authentic voices.

Druskowitz's shift from masculine pseudonyms to her own name symbolises her defiance of literary and epistemic marginalisation. She frames autonomy not as liberation from oppression but as a practice of ontological defiance—a refusal to internalise patriarchal valuations. Her plays provoke a radical reimagining of knowledge and creativity, urging women to claim sovereignty. In this unresolved tension, Druskowitz locates the enduring potential for feminist emancipation.

By composing *Lustspiele* comedies, Druskowitz rejects both tragic victimhood and false empowerment, instead using irony and farce to undermine the legitimacy of the very systems that marginalise women. By doing so, she transforms satire into a feminist tool, using laughter not to placate but to provoke.

Expectedly, Druskowitz's literary friends disapproved of her plays. Marie von Ebner-Eschenbach dismissed the dialogue in the now-lost play *Svante Sture* as being "too literary," remarking bluntly: "She still has no clue about dramatic dialogue" (Ebner-Eschenbach 1993, 158). Even sharper seems the judgment of Louise von Françoise, who wrote to Meyer about Druskowitz's satirical plays: "What we call humour is entirely absent from her disposition" (François & Meyer 1920, 264). While Ebner-Eschenbach's and von François's judgments may seem harsh, they raise the question: Was Druskowitz's penchant for dense, intellectual prose that is ill-suited to the stage, intentional as her plays are meant to deliver a more philosophical message—during which she neglected, consciously or unconsciously, some aesthetic aspects of poetic creation?

5 Helene Druskowitz's Doctoral Thesis on Lord Byron's *Don Juan*

Druskowitz's dissertation was published in 1879 in Zurich under the slightly modified title *Lord Byron's "Don Juan." Eine literarisch-ästhetische Abhandlung* (*Lord Byron's "Don Juan": A Literary-Aesthetic Treatise*). At the time, Druskowitz had not yet changed her surname, so the dissertation bears her original spelling as Druschkovich. The 58-page work is divided into four untitled chapters.

This dissertation challenges simplistic standard interpretations, rejecting notions that the poem represents either a monument to human depravity or a nihilistic epic. Instead, Druskowitz interprets it as a nuanced exploration of human weakness, conveyed through satirical humour and mockery. According to Druskowitz, Byron neither glorifies frivolity nor condemns morality outright; instead, he exposes humanity's fundamental powerlessness. She emphasises Byron's skilful use of wit, irony, and good-natured cynicism, which reveal profound insights into human nature.

Druskowitz underscores several elements in Byron's poetry. First, it is inherently subjective (Druschkovich 1879, 6): she identified this "bold subjectivism" as the defining feature of Byron's verse, noting that his poetry springs from his inner self, imbues characters with his traits, and unfolds in locations visited by him. Another essential characteristic she highlights is the *Freiheitsdrang* (yearning for freedom). This drive for freedom of thought compelled Byron to battle against the church, politics, and society, with his critiques initially directed at the Puritanism of his nation. The third distinctive quality of Byron's poetry, according to Druskowitz, is its "*Weltschmerz*, hatred of humanity, and inclination to focus on evil" (Druschkovich 1879, 10). However, she contended that these traits of the Byronic mind are not equally developed across all his works and that most of his poems retain a certain monotony.

No one, she argued, understood humanity and the world as profoundly as Byron. What he shared with his contemporaries was engagement with naturalism, which Druskowitz believed reached its apex in certain aspects of his poetry:

> After our examination, we cannot regard *Don Juan* as the 'darkest monument of human depravity,' an 'epic of Epicurean nihilism,' or a glorification of frivolity. The poem's underlying tendency is to reveal humanity's moral and natural powerlessness; however, this is achieved not through solemn or sombre means—which would necessitate inscribing Dante's *Abandon all hope, ye who enter here* over the work—but through laughter, jest, and mockery, albeit often sharp and scornful in its derision. (Druskowitz 1879, 57–58)

Her thesis was evaluated by Heinrich Breitinger, a professor of modern languages (including English), and Andreas Ludwig Kym, a professor of speculative philosophy. This dual assessment highlights the Janus-faced character of her thesis—and, by extension, much of her later work—as it oscillates between literature and philosophy. Breitinger assessed Druskowitz's thesis with the following words:

> How, then, should the present work be assessed as an *examination performance*? It cannot, admittedly, be regarded as evidence of literary-historical scholarship. Fortunately, however,

that is not its intended purpose. Nevertheless, it seems that a more thorough engagement with the *historical preliminary questions* would have significantly enhanced the *resolution* of the principal issues. The dissertation may well present itself as evidence of *education*, intellectual *rigour,* and *independent*—indeed, at times *astute*—*thinking.* To my mind, it appears *too good* to be rejected, yet *not sufficiently good* to merit a high qualification.[15]

Kym was more lenient towards Druskowitz, emphasising her independent and progressive thinking, as displayed in her doctoral thesis and written examination essay.

The thematic focus of her dissertation reveals an apparent inclination toward literature and an admiration for authors who critically engage with societal and philosophical ideas. This trajectory would later gain full momentum in her own philosophical work. Druskowitz's early scholarly interests anticipate her later radical critiques, situating her within a tradition of dissent against mainstream structures—in the case of interpreting Lord Byron's poetry, she did not rely heavily on other "standard" interpretations—which was held against her in the assessment of the thesis. Her valorisation of subversive authors aligns with her later feminist works, which similarly dismantle patriarchal and dogmatic frameworks through systematic argumentation.

6 Philosophy in Druskowitz's Oeuvre

In this volume, we present the complete texts and English translations of four of Druskowitz's five philosophical books:

– *How is Responsibility and Attribution Possible Without the Assumption of Free Will?* (*Wie ist Verantwortung und Zurechnung ohne Annahme der Willensfreiheit möglich?* 1887),
– *Modern Attempts at a Replacement for Religion* (*Moderne Versuche eines Religionsersatzes,* 1886),
– *Towards a New Doctrine* (*Zur neuen Lehre,* 1888), and

---

15 This material is found in the "Druskowitz" file preserved in the Staatsarchiv Zurich under the signature U 109 e 1. The file includes Druskowitz's letter requesting admission to the doctoral examination, her curriculum vitae, her written examination essay (*Klausuarbeit*) titled "To what extent do his predecessors influence Plato" ("Inwiefern ist Plato von seinen Vorgängern bestimmt"), Breitinger's evaluation of her doctoral thesis, Kym's evaluations of both her written essay and thesis, as well as three barely legible letters, presumably related to the official procedures of the doctoral examination process, signed by the historian Gerold Meyer von Knonau.

– *Pessimistic Cardinal Propositions, a Manual for the Freest Spirits* (*Pessimistische Kardinalsätze. Ein Vademecum für die freiesten Geister,* 1903 or 1905).

The four books collectively represent the core of Druskowitz's philosophical contributions. Their content can be categorised into two thematic groups. The first group consists of *How is Responsibility and Attribution Possible Without the Assumption of Free Will?* This book focuses particularly on the implications of moral responsibility in the absence of belief in free will. The second group comprises three works that critique and displace Christianity as the dominant spiritual, intellectual, and moral system, as well as the search for a viable alternative. The book *Modern Attempts at a Replacement for Religion* serves as a *pars destruens*, wherein Druskowitz critiques contemporary efforts to challenge religion as a foundational societal system. In the book *Towards a New Doctrine*, she provides her vision of a satisfactory alternative to religion, outlining the principles of this proposed system. Finally, in *Pessimistic Cardinal Propositions*, she extends and deepens the arguments presented in her earlier works, exploring the metaphysical and societal consequences of her positions. This categorisation highlights the dual focus of Druskowitz's *oeuvre:* a rigorous examination of specific philosophical dilemmas and a broader engagement with the socio-cultural transformations necessitated by the hoped decline of traditional religious frameworks.

A word of caution is necessary regarding the final book, *Pessimistic Cardinal Propositions*. First, the exact year of publication remains uncertain, as no date is indicated in the printed edition. Secondary literature suggests two possible years: 1903 and 1905. Both could be true. The only potential clue lies in her medical records; however, these provide limited assistance. Entries from April 1902 to 1905 describe Druskowitz as highly creative during this period, composing numerous texts, some of which, based on doctors' descriptions, can be identified as components of *Pessimistic Cardinal Propositions*. However, in her *Kankenakte,* there is a paper (folio 44) that is typewritten, with some words typed outside the margins. What remains is a touching testimony about the creation of the work:

> Declaration
> The undersigned hereby affirms that in the work *Pessimistic Cardinal Propositions*, she has given all her philosophical thoughts their precise and final expression, and solemnly promises to make no further attempt to publish a new work at her own expense.
> Dr. Helene Druskowitz
> Mauer-Öhling near Amstetten, Lower Austria
> 21 October 1905.

The second caveat pertains to the radical nature of this text. It is unquestionably the most extreme of Druskowitz's works and was published "in the same form as the manuscript," that is, without any editorial intervention or moderation of its severe expressions. The book was composed after Druskowitz had been confined to a psychiatric institution for more than fifteen years. According to her medical records, she was frequently sedated due to persistent hallucinations, which she interpreted as spiritual or mystical communications with various individuals. Additionally, she took every opportunity to acquire alcohol and reportedly consumed substantial amounts.

These circumstances may explain why certain sections of the text appear unfinished or give the impression that something is missing. Nonetheless, the originality of its content and the sharpness of its expressions testify to the author's underlying lucidity, preventing the book from being dismissed outright.

6.1 Free Will Problem

In 1887, Helene Druskowitz published a work addressing the problem of free will, entitled *Wie ist Verantwortung und Zurechnung ohne Annahme der Willensfreiheit möglich?* (*How is Responsibility and Attribution Possible Without the Assumption of Free Will?*) The book seeks to resolve a classic ethical dilemma: in what sense can we speak of moral responsibility for our actions if causal forces entirely determine us? Druskowitz contends that natural freedom does not exist, while transcendental freedom, though possible, is irrelevant to the question of responsibility. Nevertheless, she argues that the moral attribution of responsibility remains meaningful. Druskowitz initially aligns herself with Feuerbach, whose justification of the moral attribution of responsibility centres on his view that morality emerges from transforming egoistic instincts for personal happiness into moral instincts for shared happiness. According to Feuerbach, individuals achieve harmony with their own natures through love and the identification with others, leading to a sense of shared moral responsibility rather than the reliance on the concept of free will. Feuerbach argues that moral responsibility stems from the instinct for happiness, being sociable and interdependent, and individuals judge themselves based on their alignment with others' perceptions. Druskowitz appears to agree with Feuerbach on these points, although she acknowledges a serious objection: egoistic behaviour could stem from an infinite causal chain, thereby challenging the notion of moral responsibility. She suggests moving beyond causality to a higher standpoint for a valid justification of responsibility, but Feuerbach only hints at this perspective without fully developing it. Only by moving to a higher standpoint can true responsibility and moral attribution be established. This *higher standpoint* forms the core of Druskowitz's argument on free will.

According to Druskowitz, once a person understands themself as a self-conscious representative of nature, they are no longer mere automatons and are distinct from other beings. In her view, humans epitomise the convergence of natural forces, with self-consciousness being the highest expression of this unique combination. This self-consciousness, which, for Druskowitz, is exclusively human, separates individuals from the causal chain of the world's processes and makes them morally responsible for their actions. The recognition of one's responsibility emerges from this very realisation that humans are not just a link in a chain but are endowed with self-consciousness, which sets them apart from the rest of nature. This perspective presents a basis for the possibility of the moral attribution of responsibility, distinguishing humans from animals based on their capacity for moral discernment.

In consequence, responsibility arises not from free will but from humans recognising themselves as authors of their actions and representatives of nature's higher potential. This acknowledgement inspires self-improvement and counteracts egoism. Regret for wrongdoing shifts from lamenting specific actions to aspiring to become a better person, fostering long-term moral growth.

Furthermore, this *feeling of responsibility* extends beyond the individual: by holding themself accountable, a person also acknowledges the mutual responsibility that binds them to others. The individual must respect their natural limits while striving upward, with society playing a vital role in reinforcing good traits and suppressing bad ones. Evaluating actions solely through deterministic necessity overlooks nature's goal of elevating the noble and diminishing the harmful.

The consequence of this approach is that instead of justifying wrongdoing by citing a *natural disposition* or claiming that different actions could have arisen from libertarian free will, one must say: *If I had acted differently, I could have been a better person.* Druskowitz argues that this perspective has a more constructive influence on future actions than the libertarian view. At the same time, her position differs from hard determinism, which undermines the very foundation of morality: the Druskowitzian individual recognises that, as part of nature and its causal determinism, they are also *representatives of its higher potencies.*

Her conclusion emphasises that this perspective motivates individuals to strive for higher aspirations while remaining conscious of the constraints imposed by their natural dispositions, upbringing, and circumstances. Through this understanding, individuals gain a deeper appreciation of their personal worth and significance. Each person is confined to a specific sphere dictated by their physical and intellectual attributes, education, and external conditions and cannot exceed these limitations without consequence.

While Druskowitz's position on free will does not present a radically new idea, as she acknowledges, it is a variation of Schopenhauer's views, which she colourfully describes as having "put the last nail in the coffin of libertarianism." However, her argument introduces a novel aspect by incorporating elements of naturalism, hinting at an evolutionary framework, albeit in a form she understood. Although Darwin or Darwinism is not explicitly mentioned in *How is Responsibility and Attribution Possible Without the Assumption of Free Will?*, her broader works indicate that Druskowitz was not only familiar with Darwin's theory of evolution but also regarded it favourably as key to understanding society and ethics. Her reasoning begins with the *force of nature* or *the necessity of nature*, whose by-product is human self-consciousness, which distinguishes humans from animals. According to Druskowitz, humans evolved beyond animals in that, by *natural law*, they developed self-consciousness. However, she also references an inherent *goodness* in humanity that serves as a teleological principle guiding progress, though this principle is not transcendent but part of nature. Unfortunately, her arguments lack clarity in explaining what this natural goodness entails or how it relates to the laws or forces of nature.

6.2 Criticism of Religion

Druskowitz's critique of religion, particularly Christianity, is a central theme throughout her work, but two of her books focus specifically on this issue. In *Moderne Versuche eines Religionsersatzes* (*Modern Attempts at a Replacement for Religion*), published in 1886, she primarily concentrates on critiquing past and contemporary efforts to replace religion, serving as *pars destruens*. Her subsequent work, *Zur neuen Lehre* (*Towards a New Doctrine* or just *New Doctrine*), first published in 1888 and reissued in 1889 under the title *Zur Begründung einer überreligiösen Weltanschauung* (*On the Foundation of a Supra-religious World View*) should serve as *pars construens*, outlining her vision for what a replacement for religion should entail.

Druskowitz argues that Christianity persists due to its fulfilment of emotional needs, despite its waning influence as the need for fantasy diminishes. She highlights the growing rejection of religion as a significant cultural development. She posits that establishing a doctrine imbued with higher meaning and purpose for human life is a crucial task. Druskowitz believes that evolutionary theory when correctly understood, will play a pivotal role in this development. She acknowledges various thinkers—Comte, Feuerbach, Dühring, Duboc, Nietzsche, and Salter—who have attempted to replace religion with a comprehensive world view. However, she notes either the absence of a complete system or the attempt, as in the case of Nietzsche, to replace one religion with another; his philosophy, which bears resemblance to a religion. Instead, she argues that a replacement for religion should be sought in the relationship between humanity and the universe in order to establish an ideal for striving and acting as individuals in the form of perpetual advancement. According to Druskowitz, "[a] more ideal conception of things, a spiritualisation of even the least activity, a more courageous and trusting, a more joyful and higher view of life—that is what we need" (123, 253). Here, she returns to her recurring theme of advancing humanity through efforts to achieve a "higher," more spiritual way of life.

She advocates for replacing religion with a new doctrine, a world view that should supplant the belief in God and immortality with ideas grounded in modern philosophy and natural science. Unlike traditional religious faith, this new world view would offer a superior intellectual foundation based on knowledge, one that is free from reliance on a personal deity. It must command trust and respect, enrich human life with meaning, and emphasise the earth as humanity's only home. Rather than perpetuating belief in immortality, it would focus on the possibilities inherent in human development.

At the heart of Druskowitz's project lies a fundamental question: Can a higher world view, based on knowledge rather than faith, inspire the same profound and uplifting feelings as religion? Can it imbue life with greater meaning and open new horizons for human striving? She acknowledges that no philosopher has yet fully developed such a comprehensive world view, though several have made partial attempts. Religion, she argues, originates from a primitive psychological disposition that remains a potent internal force. Critical philosophy reveals that the ultimate nature of the world cannot be definitively determined, leading her to view religion as an illusion born from humanity's idealistic desire to transcend the limitations of the material world.

Religion persists because it provides a world view that resonates with the masses, and it will continue to do so as long as the emotional needs it satisfies remain unmet. For freethinkers dissatisfied with atheism, Druskowitz envisions a philosophy that, like religion, contemplates the cosmos from a higher perspective. She contends that merely dismantling religion is insufficient; an intellectually rigorous new world view must take its place.

For individuals with deeper intellectual and spiritual inclinations, the questions that religion seeks to answer become more urgent once religion is recognised as misleading. This realisation fosters a desire for a world view grounded in truth and knowledge—one that provides a higher sense of purpose and connects individuals to something greater than themselves. While atheists may deny the possibility of such a system, Druskowitz notes that attempts to formulate these world views suggest both the need and the potential for a new doctrine. It is to this audience, she argues, that the new world view must speak.

Druskowitz criticises those who continue to label a post-religious standpoint as "religion," suggesting that they have either failed to overcome old doctrines fully, misunderstood the distinction between intellectual domains, or have attempted to fuse the old and the new improperly. A genuinely new world view must grasp the fundamental problem of existence and articulate a higher purpose, as taught by critical philosophy and authentic science. This understanding will naturally lead to a set of duties and motivations for human action.

Druskowitz is clear that the new doctrine cannot be reduced to mere morality, which some thinkers have proposed as a replacement for religion. Instead, she asserts that an improvement in morality should be an outcome of the new world view, not its central tenet.

Druskowitz's worldview, in which religion is replaced by a higher organization, is based on an evolutionary theory of human progress that extends Darwin's biological evolution into the realm of consciousness and intellectual development. According to this view, humanity represents a turning point in Earth's organic development where progress can continue through intellectual and spiritual advancement rather than physical evolution, suggesting that humans are destined to transcend their current limitations through the development of higher psychic and rational capacities.

The core idea of human progress is that humanity will achieve redemption through either victorious transcendence to a higher state of being—where thinking and being coincide and reason rules—or through voluntary extinction. In her work *Towards a New Doctrine*, Druskowitz argues that the former is far more probable. This progress would occur through an immense chain of expanding consciousness, mastery over nature, moral refinement, and the emergence of new human faculties, driven by humanity's deep dissatisfaction with current existence and sublime longing for perfection.

However, in *Pessimistic Cardinal Propositions*, Druskowitz largely dismisses the possibility of such progress, especially for men, and is inclined to opt for the latter alternative.

6.3 Metaphysics and Morality

In her final book, *Pessimistic Cardinal Propositions*, Druskowitz engages with metaphysical questions and critiques traditional theological and philosophical positions.

Her argument begins with a scathing rejection of the conventional understanding of God, that is, the Christian God. The anthropomorphic portrayal of a deity, she argues, is not only grotesque and absurd but also demeaning to its very creator. She points out the inherent contradiction in the idea of a creator god who stands above the world, asking rhetorically: does not every artist or creator strive to produce something superior, rather than something inferior, to themself? After dismissing the traditional concept of a god, Druskowitz articulates her core metaphysical position, which she bases in a form of Platonism.

Druskowitz's critique targets both monism and hylomorphic dualism. She rejects monism, which recognises only the reality or substantiality of matter, for failing to address the problem of a chaotic, evil-dominated world. In her view, monism adopts an indifferent and overly optimistic perspective that ignores the horrors of existence. At the same time, she critiques hylomorphic dualism, where matter takes ontological precedence and is merely shaped by form, as this assumes a "close cooperation" between matter and form, which she finds inadequate.

Instead, Druskowitz proposes an unbridgeable divide between what she calls the *Over-Sphere* (*Übersphäre*) and matter. This term encapsulates her notion of a higher, transcendent reality, a realm beyond the material world. In her metaphysics, matter is formless, meaningless, and the source of evil, while the Over-Sphere embodies goodness, meaning, and the actual reality toward which all aspiration is directed. The relationship between these two realms is defined by privation: each is the opposite of the other, and they share nothing in common except that matter, with humans as its highest form, can intellectually apprehend the existence of the Over-Sphere and strive toward it. Despite her rejection of any concept of a transcendent deity, she does not dismiss the concept of a higher principle altogether, as embodied in her concept of the Over-Sphere.

The Over-Sphere represents the *causa finalis*, the ultimate goal toward which matter evolves. However, as long as it remains material, it can never fully attain this higher realm. She contends that the human drive towards something unattainable serves as a catalyst for development and offers a framework for understanding the world's misery—a view she frames as a form of metaphysical pessimism. The relationship between the Over-Sphere and matter is marked by deprivation: one is all that the other is not. However, there is a relationship between the Over-Sphere and matter: The Over-Sphere is the teleological goal towards which matter tends. The evolution of matter is the ascent to the Over-Sphere, which can never be reached as long as there is anything material. There is a qualitatively unbridgeable gap between matter and the Over-Sphere. This represents the gradation of Being (*Sein*): starting from the material level, it ascends over the animal, then to human consciousness (*Bewußtsein*) till it finally—and only imaginarily—comes closer to the Over-Sphere, where it suspends itself. This is also one of the main arguments against materialism: the "masterpiece" of materialism, consciousness, falls short of reaching the level of intellect (*Vernunftgrad*) necessary to grasp the Over-Sphere in its whole meaning, which lies entirely outside its capacity.

The *Pessimistic Cardinal Propositions* can also be understood as a criticism of a Nietzschean reformation of morality. However, ironically, the booklet is written in a Nietzschean aphoristic style. Combined with her sharp and brutal criticism of Nietzsche, this leads one to conjecture that the intention of the work, put in the context of criticism of Nietzsche contained in her *Modern Attempts at a Replacement for Religion* from 1886, was to "out-nietzsche" Nietzsche. This mixture of radical criticism and emulation suggests an implicit conviction that Nietzsche, in his attempts to redefine society, stopped too soon, that his project was not fully realised, and that he lost his nerve before completing it. Hers, on the other hand, is more far-reaching, more radical, and more complete, from her perspective at least (Boršić, Skuhala Karasman 2020).

To a degree, there is also something autobiographical about the central thesis of *Pessimistic Cardinal Propositions:* the dissonance between her early acclaim and later marginalisation reflects her ontological dichotomy of the Over-Sphere versus material degradation—a metaphysical framework in which she positioned herself as both architect and casualty. Even her documented struggles with addiction and emotional instability acquire symbolic resonance when contextualised within her polemics against masculine rationality, presenting a life that refused compartmentalisation of intellect and embodiment. For that reason, the *Pessimistic cardinal propositions*, with all their extreme statements, should not be read as a pathological anomaly but rather seen as a part of her existential continuum, bridging scholarly rigour and psychological fragmentation.

6.4 Radical Feminism

In her play from 1890, *The Emancipation Enthusiast*, Druskowitz already gives a tenet of her feminist stance. In this play, Druskowitz critically examines different approaches to women's emancipation in late nineteenth-century society—the play centres on the contrast between two main characters. The protagonist, Alwine Dissen, initially appears as an emancipation enthusiast but is ultimately revealed to be more performative than substantive in her feminism. Dora Hellmuth, a medical doctor who embodies genuine feminism through her professional achievements and pragmatic approach, is portrayed as a truly emancipated woman, albeit one who is notably isolated from traditional family structures. In the play,

Druskowitz expresses scepticism of superficial feminist posturing, promoting the idea that genuine emancipation requires professional competence and serious commitment. The play explores the inherent tension between feminist ideals and traditional female social expectations, emphasising substance over style in women's liberation (20–22).

This hiatus between societal expectations and female liberation is further promoted in her *Pessimistic Cardinal Propositions*. In her critique of men and patriarchy, Druskowitz builds upon a metaphysical foundation that questions the very existence and relevance of God as traditionally conceived. Her feminism is based on her metaphysical assumptions that a transcendent entity, the Over-Sphere, is fundamentally unknowable to humans, given its immaterial and inaccessible nature of the Over-Sphere—and that women are essentially closer to it than men. This is also obvious in the patriarchal portrayal of a deity as a male figure, "it is nothing but a patchwork […] rotten to the core" (153, 282). Druskowitz also makes a significant distinction between men and women in this context: men, she argues, are more closely tied to matter, whereas women, being more spiritual, are inherently closer to the Over-Sphere and thus more valuable as beings.

In addition to this metaphysical critique, Druskowitz advances a second line of argumentation rooted in cultural pessimism. She condemns the male-dominated world as fundamentally violent, chaotic, and destructive, referring to it as a "comedy of our stupid half-culture" (162, 292). She argues that the moral and existential crises that men have endured for centuries—characterised by sexual decadence and a decline in their capacity for love—have rendered them incapable of meaningful vitality or spiritual growth. In contrast, she posits that women have remained morally unscathed by these male excesses and are thus positioned to redeem men by reshaping societal values and institutions. Druskowitz envisions a future where women assume the leadership role in creating a new morality and economy. This vision manifests in her concept of an exclusively female utopia, where "cities of women" and "cities of men" are physically and socially segregated.

This idea of gender segregation is also elaborated in her book *Three English Poetesses*, where she launches a vigorous critique of marriage as an institution that suppresses women's intellectual and creative potential. Druskowitz argues that women need "space for themselves" to flourish, free from the constraints of marriage and male dominance. She reiterates this theme in *Pessimisic Cardinal Propositons*, advocating for gender-segregated cities where women can liberate themselves from the corrupting influence of men, fully develop as individuals, and advance professionally. In this speculative vision, women-only spaces are crucial for female emancipation, allowing women to establish new societal structures and values unencumbered by male interference.

Druskowitz's feminist philosophy culminates in a dystopian vision where men, left to their own devices, ultimately destroy the world while a society of women would flourish. This anti-utopian view leads her to a radical conclusion: the extinction of the human race is not only inevitable but morally desirable. Unlike many contemporary speculations about human extinction, which tend to focus on external threats such as atomic disasters, climate catastrophes, or pandemics, Druskowitz frames the extinction of humanity as a moral imperative. For her, the destruction of the human race is depicted as inherently just and legitimate, a responsibility that humanity must ultimately fulfil. This extreme conclusion aligns with her broader philosophy of metaphysical and cultural pessimism, in which the continuation of the human species is viewed not as an ideal to strive for but as an outcome to be avoided.

Druskowitz's feminist critique, particularly her advocacy for the separation of women from men and her disdain for patriarchal structures, distinctively positions her within the history of feminist thought. While her radical vision of gender segregation and human extinction diverges sharply from the more reformist currents of feminism during her time, her work highlights the profound discontent with traditional gender roles and the existential consequences of a world shaped by male dominance. This uncompromising stance, particularly her call for the complete reordering of society along gender lines, reflects her more profound philosophical pessimism and her belief in the ultimate futility of human civilisation if left under male control.

It is notable that Druskowitz does not directly reference or engage with contemporary literary works that could be characterised as misogynistic. However, a significant mention appears in her *Krankenakte* (folio 60), dated 27 April 1892. In this clinical record, a physician at the Niederösterreichische Landes-Irrenanstalt writes: "The patient describes her hallucinations as telepathic experiences; for example, she hears Professor Krafft-Ebing in the corridor, hears shuffling footsteps, and voices that forbid her to eat."

The reference is to Richard von Krafft-Ebing, the renowned psychiatrist and author of the influential *Psychopathia sexualis* (1886). In this work, Krafft-Ebing does occasionally mention food, particularly concerning rare and extreme sexual pathologies. For us, more relevant, however, can be a metaphorical invocation of hunger in the book's preface, where he quotes Schiller's aphorism: "So long as philosophy keeps together the structure of the universe, so long does it maintain the world's machinery by hunger and love." Here, "hunger" is not literal but symbolic —a primal drive paired with love, evoking fundamental human instincts.

Krafft-Ebing's text is known for pathologising female sexuality, often casting women as passive, subordinate, and lacking in erotic agency. Against this backdrop, Druskowitz's auditory hallucinations—featuring Krafft-Ebing's voice forbidding her to eat—take on a more complex, possibly psychoanalytic, dimension. The command not to eat, perceived telepathically, may symbolically represent the internalisation of patriarchal interdictions surrounding female desire and autonomy. "Hunger," when understood as both literal and libidinal, becomes a symbol for suppressed sexuality, for the forbidden impulse to assert one's own bodily and intellectual agency. The intrusion of Krafft-Ebing's voice into her psychic space can thus be read as the haunting echo of a disciplinary discourse that sought to silence and medicalise female subjectivity.

In this light, Druskowitz's experience is not merely a clinical symptom but a symbolic enactment of the conflict between the desiring self and the internalised voice of authority—a tension central to both her life and her philosophical critique of patriarchal structures.

The reception of Helene Druskowitz's radical feminist—or misandrist—positions in *Pessimistic cardinal propositions* was virtually non-existent.[16] Later authors espousing similarly confrontational perspectives, such as Valerie Solanas in her *S.C.U.M. Manifesto* (1967) or Andrea Dworkin in *Pornography* (1989), make no mention of Druskowitz. The sole known contemporary reception of Druskowitz's text was an anonymously published review in the Sunday section, *"Unser Hausfreund,"* of the newspaper *Hannoverscher Courier* on 28 February 1904. This review was prompted by the text "Maximen für Frauen," published earlier in the journal *Neue Deutsche Dichterstimmen*. This text would later become a central component of *Pessimistic Cardinal Propositions*.

The anonymous author ends his lengthy review with these remarks:

> I wished to share a curiosity. However, I have become rather anxious about it myself. Miss Druskowitz considers herself – of this, I am certain – a champion of the women's movement. Furthermore, even within her admittedly small readership, there will be those who regard her as such, who hold the women's movement accountable for what this peculiar saint concocts in her delusions. A more malicious caricature of a just, and in a certain sense even magnificent cause, has never before come to my attention. How is it possible that such elaborate works make it to press? Did the editor of the publication who accepted this opus truly have no idea what monstrous nonsense was being entrusted to him? It is a disgrace and a

---

16 Agatha Schwartz uses the term "viriphobia" to characterise Druskowitz's position, explaining it as a "heteroglossic" response to the misogynist stances of Möbius and Weininger (Schwartz 2005, 353–368; Schwartz 2008, 90–93). However, this interpretation is problematic for two reasons. First, the coinage "viriphobia" is unfortunate, as the suffix "-phobia" suggests a pathological fear of men—something that does not apply to Druskowitz. Second, Möbius's notorious misogynist work, *Über den physiologischen Schwachsinn des Weibes*, was first published in 1900, and Weininger's *Geschlecht und Charakter* appeared in 1903—at which time Druskowitz was institutionalized in a psychiatric hospital, with little or no access to books. There is no evidence that she was familiar with either author or their writings.

shame how printing ink is wasted in the German Reich nowadays. May heaven preserve us from further offspring of the intellectual lineage of the Druskowitz kind.

This overtly scornful and dismissive reaction encapsulates the profound unease provoked by Druskowitz's uncompromising tone. The review reveals not only the resistance her work encountered but also the extent to which her voice—perceived as excessive, irrational, or threatening—was marginalised in public discourse.

6.5 Ecofeminism

Although women's critiques of male aggression, belligerence, and destructivity in philosophical discourse trace back to figures like Christine de Pizan and Isotta Nogarola, Helene Druskowitz composed one of the earliest—if not the first—articulations of what might anachronistically be termed an ecofeminist position. In her *Pessimistic Cardinal Propositions*, Druskowitz condemns humanity's exploitation of nature, framing men as principal agents of ecological degradation. She writes: "Man is the most avaricious of all creatures. He has ransacked Mother Earth in every possible way, worse than a wild beast, and extracted from her all her treasures" (159, 289). Her indictment extends to men's treatment of animals, which she attributes to a "blind drive for annihilation," "lust for possession," and "gluttonous hunger" (159, 289). For Druskowitz, men represent the "lowest of all natural beings". In contrast, women "are of a more perfect and noble lineage," evident in their mythic associations with the sea and their respectful engagement with nature (15, 288). This dichotomy culminates in her vision of *Endesende*—a radical separation of genders to facilitate humanity's near-extinction, sparing only a select few who live harmoniously in isolated valleys.

Ecofeminism, broadly defined, examines intersections between the oppression of women and the exploitation of nature. The term, coined by Françoise d'Eaubonne in 1974, posits that patriarchal and capitalist systems perpetuate both gendered and environmental subjugation (d'Eaubonne 1974). D'Eaubonne's framework asserts that addressing ecological crises necessitates dismantling patriarchal structures, as the two are inextricably linked. This normative stance positions ecofeminism as a call to activism, demanding systemic change to liberate women and nature simultaneously.

A central tension within ecofeminism lies in the debate between essentialism and constructivism. Essentialist perspectives, as Buckingham notes, elevate "feminine" principles of care and cooperation as biologically innate, arguing that these traits position women as natural stewards of ecological balance (Buckingham

2015, 846). Conversely, social constructivists attribute women's affinity with nature to historical material conditions—particularly their roles in reproductive labour (e. g., cooking, cleaning) that necessitate direct interaction with natural resources (Buckingham 2015, 846).

Druskowitz's work, however, defies easy categorisation. While her valorisation of women's "noble lineage" and innate harmony with nature aligns with essentialism, her critique of patriarchal systems as structurally destructive anticipates constructivist analyses of power.

Druskowitz's proto-ecofeminist critique, though formulated a century before the term's inception, resonates profoundly with contemporary debates. Her portrayal of men as "evil and foolish devils" who pervert nature's tranquillity into a "satanic hell" (157, 287) reflects a prescient understanding of ecological interconnectedness and the gendered dimensions of environmental harm. However, her vision of *Endesende*—a utopian segregation leading to humanity's near-extinction—raises ethical quandaries. While radical, this proposal highlights a recurring theme in ecofeminist thought: the need to reframe human-nature relationships beyond exploitative paradigms.

Druskowitz's institutionalisation complicates the question of how to evaluate her position. Isolated from intellectual circles, her ideas emerged not from academic discourse but from a visceral rejection of patriarchal violence, both social and ecological. This positions her not merely as a historical curiosity but as a marginalised voice whose insights anticipate later systemic critiques.

In synthesising Druskowitz's work with modern ecofeminism, her contributions challenge us to reconsider the boundaries between essentialism and constructivism. Rather than opposing frameworks, they might instead represent complementary lenses for understanding the multifaceted ties between gender and ecology. As Buckingham (2015) suggests, the goal is not to resolve this tension but to harness it—recognising that both biological affinities and socio-historical conditions shape humanity's relationship with nature. Druskowitz's polemics, though extreme, remind us that the stakes of this reckoning are nothing less than the survival of life itself.

Even from this angle, Druskowitz's writings offer provocative ideas which can be read as a foundation for ecofeminist thought. By linking male destructiveness to ecological collapse and envisioning a world where feminine principles restore balance, she transcends her era's limitations to speak to enduring crises. Her work invites contemporary scholars to grapple with the interplay of biology, power, and ethics in forging sustainable futures. While her radical solutions may unsettle modern sensibilities, they underscore a truth central to ecofeminism: the liberation of women and the healing of nature are inseparable endeavours. In this light,

Druskowitz's voice—forged in isolation and defiance—remains a vital call to reorient humanity's place within the natural order.

7 Influence

Helene Druskowitz's academic training at the University of Zurich encompassed a rigorous classical education, culminating in a doctoral thesis on the English poet Lord Byron and an oral examination spanning philosophy and the ancient Greek language. Despite this foundation in antiquity, her philosophical corpus exhibits a striking disengagement from classical thought. Plato is referenced only once in her *Pessimistic Cardinal Propositions* as "great Plato" (162, 293), while Aristotle remains conspicuously absent from her writings. With rare exceptions—such as her cursory engagement with the *Bhagavad Gita* (53, 175 – 176)—the earliest thinkers she substantively engages are Immanuel Kant and Arthur Schopenhauer, whose critiques of free will and metaphysical systems profoundly shaped her work. Besides them, Druskowitz's oeuvre predominantly engages with philosophers and thinkers of her era, reflecting a deliberate privileging of modern intellectual currents over classical traditions.

7.1 Discussing Free Will

Helene Druskowitz's critique of free will, as articulated in her book *How is Responsibility and Attribution Possible Without the Assumption of Free Will?*, engages critically with three pivotal figures: Immanuel Kant, Arthur Schopenhauer, and Paul Rée. Her analysis situates itself within the late nineteenth-century philosophical discourse, interrogating the coherence of moral responsibility amidst a deterministic framework.

Kant's conception of the transcendental subject profoundly shaped Druskowitz's intellectual milieu. For Kant, freedom is a transcendental idea—a necessary postulate of practical reason that enables moral responsibility despite the deterministic causality governing phenomena. Druskowitz, however, rejects Kant's bifurcation of the noumenal and phenomenal realms, arguing that his transcendental idealism inadvertently perpetuates metaphysical obscurity. By positing freedom as a regulative principle rather than an empirical reality, Kant's framework, in her view, fails to reconcile the antinomy between determinism and moral accountability. This tension underscores her broader critique of transcendental philosophy as insufficiently grounded in material and psychological causality.

Druskowitz credits Schopenhauer with systematically dismantling the illusion of free will. His distinction between the will-in-itself and its phenomenal manifestations provides the cornerstone of her argument. Schopenhauer asserts that while the will is free, its empirical instantiation—human agency—is bound by the principle of sufficient reason. Druskowitz expands this insight, emphasising that the individual, as a temporal manifestation of the will, cannot act *ex nihilo*; antecedent conditions causally determine every decision. She concurs with Schopenhauer's observation that the "philosophically raw man" misattributes spontaneity to freedom, conflating subjective experience with metaphysical independence. For Druskowitz, Schopenhauer's rigour in exposing this fallacy renders his work indispensable to any coherent theory of determinism.

Paul Rée's influence on Druskowitz is both substantive and polemical. A staunch determinist, Rée rejected free will as a vestige of theological and metaphysical dogma, attributing human behaviour to egoistic drives shaped by evolutionary and environmental factors. Druskowitz engages Rée's naturalism but contests his reduction of moral phenomena to biological determinism. While she accepts his premise that actions arise from causal chains—*ex nihilo nihil fit*—she diverges in her account of responsibility. For Rée, moral judgments are socially constructed tools of retribution, devoid of metaphysical grounding; Druskowitz, however, reinterprets responsibility as a pragmatic construct necessitated by social cohesion, even in the absence of libertarian freedom. This recalibration allows her to preserve ethical discourse without recourse to transcendental or agential metaphysics.

Druskowitz's originality lies in her synthesis of these thinkers. From Kant, she retains the imperative to reconcile determinism with moral practice, albeit rejecting his transcendental resolution. From Schopenhauer, she adopts the ontological primacy of causal necessity while critiquing his pessimism as ethically inert. From Rée, she borrows the naturalistic critique of free will but rejects his nihilistic conclusions about moral value.

7.2 Discussing Criticism of Religion

In *Modern Attempts at a Replacement of Religion*, Helene Druskowitz interrogates post-theistic frameworks proposed by Ludwig Feuerbach, Auguste Comte, and John Stuart Mill, rejecting their attempts to reconstitute religion on atheistic or anthropocentric grounds. While acknowledging Comte's *Système de politique positive* as a unique contribution, she critiques its residual teleological optimism and failure to transcend anthropomorphic projections. Feuerbach's reduction of morality to intersubjective relations—rooted in the "need for others' happiness"—is similarly dismissed for neglecting the individual's intrinsic relationship to truth and self-constitution. For Druskowitz, morality encompasses not merely social utility but also the cultivation of intellectual conscience and fidelity to truth as ends in themselves.

Friedrich Albert Lange's proposal to retain Christianity as allegory is scrutinised for its psychological naïveté: Druskowitz argues that symbolic engagement with religious ideas, without genuine faith, collapses into intellectual dishonesty. Enlightened individuals, she contends, cannot sustainably envy believers' certitude without confronting their failure to articulate a coherent secular alternative.

Druskowitz's analysis of Friedrich Nietzsche's *Thus Spoke Zarathustra* centres on its formal mimicry of religious texts, which she interprets as a hubristic attempt to position the Übermensch as a salvific ideal. While acknowledging the work's literary innovation, she dismisses its philosophical coherence, arguing that the Übermensch represents an intermediate stage, rather than the ultimate stage in ethical evolution. Julius Duboc's *Optimism as a World View* receives similarly mixed appraisal. Though lauded for emphasising the world's immeasurable mystery, it is faulted for neglecting the ontological "primal grounds" of being and failing to delineate the psychological impact of existential indeterminacy.

Within the limited secondary literature addressing her work, Druskowitz is frequently situated within the orbit of Friedrich Nietzsche's philosophical project. While Nietzsche's thought arguably presented a potential catalyst for her radical disillusionment, her intellectual lineage reveals more profound affinities with now-obscure figures, including the German polemicist Eugen Dühring (1833 – 1921) and the American ethical philosopher William MacIntyre Salter (1853 – 1931). Dühring's anti-metaphysical materialism and critiques of religious institutions resonate in Druskowitz's construction of an "Over-Sphere" as a post-religious ideal. At the same time, Salter's fusion of moral philosophy with quasi-religious fervour informed her vision of ethical reform. This selective engagement underscores her rejection of canonical authority in favour of thinkers whose radicalism aligned with her feminist and anti-patriarchal imperatives.

Dühring is now (in)famous for two main reasons: his critique of Marxism—particularly his intellectual conflict with Friedrich Engels, which prompted Engels's influential book *Anti-Dühring* (1878)—and his virulent antisemitism. The latter went systematically beyond the casual prejudices of his era and contributed to the ideological foundation of National Socialism in Germany. While more influential thinkers have largely eclipsed Dühring and he is now rejected for his racist views, in his time, he represented a significant alternative intellectual current in socialist and philosophical thought, challenging dominant paradigms and fostering critical discourse.

For Druskowitz, Dühring's philosophy offered an example and inspiration for a "higher world view, perception of life and knowledge, and view of humanity." She particularly admired his synthesis of philosophy as a scientific discipline with a deeply personal commitment. Most notably, she valued Dühring's rejection of religion and his advocacy for women's right to education. Nevertheless, she expressed reservations about his "brazen severity" (Druskowitz 1889, 8) and openly distanced herself from several of his positions. At the outset of her book, she declared: "Since I cannot regard all his reformative ideas and suggestions as correct or decisive, I will freely challenge him where his assertions or proposals seem inadequate or excessive to me" (Druskowitz 1889, 1). Specifically, Druskowitz dissociated herself from his ultimately materialistic world view, which included the doctrine of the absolute sovereignty of reason, his interpretation of infinity, and his derivation of motion from matter's initially static state (Druskowitz 1889, 2). She also explicitly rejected his virulent antisemitism (Druskowitz 1889, 9–10, 87–93). Elements of these critiques are also found in other works by Druskowitz, included in this volume.

As for Macintyre Salter, his philosophy is today almost completely forgotten; major philosophical databases show practically no secondary literature on him except for his analyses of Nietzsche's philosophy. Today, he is primarily remembered as one of the founders of the Ethical movement, a once-famous alternative to a non-theistically ethical organisation that people like Albert Einstein and Eleanor Roosevelt frequented.

Druskowitz expressed admiration for William Mackintire Salter's lectures on ethical religion, which appeared in German as *Die Religion der Moral* in 1885, four years before their English edition, *Ethical Religion*. Salter's philosophy, as Druskowitz regarded it, was distinguished by its emotional intensity and rhetorical eloquence. Salter's moral philosophy elevates ethics to a transcendent, quasi-religious plane, positing that humanity's "higher nature," though rarely awakened, has the potential to inspire justice and nobility independent of theistic belief. For Salter, morality is not a social convention but an expression of a cosmic law—an objective and universal principle of righteousness that exists irrespective of human opinion or cultural contingency.

His lectures are marked by an idealistic impulse, calling for the moral elevation of society rather than accommodation to existing norms. Though Salter did not produce a comprehensive philosophical system, his intellectual influence stemmed from his capacity to galvanise audiences. His ethical appeal derives not from abstract theorising but from the warmth of his rhetorical expression and his insistence on the transformative potential of moral enthusiasm.

Druskowitz also praised Salter's personal life as a testament to his philosophical convictions. His integrity of character, the harmony of his familial relations, and his expanding influence within the ethical culture movement exemplified for her the lived embodiment of his ideals. In contrast to more academically rigorous figures such as Felix Adler, Salter's accessible prose and affective power made his work particularly resonant across transatlantic contexts. His writings contributed significantly to the broader ethical movement that sought to reframe moral obligation without recourse to religious dogma, thereby aligning with Druskowitz's secular-humanist orientation.

In *Towards a New Doctrine*, Druskowitz re-engages with Lange's symbolic hermeneutics, rejecting Spencerian compatibilism while affirming Dühring's rigid demarcation between religious and scientific epistemologies. Charles Darwin's evolutionary theory informs her teleological vision, yet she critiques its biological determinism via Carl du Prel's *The Philosophy of Mysticism*, which posits metaphysical limits to material progress. While du Prel locates nascent higher consciousness in abnormal mental states (e.g., somnambulism, visions), Druskowitz rejects this, asserting that future psychic organs may emerge independently of observable traits. Druskowitz emphasises conscious intellectual and moral efforts as prerequisites for unlocking latent capacities, framing humanity as a "transitional type" destined for a superior ontological order. Philipp Mainländer's apocalyptic pessimism—forecasting humanity's voluntary extinction through ennui—is cautiously endorsed as a logical terminus for societies estranged from transcendent ideals.

8 Conclusion

Although Helene Druskowitz's influence on twentieth-century thinkers and philosophers remains mainly unrecognised, particularly among American, British, or French scholars specialising in free will, radical feminism, or ecofeminism, her work presents intriguing anticipations of various philosophical movements that merit scholarly examination. While it is improbable that later thinkers of these movements were directly acquainted with Druskowitz's writings, her insights reveal a prophetic quality, positioning her as a significant figure in the intellectual landscape.

Druskowitz's ideas, particularly regarding free will, find resonance in contemporary philosophical discussions of semi-compatibilism. Semi-compatibilism is a nuanced position within the free will debate that seeks to reconcile the concept of moral responsibility with the truth of determinism. Unlike traditional compatibilism, which argues that free will and determinism are compatible, semi-compatibilism focuses specifically on moral responsibility, asserting that it does not depend on an agent's ability to do otherwise (the principle of alternative possibilities). Instead, semi-compatibilists, such as John Martin Fischer, emphasise the importance of reasons-responsiveness and the coherence of an agent's actions with their motivations and values within a deterministic framework. Druskowitz's exploration of moral responsibility within the bounds of causality echoes this perspective. Her writings suggest that individuals can be held accountable for their actions even if those actions are determined by prior causes, as long as they stem from an agent's reflective endorsement or alignment with their values. This alignment between Druskowitz's emphasis on moral accountability under causal constraints and the core tenets of semi-compatibilism underscores her prescience in addressing themes that continue to shape contemporary debates on free will and moral agency.

Druskowitz's critiques of patriarchal structures and her expressions of misandry echo the arguments advanced by radical feminists several decades later. Her insistence on women's potential to lead the creation of a new morality and societal structure underscores a transformative vision that parallels radical feminist calls for societal overhaul. This alignment suggests that Druskowitz's work could provide a valuable historical context for understanding the evolution of feminist thought, particularly in its critique of male dominance and its implications for societal welfare.

Additionally, Druskowitz's condemnation of male-led environmental degradation resonates with the ecofeminist movement that emerged in the late twentieth century. Ecofeminists draw connections between the exploitation of women and the exploitation of nature, arguing that patriarchal structures contribute to ecological crises. Druskowitz's foresight in addressing the destructive tendencies of men towards both women and the environment reflects a nuanced understanding of the interplay between gender and ecological issues, positioning her work as an early precursor to ecofeminist discourse.

In conclusion, while Druskowitz may not have directly influenced subsequent generations of thinkers, her writings offer profound insights that intersect with significant philosophical movements of the twentieth and twenty-first centuries. Her exploration of free will, radical critiques of patriarchy, and recognition of the ecological ramifications of male dominance provide fertile ground for further scholarly exploration, situating her as a pivotal figure whose ideas warrant renewed attention in contemporary discussions of feminism, ethics, and environmental philosophy.

Druskowitz's Bibliography

While several books and dramatic works can be definitively attributed to Druskowitz, some texts and titles are of dubious authorship or have been mistakenly ascribed to her. Moreover, several works mentioned in nineteenth- and early twentieth-century almanacs and lexicons are no longer extant. This can be attributed to several factors. First, Druskowitz herself likely destroyed some of her documents along with her literary works. Second, the few surviving personal letters, scattered across various archives, are often written in an almost indecipherable hand, making it difficult to trace her writings. Additionally, evidence suggests that she concocted various fanciful stories about her background and probably also her literary achievements.[17] Finally, Druskowitz wrote her philosophical and literary critical works, as well as some of her plays (*The Woman Pedagogue*), under her name. However, she published some of her plays under multiple pseudonyms: E. René, Erich René, and Adalbert Brunn. Secondary literature also quotes some other pseudonyms that we were unable to identify (H. Foreign, Erna von Calagis, H. Sakkorausch, H. Sakrosankt).

During her lifetime, several bibliographic compilations of Druskowitz's writings were attempted, yet these lists are neither reliable nor exhaustive. As a result, tracing her complete oeuvre poses considerable challenges. As already mentioned, one notable factor contributing to this difficulty is her use of multiple pseudonyms. Furthermore, Druskowitz probably destroyed a substantial number of her works during her prolonged periods in psychiatric institutions, further complicating efforts to compile an accurate inventory of her writings.

The existing lists of her works encompass those for which authenticity can be confidently established.

Plays

Sultan und Prinz, Verlag der Wallishausser'schen Buchhandlung, Wien, 1881. Published under the pseudonym E. René.

---

17 For instance, she not only changed her surname from Druschkovich to Druskowitz but also adopted the prefix "von," likely to suggest noble lineage. The reasons behind this shift remain speculative. Perhaps she felt a sense of inadequacy within the aristocratic circles she frequented, as she came from a prosperous but non-aristocratic family. Alternatively, it might have been an extension of her philosophy, as articulated in *Pessimistic Cardinal Propositions*, where she described women as the more noble and "aristocratic gender." While the exact moment she began signing her name as "von Druskowitz" is unclear, she indeed continued using this name until her death.

Der Präsident vom Zither-Club, Alwin Arnold, Dresden – Blasewitz, [1884]. Published under the pseudonym Erich René.

Aspasia, Rudolph Petzold, Dresden, 1889. Published under the pseudonym Adalbert Brunn. This play was published under the name *Die Emancipations-Schwärmerin* the following year, along with three other plays.

Die Emancipations-Schwärmerin, Rudolf Petzold, Dresden, 1890. 1–80, 111–112. Published under the name Dr. Phil. Helene Druskowitz (Adalbert Brunn).

Er doziert, Rudolf Petzold, Dresden, 1890. Published in the same volume with *Die Emancipations-Schwärmerin*, 81–90.

Eisamkeit – das einzige Glück, Rudolf Petzold, Dresden, 1890. Published in the same volume with *Die Emancipations-Schwärmerin*, 91–100.

Unerwartet, Rudolf Petzold, Dresden, 1890. Published in the same volume with *Die Emancipations-Schwärmerin*, 101–110.

Die Pädagogin, Metzger & Wittig, Leipzig, 1890.

International, Metzger & Wittig, Leipzig, 1890.

Literary Criticism

Percy Bysshe Shelley, Robert Oppenheim, Berlin, 1884.
Drei englische Dichterinnen, Robert Oppenheim, Berlin, 1885.

Philosophical Texts

Über Lord Byrons "Don Juan", Zürcher u. Furrer, Zürich, 1879.
Moderne Versuche eines Religionsersatzes, George Weiß, Heidelberg, 1886.
Wie ist Verantwortung und Zurechnung ohne Annahme der Willensfreiheit möglich?, Georg Weiß, Heidelberg, 1887.
Zur neuen Lehre, Georg Weiß, Heidelberg, 1888.
Eugen Dühring. Eine Studie zu seiner Würdigung, Georg Weiß, Heidelberg, 1889.
Zur Begründung einer überreligiösen Weltanschauung (this is a reprint of the *Zur neuen Lehre*), Georg Weiß, Heidelberg, 1889.
["Maximen für Frauen," published in *Neue Deutsche Dichterstimmen* in 1904, refered to by an anonymous reviewer in "Unser Hausfreund" in the newspaper *Hannoverschen Courier* 689 of 28 February 1904, 5508.]
Pessimistische Kardinalsätze. Ein Vademecum für die freiesten Geister, Herrosé Ziemsen, Wittenberg, [most likely 1905.]

Newspaper Texts, Poems, Manuscripts

"In wiefern ist Plato von seinen Vorgängern bestimmt?", *Staatsarchiv Zürich*, sign. U 109 e 1. 1878. Klausurarbeit, 20 handwritten pages.
"Louise von François", *Neue Illustrirte Zeitung* 22/I, 26 Februar 1882, 346.
"Conrad Ferdinand Meyer", *Neue Illustrirte Zeitung* 47/II, 20 August 1882, 739.

"Neulicht. Praedikte. Neue Augabe." In: Briefe und Schreibmaschinmanuskript an Marie von Ebner-Eschenbach aus der Zeit vom 07.09.1882 bis 08.09.1914. *Nachlass Marie von Ebner-Eschenbach*, Bibliothek I.N. 61140/6, ID-Nr. AC15956267, 4 handwritten pages without folio numbers, possibly 1882.

"Shakespeare's Vorläufer in Indien und andere indische Dramatiker", *Dramaturgische Blätter und Bühnen-Rundschau*, XVII/49, 9 December 1888, 638–639, and XVII/50, 16 December 1888, 651–652.

"Ein neuer Philosoph für das Volk (William Macintire Salter)", *Deutschland* 2, 12 October 1889, 27.

"Lenzstimmung", *Zeitgenosse* 1, 1890/91, 251.

"An Therese Malten als 'Armide'", *Deutsches Dichterheim* I/2, ed. Paul Heinze, 1891, 27. A poem.

"Welch' ein Schrei!", a poem dedicated to Therese Malten, composed probably around 1891. Our copy is from the newspaper *Hannoverscher Courier*, 15 June 1898, page 2.

"Letzer Wille". 1907. *Krankenakte*. Niederösterreichisches Landesarchiv in St. Pölten, sign. HPA MÖ, AZ: 8340 Druskowitz, four handwritten pages, no folio numbers.

"Philosophischer Rundfragebogen". *Krankenakte*. Niederösterreichisches Landesarchiv in St. Pölten, sign. HPA MÖ, AZ: 8340 Druskowitz, one typewritte page, no folio numbers.

"Erklärung". *Krankenakte*. Niederösterreichisches Landesarchiv in St. Pölten, sign. HPA MÖ, AZ: 8340 Druskowitz, 3 handwritten pages, no folio numbers.

"Flüsternde Wände!". *Krankenakte*. Niederösterreichisches Landesarchiv in St. Pölten, sign. HPA MÖ, AZ: 8340 Druskowitz, 11 handwritten pages, 28r–33v.

Spuria

Contemporary lexica and almanacs—such as those compiled by Kürschner, Degener, and Brümmer—list several additional works attributed to Druskowitz that we have been unable to locate. It is possible that some of these texts were published in various Austrian and German newspapers or literary journals.

Furthermore, various secondary sources reference her founding of two women's journals, *Der Heilige Kampf* and *Der Fehderuf*, yet we have not been able to locate any extant issues. It is plausible that Druskowitz proposed the publication of these journals to several publishers but that these efforts ultimately did not come to fruition, as indicated by some letters in *Krankenakte*.

The following texts are attributed to Druskowitz, none of which we were able to locate:

An essay on Giacomo Leopardi, 1881 (Ebner-Eschenbach 1993, 118)
A play *Svante Sture*, 1881 (Ebner-Eschenbach 1993, 158)
Die Grundlagen des ästhetischen Urteils, 1886.
Über die ästhetische Erzieung, 1886 (Ebner-Eschenbach 1993, 604)
Die Unhaltbarkeit des Utilitarismus, 1888.
Die Studentinnen, 1889.
Léonie. Dramolet. 1890 or 1891.
Neue tragische Themen, 1899.
Blanca, 1899.
Die Wege des Todes, 1899.
Rätsel, 1899.
Meine Erfahrungen in der Deuteroskopie und Telepathie, 1899.

An essay on Therese Malten (Ebner-Eschenbach 1995, 38)
Der freie Transszendentalismus oder die Überwelt ohne Gott (Das Übergöttliche), 1900.
Der Kultus der Frau, 1900.
Das Männerproletariat oder die Fällung des Mannes als Tier und Denker, 1900.
Teilung der Städte nach den Geschlechtern (Überwindung des Weltpessimismus), 1901.
Die Frau und der Tod, 1902.
Gegensätze im Sein, 1902.
Ethischer Pessimismus, 1903.

Bibliography

Boršić, Luka. 2018. "Helene Druskowitz i Friedrich Nietzsche". *Prilozi za istraživanje hrvatske filozofske baštine* 44/2, 395–426.

Boršić, Luka, Skuhala Karasman, Ivana. 2020. "Meet Helene Druskowitz". *Prolegomena* 19/2, 177–195.

Brown, Malcolm. 1987. "Friedrich Nietzsche und sein Verleger Ernst Schmeitzner. Eine Darstellung ihrer Beziehung". *Archiv für Geschichte des Buchwesens* 28, 215–291.

Brümmer, Franz, ed. 1913. *Lexikon der deutschen Dichter und Prosaisten vom Beginn des 19. Jahrhunderts bis zur Gegenwart.* Leipzig: Reclam.

Buckingham, Susan. 2015. "Ecofeminism". *International Encyclopedia of the Social & Behavioral Sciences*, 2nd ed., vol. 6. http://dx.doi.org/10.1016/B978-0-08-097086-8.91020-1, 845–850.

Chambers, Helen. 2011. "Reading and responding to English Women Writers: Annette von Droste-Hülsoff, Marie von Ebner-Eschenbach and Helene Druskowitz." *Women's Writing* 18.1, 86–102.

Colvin, Sarah. 2003. *Women in German Drama: Playwrights and Their Texts, 1860–1945.* New York: Camden House.

d'Eaubonne, Françoise. 1974. *Le feminism ou la mort.* Paris: P. Ouray.

Dahme, Lena F. 1936. *Women in the Life and Art of Conrad Ferdinand Meyer.* New York: Columbia University Press.

Degener, Herrmann A. L., ed. 1905. *Wer ist's? Zeitgenossenlexikon enthaltend Biographien nebst Bibliographien.* Berlin, Leipzig: Degener.

Druskowitz, Helene 1884a. "Brief an Conrad Ferdinand Meyer". In: *Conrad Ferdinand Meyer Nachlass*, Zentralbibliothek Zürich, MS CFM 331.7.

Druskowitz, Helene 1884b. "Brief an Conrad Ferdinand Meyer". In: *Conrad Ferdinand Meyer Nachlass*, Zentralbibliothek Zürich, MS CFM 331.8.

Druskowitz, Helene 1981. "Brief an Nietzsche". In *Nietzsche Briefwechsel. Kritische Gesamtausgabe. Briefe an Nietzsche. Briefwechsel. Dritte Abteilung. Zweiter Band.* Hrsg. Giorgio Colli und Mazzino Montinari, unter Mitarbeit von Helga Anania-Hess. Berlin, New York: Walter de Gruyter.

Ebner-Eschenbach, Marie. 1993. *Kritische Texte und Deutungen – Tagebücher III.* Edited by K. K. Polheim and N. Gabriel, Tübingen: Max Niemeyer Verlag.

Ebner-Eschenbach, Marie. 1995. *Kritische Texte und Deutungen – Tagebücher IV.* Edited by K. K. Polheim and N. Gabriel, Tübingen: Max Niemeyer Verlag.

Ebner-Eschenbach, Marie. 1996. *Kritische Texte und Deutungen – Tagebücher V.* Edited by K. K. Polheim and N. Gabriel, Tübingen: Max Niemeyer Verlag.

eKGWB/BVN = Friedrich Nietzsche. Digitale Kritische Gesamtausgabe. Werke und Briefe [Friedrich Nietzsche, Digital critical edition of the complete works and letters, based on the critical text by G. Colli and M. Montinari, Berlin/New York, de Gruyter 1967–, edited by Paolo D'Iorio], supported by Nietzsche Source, www.nietzschesource.org, 2009–.

von François, Louise and Meyer, Conrad Ferdinand. 1920. Ein Briefwechsel. Edited by A. Bettelheim. Berlin, Leipzig: Vereinigung wissenschaftlicher Verleger Walter de Grünter.

Gronwold, Hinrike. 1992. Helene Druskowitz 1856–1918 – "Die geistige Amazone". *WahnsinssFrauen*. Edited by Sibylle Duda and Luise F. Pusch, Frankfurt am Main: Suhrkamp, 96–122.

Janz, Curt Paul. 1978. *Friedrich Nietzsche, Band 2: Die zehn Jahre des freien Philosophen*. München: Hanser.

Kohut, Adolf. 1889. "Zwei Fräuleins Doctor". *Im Boudoir – Beiblatt der "Wiener Mode"*, II/17, 21–22.

Kraepelin, Emil. 1883. *Compendium der Psychiatrie*. Leipzig: Verlag von Ambr. Abel.

Kürschner, Joseph, ed. 1887, 1889, 1891, 1900, 1901. *Deutscher Litteratur-Kalender*. Leipzig: Göschen.

Merz, Claudia. 2011. Das satirische Schreiben von Helene Druskowitz als Spiegel der Bildungssituation am Ende des 19. Jahrhunderts. Universität Wien: Diplomaarbeit. Available at: https://services.phaidra.univie.ac.at/api/object/o:1277366/preview

Meyer, Conrad Ferdinand. 1884. Rezension von: Helene Druskowitz: Percy Bysshe Shelley, *Magazin für die Literatur des In- und Auslandes*. (Also in: Meyer, Conrad Ferdinand. 1985. *Sämtliche Werke*, vol. 15: Clara. Entwürfe zu Erzählungen. Kleine Schriften. Edited by H. Zeller and A. Zäch. Bern: Benteli-Verlag, 270–273).

Montinari, Mazzino. 2014. "Nietzsche – Hillebrand". In: *Studia Nietzscheana*, http://www.nietzschesource.org/SN/montinari-2014.

Nachbaur, Petra. 1999. "Der Wahnwitz des ‚Frl. Dr.' Helene Druskowitz, Emanzipations-Satirikerin der Jahrhundertwende". In: *Satire – Parodie –Pamphlet – Caricature en Autriche à l'époque de François-Joseph (1848–1914)*. Edited by Gilbert Ravy and Jeanne Benay. Rouen: Publications de l'Université de Rouen, 173–194.

Nietzsche, Friedrich. 2000. *Franz und Ida Overbeck Briefwechsel*. Stuttgart, Weimar: Metzler.

Nietzsche, Friedrich. 2006. *Thus Spoke Zarathustra*. Translated by Adrian del Caro and edited by Robert Pippin. Cambridge: Cambridge University Press.

Rehm, Hermann. 1901. "Frauenstudium." Vortrag gehalten auf dem II. bayerischen Frauentag zu Nürnberg am 12. April. Ansbach: Druck und Verlag von C. Brügel & Sohn.

von Salis-Marschlins, Meta. 1897. *Philosoph und Edelmensch. Ein Beitrag zur Charakteristik Friedrich Nietzsche's*. Leipzig: C. G. Naumann.

Schwartz, Agatha. 2005. "Austrian Fin-de-Siècle Gender Heteroglossia: The Dialogism of Misogyny, Feminism, and Viriphobia. *German Studies Review* 28/2, 347–366.

Schwartz, Agatha. 2008. *Shifting Voices. Feminist Thought and Women's Writing in* Fin-de-siècle *Austria and Hungary*. Montreal & Kingston, London, Ithaca: McGill-Queen's University Press.

Translators' Notes

For the transcription of the original texts, we relied on the original published editions of Druskowitz's works. To the best of our knowledge, no drafts of her manuscripts have survived. Even if any of her handwritten drafts were extant, they would likely be of limited utility due to the near illegibility of her handwriting. While she occasionally utilised a typewriter, only two or three such documents have been preserved, none of which pertain to the works under consideration.

In transcribing the German texts, we adhered to modern German orthographical conventions. However, we refrained from altering Druskowitz's style, regardless of how antiquated it may occasionally appear today (e. g., the use of the "e-Dativ"). Obvious typographical errors were silently corrected. For other editorial interventions, square brackets were employed, while braces indicate the pagination of the original editions.

The translation posed distinct challenges. Druskowitz was not a professional academic philosopher and did not identify as such; she regarded herself primarily as a philosopher-artist—one might add, with redemptive aspirations and (anti-)utopian ideals. This is reflected in her language and style, which are neither terminologically consistent nor strictly academic in nature. For instance, her citations are sometimes unreferenced or inaccurately attributed and paginated. Besides German, she employed French, with occasional Latin and, in one instance, an Ancient Greek phrase. Nevertheless, she favoured German translations of non-German philosophers despite her fluency in multiple languages, including English.

We approached Druskowitz's citations of other philosophers in the following ways.
a. Whenever feasible, original English texts were identified if Druskowitz referenced English or American philosophers (e. g., Mill, Salter, Thoreau) and their texts were quoted. We prioritised editions contemporary to Druskowitz, particularly those that may have informed the German translations she used.
b. For non-German philosophical works, we used contemporary English translations (e. g., Auguste Comte's *System of Positive Polity or Treatise on Sociology*, published in 1851). However, since nineteenth-century translations often paraphrase rather than faithfully translate, significant divergences were noted.
c. For German philosophers and poets (e. g., Kant, Nietzsche, Schopenhauer, Goethe), we used modern English translations that closely adhere to the originals.

d. In rare cases where Druskowitz likely translated passages herself without acknowledgement, we either retained the original English text (59, Spencer) or provided detailed explanations (53, *Bhagavad Gita*).
e. We translated other sources, particularly French ones, for which we were unable to find existing English translations. We marked these translations as our own.

Regarding terminological issues, the following solutions are noteworthy.
a. For the term *Mensch*, we used "human(s)" (with necessary grammatical changes in the sentence), "human being", and "individual", avoiding the older practice of translating it as "man" since the gender differentiation is of crucial importance in Druskowitz's philosophy.
b. The term *Zurechnung* and related verbs posed a challenge. The noun can be translated as "imputation," emphasising the ascription of moral or legal responsibility for an action; "attribution," which focuses on assigning causality or responsibility and is often used in a broader, less formal sense; or "accountability," relating to holding someone responsible for their actions, typically tied to the capacity for free and rational decision-making. We opted for "attribution" as the broadest term, encompassing the notion of causally attributing responsibility for an action and related concepts.
c. *Übersphere* is "Over-sphere", *Geist* is "spirit" or "mind", depending on the context.
d. We render some crucial epistemological terms as follows: *Erkenntnis* (and cognates) as "cognition" or, if not used in the Kantian sense, as "recognition", "knowledge"; *Verstand* as "understanding" or "intellect", *Vernunft* as "reason", *Gemüt* as "mind".
e. To properly render Druskowitz's term *Geschlecht* and its cognates, we have instituted a terminological distinction between "gender" and "sex." This interpretive choice is indispensable for a nuanced understanding of her final work, *Pessimistic Cardinal Propositions*, in which the problematic of gender emerges as a central philosophical theme. Our framework, however, should not be confused with a Beauvoirian one. For us, "gender" denotes the categorical distinction between men and women, a reality that Druskowitz understands as transcending mere biological determination. In contrast, "sex" is employed in a more restricted sense, referring specifically to anatomical organs, physical constitution, or bodily activity.
f. A deliberate orthographic distinction has been established throughout this translation between "god" and "God." This choice is intended to reflect the tenor of Druskowitz's philosophy. Her pungent atheism and philosophical contempt for divinity in the abstract are conveyed by the lowercase "god."

The capitalized "God," by contrast, is reserved for those instances where she engages with a specific theological entity, principally the God of Christian doctrine. However, this distinction is not always clear.

g. The prose of Helene von Druskowitz is characterized by a stylistic idiosyncrasy wherein she eschews both a consistent technical terminology and a fixed philosophical lexicon. This stylistic feature is often compounded by labyrinthine sentence structures that demand careful interpretive labour to reveal their precise meaning. Given these challenges, our guiding principle has been to preserve semantic integrity rather than to maintain literal equivalence. Therefore, where her syntax proved convoluted, we did not hesitate to restructure a single sentence into several more lucid statements, believing this to be the most faithful method for conveying her original thought.

How Is Responsibility and Attribution Possible Without the Assumption of Free Will? An Investigation by Dr H. Druskowitz

1

{1} The following points of view must be distinguished regarding responsibility and attribution:
1) responsibility and attribution are upheld based on the assumption of natural free will;
2) natural freedom is denied, and responsibility and attribution are based on the assumption of transcendental freedom;
3) natural and transcendental freedom is denied, and thus also the existence of responsibility and the justification of attribution;
4) the existence of responsibility and the justification of attribution are upheld, even though both natural and transcendental freedom are denied (or the assumption of the latter is regarded as meaningless for the judgement of empirical humans, as we do). An explanation of responsibility and attribution is sought in another direction—it remains to be seen in which.

We take this last standpoint. The same has already been asserted by Ludwig Feuerbach, for example, however without being able to come to terms with his justification of responsibility {2} and attribution, to which we shall return during our presentation.

However, before we criticise Feuerbach's attempt and then present our view, we want to demonstrate the untenability of the first three viewpoints listed above.

Firstly, the illusion of natural free will.

The doctrine of free will, or free personality, was already a component of Buddhism and even Brahmanism in the Orient.

So it says in the *Bhagavad Gita*, the Brahma theodicy:

> The Lord of the world does not create the state of action, nor even deeds
> Nor striving, nor fruit of works. *The individual will prevail,*
> *The Lord gives no one his sins and his good deeds.*[1]

---

[1] [Druskowitz indicates this as verse 14 of the *Bhagavad Gita*. It probably refers to Part 14 of the Fifth Discourse. The German translation is probably Druskowitz's own. However, more critical

According to both Brahmanic and Buddhist views, humans are considered the free authors of their deeds, and their future fate is determined by their will, which is regarded as free.

In the Occident, the doctrine of free will was first established by Christian theology and a pseudo-philosophy based on Christian theological views, and the problem was characterised particularly sharply by the technical expression: *liberum arbitrium indifferentiae*. Luther, therefore, called this doctrine a "theological figment of the imagination" in opposition to Erasmus. It is clear {3} enough what was meant by it. On the one hand, it was intended to prove that the Creator of the world was not involved in the existence of evil and that this was only the fault of humans; on the other hand, however, it was believed that through it, humans could be more sharply distinguished from animals and characterised as godlike beings.

The Greeks and Romans had little concern with the question of whether the will was free or not and were far from having arrived at the widespread view of the subject that has been achieved by Christian theology.

However, Christian theology would have been just as unable to assert that human will is free as Indian theology and philosophy could, had it not been for the points of reference for free will found in the common human consciousness. Nevertheless, theology and philosophy have presented a delusion as a general law, a delusion to which ordinary human consciousness succumbs in some instances, under certain circumstances.

According to Kant, freedom of the will means the faculty to initiate a series of changes "spontaneously [from one's self]". Schopenhauer, in his excellent and beautiful treatise on the freedom of the will, says: "A free will, then, would be of a kind that was not determined by grounds, and—since everything that determines another must be a ground, and in the case of real things a real ground, i.e. a cause—it would be of a kind that was determined by nothing at all; {4} its particular manifestations (acts of will) would thus have to come forth simply and originally out of itself, without being brought about necessarily by preceding condi-

---

translations of the *Bhagavad Gita* have different translations. E.g. Richard Garbe's standard German edition from 1905 reads *ad loc.:*

14. Nicht die Tätigkeit, nicht die Werke der Welt bringt der Herr [d.h. der Geist] hervor, [auch] nicht den Zusammenhand zwischen den Werken und ihren Früchten; sondern [nur] die Natur wirkt. (94)

Similarly, in Sivananda's translation, part 14 reads:

Neither agency nor actions do the Lord create for the world, nor union with the fruits of actions. But it is Nature that acts. (2003, 112)

Both translations diverge significantly from the one by Druskowitz.]

tions, that is, without being determined by anything at all in accordance with a rule" (Schopenhauer 2009, 36). Paul Rée has a very precise description in his work *The Illusion of Free Will, Its Causes and its Consequences* (1885)—a treatise whose results are indeed nothing new, but which is a masterpiece in terms of clarity and conciseness of presentation—by saying that the will is free means that every act of will is an "absolute beginning", or "every act of will is an initial link and not an intermediate link, [and] is not the effect of preceding causes" (Rée 1885, 24).

However, none of the offered definitions of the concept of free will says what it means when understood as an inner perception. As such, however, it signifies the sovereign actuation, the direct revelation of the ego. We shall see later how the ego arrives at the assumption that it sets itself in the act of will without causal determination.

However, one indeed finds oneself at a loss when considering this independence of acts of will from preceding causes because the law of causality constitutes the essential form of our cognition, and all phenomena, whether of a physical or psychological nature, are subject to it.

Thus, Kant says: "The law of nature that everything that {5} happens has a cause, that since the causality of this cause, i.e., the *action*, precedes in time and in respect of an effect that has *arisen* cannot have always been but must have *happened*, and so must also have had its cause among appearances, through which it is determined, and consequently that all occurrences are empirically determined in a natural order—this law, through which alone appearances can first constitute one *nature* and furnish objects of one experience, is a law of the understanding, from which under no pretext can any departure be allowed or any appearance be exempted; because otherwise one would put this appearance outside of all possible experience, thereby distinguishing it from all objects of possible experience and making it into a mere thought-entity and a figment of the brain" (Kant 1998, 538). And: "Every action, as appearance, insofar as it produces an occurrence, is itself an occurrence, or event, which presupposes another state in which its cause is found; and thus everything that happens is only a continuation of the series, and no beginning that would take place from itself is possible in it. Thus, in the temporal succession, all actions of natural causes are themselves, in turn, effects, which likewise presuppose their causes in the time series. An *original* action, through which something happens that previously was not, is not to be expected from the causal connection of appearances" (Kant 1998, 539).

Just as every physical, chemical or biological process, so every thought, every wish, every action, be it the most significant or the most insignificant, is causally determined, the necessary product of the given inner and outer factors, and only specific thoughts, wishes and actions can appear under {6} given inner and outer circumstances. Indeed, as has often been shown, it may well be said that the most insignificant external and internal process was founded in the original position of the atoms and that the entire world process would have had to proceed somewhat differently had any actual process, which may be thought of as maximally insignificant, not occurred. Furthermore, just as the individual actions, so also the characteristics from which the actions spring are necessarily conditioned and determined, a truth which Goethe has expressed very beautifully in verse:

> As on the day you were granted to the world,
> The sun stood to greet the planets,
> You likewise began to thrive, forth and forth,
> Following the law that governed your accession.
> You must be so, you cannot flee yourself,
> Thus sibyls long ago pronounced, thus prophets,
> And neither time nor any power can dismember
> Characteristic form, living, self-developing. (Wetters 2014, 201)

Even if philosophers had long recognised the lack of freedom of the will, Schopenhauer deserves credit for having definitively established this truth for all thinkers.[2]

{7} The view that the will is free, or that the ego manifests itself sovereignly, is expressed in two formulae, one of which is: "I can do what I will," and the other:

---

[2] Among modern poets, no one has grasped the concept of necessity so energetically as the English poet Shelley in his youthful poem "Queen Mab". Here it is said of the spirit of the world that it determines according to "irresistible law":
"The place each spring of its machine shall fill;
So that, when waves on waves tumultuous heap
Confusion to the clouds, and fiercely driven
Heaven's lightnings scorch the uprooted ocean-fords -
Whilst, to the eye of shipwrecked mariner,
Lone, sitting on the bare and shuddering rock,
All seems unlinked contingency and chance –
No atom of this turbulence fulfils
A vague and unnecessitated task
Or acts but as it must and ought to act.
Even the minutest molecule of light,
That in an April sunbeam's fleeting glow
Fulfils its destined though invisible work,
The universal Spirit guides […]."
   And later:
"Spirit of Nature! all-sufficing Power,
Necessity! thou mother of the world!"

"I could have acted differently than I actually did." They express that an act was done without compelling reasons out of the free self-determination of the agent. The latter formula follows from the former, although it is not originally contained in it.

Schopenhauer rightly points out that in the formula "I can do what I will," proclaimed by self-consciousness, there is still no determination about the willing itself. "Anyone's *self-consciousness* proclaims very clearly that he can do what {8} he wills. Since even entirely opposed actions can be thought of as *willed* by him, it follows to be sure that he can also do opposed things *if he will.* The unrefined understanding, however, confuses this with his ability to oppose things in a given case and calls this *freedom of the will.* Except that his being able to *will* opposed things in a given case is by no means contained in the above pronouncement, but rather merely that, out of two opposed actions, if he *wills this one*, he can do it, and if he *wills that one*, he can do it too: but whether he *could will* the one as much as the other in the given case remains unresolved by this and is the object of a deeper investigation than can be decided through mere self-consciousness" (Schopenhauer 2009, 47). Schopenhauer also rightly emphasises that it is difficult to make it at all clear to the philosophically crude person what the problem of free will is actually about and that, when he finally begins to understand, he falls into uncertainty and confusion and "will prefer to take refuge from it once more behind his theme 'I can do what I will' and fortify himself there against all grounds and all reasoning" (Schopenhauer 2009, 48).

This misinterpretation of the formula "I can do what I want" could not occur if cause and effect were not often so far apart in human behaviour. In the case of animals, where the connection between cause and effect is apparent in most cases, no one thinks of freedom of will, whereas in humans, "the cause and its effect {9} diverge from one another more and more, separate from one another more clearly and become more heterogeneous, with the cause becoming less and less material and palpable, so that less and less seems to lie in the cause and more and more in the effect. Because of all of this put together, the connection between cause and effect loses in immediate graspability and intelligibility" (Schopenhauer 2009, 48).

P. Rée seems to hold the view that it was reserved for him to show why the will appears to be free. The first sentence of his treatise reads: "That the human will is not free has been demonstrated by philosophers. But whence then does it appear to be free?" (Rée 1885, 1). From these words, however, it is clear that Rée, even if he considers the lack of freedom of the will itself to be proven, nevertheless regards it as his responsibility to investigate the causes of the illusion of free will. However, instead of offering something new, Rée presents far less than what a philosopher, namely Schopenhauer, had already taught long before him in that excellent treatise—though Rée does not even mention it—even though, as we shall soon show, Schopenhauer does not fully satisfy on this point.

Schopenhauer emphasises, as we have seen, the deception that arises from the possibility of different kinds of action, which is then confused with the freedom of the will; as a second point, he then emphasises that the causes of actions often remain hidden because of their immaterial nature, {10} which gives rise to the erroneous opinion that there are no causes. On p. 62, he then says: "This error is supported quite specifically by the false interpretation of the pronouncement of self-consciousness 'I can do what I will' that we examined at length in the first chapter, especially if it is heard when, as always, various motives are exerting an influence and are merely soliciting and excluding one another for the time being. So this taken together is the source of that natural illusion out of which grows the error that in our self-consciousness there is the certainty of a freedom of our will [...]" (Schopenhauer 2009, 62).

While Schopenhauer thus identifies 1) the deception produced by the formula "I can do what I will" and 2) the error that actions could exist without causes as sources of the illusion of free will—albeit without correctly linking these moments and, above all, without investigating the actual cause of that incorrect interpretation of the statement of self-consciousness: "I can do what I will"—Rée only focuses on the second aspect and concludes: "Our willing (of any action) is always causally determined, but it seems free (from causes); it seems to be an absolute beginning. *Where does this appearance come from? We do not perceive the causes by which our volition is conditioned,* and therefore we think that it is not causally {11} conditioned at all" (Rée 1885, 17 [our translation]). Suppose even Schopenhauer, in explaining the illusion in question (without uncovering its deepest cause), did not sufficiently distinguish between *causa* and *condicio*. In that case, Rée entirely conflates the *condicio* with the *causa*. The fact that we do not perceive the causes of actions can only be the *condicio* of our deception about the nature of the origin of our willingness, while the *causa* of this deception, even if not its deepest, is that false interpretation of the statement of self-consciousness: "I can do what I will." Through understanding the reasons for an action, a person is indeed led to consider the action as necessary. In contrast, a lack of insight into the reasons for an action can only be a condition, not the determining ground, for why one believes they could have acted differently. Even the explanation that Schopenhauer gives of the illusion of freedom of will, as we have already remarked, cannot suffice, for Schopenhauer not only fails to connect the two moments he emphasises correctly, but he also leaves unexplained how humans arrive at the false interpretation of the statement of self-consciousness: "I can do what I will," how they arrive at the assumption that they exercise free self-determination, or in other words, that the ego sets itself sovereignly, in free activity.

Herbert Spencer has attempted to explain this, although his explanation does not seem to be correct to us.

{12} Herbert Spencer, in his *Principles of Psychology*, says: (I p. 523)[3] "Considered as an internal perception, the illusion [of free will, Druskowitz's addition] results from supposing that at each moment the *ego*, present as such in consciousness (I exclude the implied, but unknown, substratum which can never be present), is something more than the aggregate of feelings and ideas which then exists. When, after a certain composite amount of emotion and thought has arisen in humans, they act, they commonly assert that *they* are determined to act, and by speaking as though there was a mental self *present to their consciousness*, yet not included in this composite amount of emotion and thought, they are led into the error of supposing that it was not this composite amount of emotion and thought which determined the action. While it is true that they determined the action, it is also true that the aggregate of their feelings and ideas determined it since, during its existence, this aggregate constituted their entire consciousness —that is, constituted their mental self. — Either the *ego*, which is supposed to determine or will the action, is present in consciousness, or it is not. If it is not present in consciousness, it is something of which we are unconscious—something, therefore, of whose existence we neither have nor can have any evidence. If it is present in {13} consciousness, then, as it is ever present, it can be at each moment nothing else than the total consciousness, simple or compound, passing at that moment. It follows, inevitably, that when an impression received from without makes nascent certain appropriate motor changes, and various of the feelings and ideas which must accompany and succeed them, and when, under the stimulus of this composite psychical state, the nascent motor changes pass in actual motor changes; this composite psychical state which excites the action, is at the same time the *ego* which is said to will the action. Naturally enough, then, subjects of such psychical changes say that they will an action; since psychically considered, they are at that moment nothing more than the composite state of consciousness by which the action is excited. Therefore, to say that the performance of the action is the result of free will is to say that the subjects determine the coherences of the psychical states which arouse the action. As these psychological states constitute the subjects at that moment, this means nothing else than that these psychological states determine their coherences, which is absurd. Experi-

---

3 [We could not find a German translation of Spencer's *Principles of Psychology*, which means that Druskowitz most likely translated the portion of the text herself, as she otherwise indicated the translators when using existing translations. This passage is based on the third edition of Spencer's *Principles of Psychology* (1886). The pagination given by Druskowitz is wrong: the text is to be found on pp. 500–502.]

ences have determined their coherences—the greater part of them, constituting what we call natural character {14} of humans, by the experiences of antecedent organisms, and the rest by their own experiences. The changes which at each moment take place in their consciousness, and among others those which they are said to will, are produced by this infinitude of previous experiences registered in his nervous structure, cooperating with the immediate impressions on his senses; the effects of these combined factors being in every case qualified by the physical state, general or local, of his organism." —

One can only agree with the last sentences of this passage. However, we consider erroneous the assertion that the ego is equivalent to the respective aggregate of feelings and representations of which the individual becomes conscious, as well as Spencer's explanation of the illusion of self-determination. How unjustified the identification of consciousness with the ego itself is, an identification recently made again by Th. Ribot in his book *Les maladies de la personnalité* arrives at this conclusion through the simple consideration that that which has consciousness cannot itself be consciousness. Without wishing to enter into the complex problem of the essence of the ego, we can nevertheless assert this much: that the ego is the unified bearer of all the states of consciousness of which an individual is capable and that the respective state of consciousness always forms only an insignificant partial section of the great domain of the ego, which remains unconscious except for {15} that section. Suppose the ego is the bearer of the states of consciousness. In that case, its states are entirely subject to the law of causality, and it is not in the power of the ego, which is only the bearer of the states, to determine the content of consciousness at any given time. Since the feeling of the ego accompanies all states of consciousness and since the ego feels all states as its own states, the illusion of the sovereignty of the ego arises, according to which a human thinks that the ego determines the content of consciousness by itself, that it determines the acts of will that come to consciousness, or that these are nothing other than a sovereign revelation of the ego.

Thus, the process and the relation of the moments which lead to the illusion of natural freedom of the will are as follows: the ego, feeling all states of consciousness as its own states, as partial expressions of its domain, believes that it sovereignly determines them, whereas it is only their bearer. This, however, leads to the misinterpretation of the formula "I can do what I will," but this confusion only occurs on the condition that the motives of the will do not emerge clearly and intensely enough. We shall soon return to the latter point.

2

{16} It is peculiar that Kant did not recognise the illusion to which people succumb regarding the will—at least in many cases, though, as we believe, not always—but instead held the view that people perceive the *necessity of actions yet still attribute [responsibility] for them.*

Thus, he says: "[O]ne may take a voluntary action, e.g. a malicious lie, through which a person has brought about a certain confusion in society; and one may first investigate its moving causes, through which it arose, judging on that basis how the lie and its consequences could be imputed to the person. With this first intent one goes into the sources of the person's empirical character, seeking them in a bad upbringing, bad company, and also finding them in the wickedness of a natural temper insensitive to shame, partly in carelessness and thoughtlessness; in so doing one does not leave out of account {17} the occasioning causes. In all this one proceeds as with any investigation in the series of determining causes for a given natural effect. Now even if one believes the action to be determined by these causes, one nonetheless blames the agent, and not on account of his unhappy natural temper, not on account of the circumstances influencing him, not even on account of the life he has led previously; for one presupposes that it can be entirely set aside how that life was constituted, and that the series of conditions that transpired might not have been, but rather that this deed could be regarded as entirely unconditioned in regard to the previous state, as though with that act the agent had started a series of consequences entirely from himself. [...] [n]ow, in the moment when he lies, it is entirely his fault" (Kant 1998, 544). And elsewhere: "[H]e [a human being] *explains* his misconduct by certain bad habits, which by gradual neglect of attention he has allowed to grow in him to such a degree that he can regard his misconduct as their *natural* consequence, yet this cannot protect him from the reproach and censure he casts upon himself" (Kant 2015, 80).

Paul Rée agrees with Kant that people explain actions but still attribute [responsibility] for them, but wants to distinguish between "explaining an action" and "regarding it as an effect". Human beings do the former but not the latter. For if they did, they would cease to attribute [responsibility] for actions, since according to Rée, regarding an action as an effect and attributing responsibility for it are mutually exclusive, and no one who understands the causal conditionality of an action {18} still attributes it to another as guilt or merit. "They see the motives but not the cause," says Rée. It should be noted here that Rée differentiates the concepts of "motive" and "cause" quite arbitrarily. The cause is only the more general concept, which, however, does not include the thought of necessity to a more intensive degree than motive. Motive, however, is a mental cause.

Kant is certainly wrong when he attributes the cognition of the necessity of actions to people in general. People often "explain" actions to themselves without recognising them as causally determined. However, it is equally erroneous to maintain that people as a whole, except for a few philosophers, never understand actions as necessary and always fall prey to the illusion that instead of an action actually committed, another, indeed a diametrically opposed one, can always be performed. This is what, for example, Rée, maintains.

He seeks to substantiate this assertion by showing how, in his opinion, people would judge a morally indifferent act: "Someone comes running by in furious haste. 'Why is that man running so?' people ask. They learn that he is running towards the railway station, where a train is just about to leave. Now they have explained the running. However, have they realised the causal conditionality of it? By no means, as can easily be demonstrated, ask them about it. People will reply: 'The {19} man runs because the intention of not missing the train has influenced his will. He could have willed and acted differently; at the moment when he began to run, he could have taken a carriage instead or given up on using the train and turned back.' In other words, they inquire about the motives of the action, i.e. they explain it to themselves. They do not see that the motives, together with the other thoughts, sensations, and impressions, made walking a necessary result at that moment; that things should have been arranged somewhat differently from eternity if he had taken a carriage instead of walking" (Rée 1885, 46–47 [our translation]).

Granted that they are unable to grasp these thoughts, the words that Rée puts into the mouths of the observers of the running man will, in any case, only be uttered by the most unintelligent and unimaginative among them. Only a thoughtless and completely unimaginative person will consider it possible that someone who is running with "furious haste" towards a specific goal could just as well renounce the same and turn back, and even the thought that the man could have taken a carriage when he began to run will only occur to the more unthinking among the spectators. For the more prudent humans are, the nearer they approach the point of regarding the given things as necessary, though they are still far from giving a philosophical expression to their views. Conversely, the more short-sighted and superficial humans are, {20} the more inclined they are to suppose that things might have turned out differently from what they did, that things might have been done differently from what was actually done.

Nevertheless, some situations have so compelling a character that even the superficial judge perceives what must necessarily arise from them, and the cause of many an action stands out so markedly that no one doubts that it could have produced only the effect which it actually produced and no other.

The awareness of the necessity of certain decisions and actions is already expressed in the use of language, for example, in expressions such as "to feel urged or driven," "to be morally compelled," and so on. We acknowledge that those who use these terms are often unable to grasp their meaning fully, but by using them, they demonstrate that they are at least on the right track in judging actions from the best or most possible perspective. Who, even with a modest power of judgement, will think it possible that someone could just as well have refrained from an act which they committed in the highest affect? In such a case, everyone recognises that the offender was carried away by his passion, and least of all, will they, who are about to perform an act infused with passion, admit that they could just as well perform another or even a diametrically opposed one. {21} Suppose a man is about to rush into a burning house in order to save a sick man who has remained behind and who is his friend. Will the man at that moment be able to say that he might as well go to the club or home instead of rushing into the burning house? We do not think it is possible.

Only in the case of minor decisions and relatively emotionless acts of will, where the motives are less intense, or where humans act in complete harmony with their essence so that they do not at all have the feeling of *being necessitated*,[4] the illusion will arise only in the more prudent and deeper-seeing person that they have acted, as it were, "of their own accord" out of free self-determination.

Thus, in recognising the {22} necessity of volitional acts, it depends, firstly, on the degree of the capacity of someone who judges, and it is quite erroneous to allow all humans, except for some philosophers, to manifest the same degree of lack of insight into the necessity of volitional acts. Secondly, it depends on the degree of clearness and intensity with which the motive of an action emerges. For the more clearly and intensely it manifests itself, the more easily is the necessity of an action recognised; and conversely, the more obscure the motive of an action, the more easily even the more prudent person falls prey to the illusion of freedom of will.

---

4 We agree with Schopenhauer when he has a man he imagines standing on the street say (2009, 62–63): "It is six o'clock in the evening, the day's work is ended. I can now go for a walk, or I can go to the club; I can also climb the tower to see the sun going down; I can also go to the theatre; I can also visit this friend, or again that one; yes, I can even run out of the gate into the wide world and never return. All of that is solely up to me, I have total freedom over it; and yet I am doing none of that now, but am going home with just as much free will, to my wife." The man therefore considers it possible that instead of going home, he could just as well go to those other places, because he is obviously in a dispassionate state. However, if at the moment he steps onto the street, someone were to rush up to him with the news that his wife was struggling with death at home, he would obviously consider only one thing possible, namely to hurry home.

However, we must admit that many may understand the necessity of the acts of the will in numerous given cases, but there are still only a few who have grasped the law of causality as a general one that operates without exception and to which every external and internal process is subject. Yet it is to be hoped that with the broader dissemination of philosophical writings, the number of those who have arrived at the knowledge in question will also grow, even if more general progress in this respect is likely to be slow. The recognition of the lack of freedom of the will not only presupposes a certain degree of philosophical ability—and one often experiences the strangest disappointments even in clever people who understand very well the necessity of certain acts of the will in practical life, as soon as one tries to make the problem clear to them in its general form—but there is also another reason which makes people {23} inaccessible to the insight into the necessity of all acts of the will: the assumption of freedom of the will obviously flatters their arrogance and they believe that one wants to deprive them of a privilege they enjoy over other living beings if one tries to make it clear to them that the freedom of the will, the sovereignty of the ego, belongs to the realm of illusions. They do not realise that even if they are entirely subject to the law of causality, there is, as we shall see, another higher point of view from which humans can and must be judged.

3

{24} One thing is sure: no matter how deeply convinced we may be of the causal determination of all thoughts, desires, actions, and even character itself, no matter how thoroughly we may understand that both the noblest and the basest deeds arise not from free choice but necessarily from natural disposition and the immediate circumstances of their authors, we nevertheless continue to regard a virtuous act as merit and a wicked one as guilt.

We have seen from the quotations given earlier that this was Kant's view.

Schopenhauer says in his often-mentioned treatise (2009, 105): "For there is one more fact of consciousness that I have entirely neglected so far, so as not to disturb the progress of the investigation. This is the wholly clear and sure feeling of *responsibility* for what we do, of *accountability* for our actions, which rests on the unshakeable certainty that we are *the doers of our deeds*. Because of this consciousness, it never occurs to anyone {25}—not even one who is wholly convinced of the necessity with which our actions occur as expounded above—to exculpate himself for a transgression by way of this necessity and to shift the blame from himself to the motives because once they occurred, the deed was inevitable." —

Rée, of course, would like to deny this fact of self-consciousness. Rée maintains—and he is only the most astute and boldest representative of a group of like-minded thinkers—as we have already emphasised, that one no longer attributes merit or guilt to an act as soon as one ceases to regard it as an absolute beginning and recognises its causal determination. At the end of *The Illusion of Free Will*, he says: "In reality, it is like this: actions that are naturally necessary are nevertheless attributed [responsibility] because their necessity is not recognised. As soon as this commonly overlooked aspect of the action is perceived, the attribution [or responsibility] ceases. Therefore, to explain attribution, it is not necessary to assume that actions *are free*; attribution is explained by the fact that people *perceive* actions *as if they are free*. It is characteristic that Kant never mentioned the illusion of free will: he thought that all people saw natural necessity but still attributed [responsibility to] actions; therefore, actions must be free. In reality, almost no one sees this necessity, hence the attribution." [Rée 1885, 54, our translation.]

According to Rée and his followers, as soon as someone becomes convinced of the necessity of acts of will, the ethical distinction between good and evil ceases to exist for them. {26} Consequently, there is neither virtue nor vice, neither merit nor guilt. Humanity sinks to the level of an automaton. If you are wise, Rée might advise a disciple of his teaching, and wish to present yourself as someone thoroughly imbued with an understanding of the law of causality, then you must, for instance, only show sympathy, not admiration, for a person who sacrifices themselves in the service of truth. Admiration would imply the false notion that this self-sacrificing individual is the free originator of their actions. In fact, you may even regard that self-sacrificing individual with a superior smile since you realise that the force in them, which drives their selfless actions, is itself just a fortunate effect of preceding causes—something that they might entirely overlook. On the other hand, you should harbour nothing but antipathy toward an evildoer, not that feeling known as "moral indignation," for this is a wholly illogical affect, as it attributes an action to its perpetrator when every action is merely an effect, since it imputes an action to its performer, whereas every action is merely an effect, and effects cannot be attributed to anyone. If a person's hostility is directed towards you, you must accept it calmly, without a surge of anger. Do not find satisfaction in the fact that your enemy or wrongdoer is overtaken by fate. And if you respond to them and put them in their place, do so solely to deter them from further excesses, as all punishment is justified only as a deterrent. Holding someone accountable for their harmful actions is as foolish as holding a {27} wild animal accountable. — But as you judge others, so you must judge yourself and realise that you cannot act in a good or evil way, neither moral nor immoral, since all these predicates presuppose the illusory concept of freedom of the will. Respect the rights of others and, even more, try to promote them because it is wiser and more profitable to do so, but not because it is good or moral.

Such, roughly speaking, would be the way Rée might speak to a disciple of his teaching. —

What would be the consequences of a consistent view of all human characters and actions as mere effects only? None that are favourable, as is easy to demonstrate. For evidently, only a modest minority of the most moderate and wisest people would be able to view the actions of their fellow humans *sub specie necessitatis* and cease to oppose the excesses, baseness, crude selfishness and malice with the weight of moral indignation. Meanwhile, their less moderate and wise fellow humans would likely be provoked by this sense of superiority and respond with even greater malice. Thus, the prospect opened up by the possible spread of this view of humanity among a small minority is by no means an inviting one. This is not to say, however, that it would be undesirable for the recognition of the illusion of free will to spread more and more, rather, what is undesirable is that, having arrived at this knowledge, one should remain fixed there and judge all of humanity solely {28} from the standpoint of that very cognition. Supposing the conviction that characters and actions are merely effects could become a common good of humanity—which is, admittedly, the illusion of illusions, as it implies the complete victory of intellect over feelings and affects—this ideal of humanity would not even be beautiful or desirable. On the contrary, one turns away with instinctive aversion from the image of this humanity that would have forfeited all greatness and poetry, along with feelings and affects.

Apparently, Rée and his followers are right; apparently, an act that is not committed out of free self-determination but under an impulse that is, in turn, conditioned by an infinite causal chain should not be attributed to its perpetrator as guilt. Nevertheless, our feeling resists regarding humans only as automata, only from the point of view of causal determinism. Anyone who has not entirely lost their sense of dignity will, even if they are firmly convinced of the lack of freedom of the will, still feel pangs of conscience and remorse when they are carried away by passion to commit an unjust act and will firmly reject any exoneration offered by others who have likewise grasped the law of causality. We must therefore say, with Kant and Schopenhauer, that even when convinced of the lack of freedom of the will, humans are still internally compelled to hold on to responsibility and attribution.

{29} But how can this phenomenon be explained? Should it not be possible to find a justification for this feeling?

According to Kant, the deeply rooted feeling of responsibility in humans can only be explained by the fact that humans, although subject to the iron law of causality as empirical characters, are free in another, higher respect. By his fundamental distinction between appearance and thing-in-itself, Kant regards humans as citizens of two worlds: the empirical and the transcendental or intelligible world. While humans, as citizens of the empirical world, are not responsible for their actions due to the necessity of all their deeds, they are responsible as citizens of the transcendental world, where the law of causality does not apply and where humans appear as the free authors of their actions. Feuerbach, for this reason, called free will "an empty tautology of the thing-in-itself," while Schopenhauer considered Kant's account of the relationship between the empirical and intelligible character to be "the most beautiful and deeply thought-out" concept ever produced by this great mind, indeed by any human being. Kant now expressly describes the intelligible character as reason and allows it to manifest itself *at all times* in the empirical character. In contrast, Schopenhauer describes *the will*, rather than *reason*, as the bearer of the transcendental character, allowing the empirical character to be determined *once and for all* by the transcendental character. Therefore, Schopenhauer's justification of responsibility and attribution {30} is not only a further development but rather a remodelling of Kant's doctrine, although Schopenhauer makes no mention of the gulf that actually exists between his and Kant's doctrine on this point. — After presenting Kant's distinction between the empirical and transcendental character, he says (2009, 108–109): "This way leads, as is easy to see, to the point that we have to seek the work of our *freedom* no longer in our individual actions, as the common view does, but in the whole being and essence (*existentia et essentia*) of the human being himself, which must be thought of as a free deed that merely presents itself for the faculty of cognition, linked to time, space and causality, in a plurality and diversity of actions—actions which nonetheless, precisely because of the original unity of what presents itself in them, must all bear exactly the same character and so appear as strictly necessitated by the motives by which they are called forth and individually determined on each occasion. Consequently, *operari sequitur esse* stands firm without exception for the world of experience. Each thing operates following its own constitution, and its consequent operation as a result of causes reveals this constitution. Each human being acts according to how they are, and the corresponding necessary action on each occasion will be determined, in the individual case, solely by motives. Thus *freedom*, which cannot be encounterable in the *operari*, *must reside* in the *esse*. In all ages, it has been a fundamental error, a backwards shift, to assign *necessity* to the *esse* and *freedom* to the {31} *opera*te. Quite the reverse, *freedom resides in the* esse *alone*, but from it and the motives the *operari* follows with necessity: and *in what we do, we recognize what we are*. On this, and not on the alleged *liberum arbitrium indifferentiae*, rests the consciousness of responsibility and the moral tendency of life."

The objection has been repeatedly made, especially against Kant's doctrine of transcendental freedom, [arguing] that the appearance of a first beginning in the world governed by the law of causality is entirely incomprehensible. However, this objection seems to be based on a misunderstanding. The objection to Kant's and Schopenhauer's doctrine of transcendental freedom is that humans can only be judged as empirical subjects within the empirical world, and it is entirely unjustified to apply ethical concepts in a transcendental sense to something that completely eludes our judgment. Although the existence of goodness in the human world may lead us to infer a predisposition for it in the fundamental grounds of the world *as it appears to us*, we must never hold the empirical human being accountable for their *substratum*. We can undoubtedly say that nature itself calls upon us to do good, that in this lies our perfection or at least one aspect of our perfection, but not that the ethical distinction is to be transferred to the metaphysical background, which we cannot characterise in any way.

4

{32} Before we express our view of the extent to which moral attribution and responsibility can be conceived as possible, even without the assumption of both natural and transcendental freedom, let us turn to Feuerbach's attempt to justify attribution and responsibility.

Feuerbach considers the will to be identical with the drive for happiness. However, this drive for happiness comes into conflict with itself. It ultimately creates suffering instead of happiness for the individual if it fails to respect and promote the drive for the happiness of others—if the egoistic drive for happiness does not transform into a moral drive for happiness. "Morality recognises no happiness for itself without the happiness of others, acknowledges and desires no happiness that is isolated and independent of the happiness of others or even consciously and wilfully aimed at their unhappiness; it knows only a sociable, shared happiness."[5] However, a person arrives at the idea of the necessity of others' happiness through the feeling of identification brought about by love. The realm of love or morality is the actual realm of freedom—that is, the harmony of humans with the fundamental trait of their nature, the {33} drive for happiness, which only reaches its goal when it appears as a moral drive for happiness. Moral responsibility lies in the feeling of identity, of love, and not in the illusory notion

---

5 [Druskowitz does not quote the source of Feuerbach's passage. It is to be found in his treatise "Noth meistert alle Gesetze und hebt sie auf" (1874, II 291).]

of free will.[6] Accordingly, a human being judges themself entirely based on the consciousness of their fellow human beings. One is a moral "monster" if one does not feel hatred and contempt for oneself because of an action for which others hate and detest them. Because an evil act is contrary to the general will, the author feels remorse and regards it as accidental. In contrast, the indignation felt by the injured parties and the retribution they take is only the natural counter-reaction of their impaired drive for happiness.

"Painful coercive measures indeed most flagrantly contradict the drive for happiness, but only with that of the sufferer, not with that of the person exercising it. Nevertheless, whoever does not recognise and respect the drive for the happiness of others willingly and in good faith—indeed {34} even directly violates it – must accept that they will exercise their right of retribution against him, the right of Rhadamanthus, the fearsome judge of the underworld. [...] We make no superhuman demands on you, incorrigible egoist, we even recognise your egoism, we only demand that you also recognise our egoism" (Feuerbach 1874, 290 [our translation]).

Moreover, we must insist on this demand even if we are convinced of the psychological necessity of all acts of the will. "As long as humans live in society, that is, under laws and rules of conduct toward one another, they will adhere to the distinction between those who are not accountable and those who are accountable for their actions, even though the actions of the latter arise from psychological necessity, not pathological necessity" (Feuerbach 1874, 187 [our translation]).

However, the objection remains that basing responsibility and attribution on the feeling of identity is flawed. In the case of a reprehensible act, for example, the perpetrator's drive for happiness may have asserted itself at the expense of another's drive for happiness simply because the perpetrator's egoism was stronger than their altruism. This abnormal egoism, in turn, must be viewed merely as the effect of an infinite causal chain.

Thus, it must be shown that considering humans from the standpoint of the law of causality is merely a transitional stage from which one must advance to a higher standpoint, and only when this {35} higher standpoint is reached is a valid justification of responsibility and attribution possible.

---

6 "'Conscience is the *alter ego*, the other ego in the ego ...' my ego that takes the place of the injured you ... The imagined, visualised image of the other that keeps me from doing him evil or torments and persecutes me if I have already done him evil ... Conscience comes from knowledge or is connected with knowledge ... Conscience is shared knowledge [*Mitwissen*]. So much is the image of the other interwoven into my self-consciousness, into my self-image, that even the expression of the most intrinsic and most intimate is conscience, an expression of socialism, of communality" (Feuerbach 1874, II 320 [our translation]).

Feuerbach touched upon the standpoint we mean, and in the following section, we will outline it along with the consequences that arise from it, but he did no more than this.

5

{36} It is undoubtedly important to realise that the sense of sovereignty of the self, by which the self believes to manifest itself in acts of will without causal conditionality, is entirely illusory. Instead, all human feeling, thinking, and action should be seen as necessarily determined by an infinite series of preceding causes—that is, as an effect. However, one must not remain stuck with this view of humans; it is only a precursor to a higher perspective. The individual is more than just an intermediary link in the infinite causal chain of the world process; it is simultaneously an independent, self-contained expression of certain aspects of real nature (considered as the pinnacle of all forces). Indeed, it is an expression endowed with self-consciousness, a manifestation equipped with self-awareness of specific qualities and potentials of nature. The natural force that the individual appears to represent must be considered something independent. As soon as the individual is understood as a self-aware representative of certain {37} aspects of independently conceived nature, it ceases to be merely an automaton and instead appears as a being that is, in a certain sense, independent. Insofar as it appears in this way, it is also a responsible and morally accountable author of its actions.

Now, all things are expressions and manifestations of certain qualities of being. Nevertheless, we must differentiate in how we relate to the useful animal or the noble human being, to the wild beast or the evil, wicked person. Both the good and the bad animal are also manifestations of the corresponding potencies of nature, without our attributing to the former its behaviour as merit and to the latter its own as guilt, or at least not in the way we must do towards human beings. The difference which we must make between humans and animals concerning the manifestation of good or bad traits of character is determined precisely by the moral discernment which belongs to humans—at least to mentally healthy, mature, and civilised humans—which animals lack or possess only to a minimal degree, even in the most intelligent species. If humans feel themselves to be the representative of certain qualities of nature concerning their character, then they also consider themselves responsible for their actions. For what is the feeling of responsibility other than acknowledging oneself as the author of one's actions? Moreover, human beings are the author of their actions, even when considered as an expression of a specific aspect of nature, even without the presupposition of {38} freedom of will. Because humans are aware of how they act and represent themselves, the reactions of their fellow humans to their actions must assume a different character than the reactions humans have toward the behaviour of animals or raw natural forces. Because humans consider themselves responsible from this standpoint, they are also held responsible by others. The love we show to all the harmonious forces revealed in nature takes on the character of moral reverence toward the good deeds of a human. In contrast, the hatred we bear against the destructive forces of nature takes on the character of moral indignation against the evil actions of a human. We revere the consciously good in a good person, and we are indignant at the consciously evil in a bad person.

Responsibility and attribution, thus, do not cease to exist with the rejection of the assumption of a sovereign activity of the ego in the act of will but are founded in the significance of the individual as a self-conscious representative of specific potencies of nature. If the individual in its totality as well as in its individual thoughts, feelings and acts of will is also to be regarded as an effect of previous causes, it is nevertheless at the same time more than this: namely a self-conscious partial expression of certain powers of nature conceived as independent, which as such feels responsible for its actions and is therefore also held responsible by the world.

{39} By considering oneself as a representative, an expression of certain powers of nature, as a defined, independent entity of a specific character that is simply what it is, a powerful drive can emerge in the individuals to elevate themselves from a lower to a higher level, thereby creating a strong counter-motivation against the excesses of egoism. Anyone who has elevated themselves to the standpoint we have described, if carried away by passion into an act of injustice, will not exclaim, "If only I had acted differently!" as only someone who has not yet reached a complete cognition of the necessity of all acts of will would do. Nor will they, like someone who has reached this cognition but not gone beyond it, excuse themselves by saying, "I could not have acted otherwise; my action was the necessary consequence of my nature, which I did not create myself." Instead, they will exclaim, "If only I had been able to act differently, if only I could have been a better person!"—a regret that will have a much more lasting influence on the person's future behaviour than the regret stemming from the assumption of free will. An individual who understands this standpoint will never resort to the unworthy excuse that they did not create their evil inclinations because they recognise that they are what created them, or at least a part of it, and that nature itself calls upon them to become {40} a representative of its higher potentials. — While this perspective encourages a person to strive upward, it also teaches them to respect the limits set by their natural disposition, upbringing, and external circumstances, allowing them to recognise their worth and significance increasingly. Every person, according to their physical and intellectual makeup, education, and external circumstances, is allotted a particular sphere that they cannot exceed without consequence.

Furthermore, only by society reacting in a certain way to the individual's behaviour and not regarding the individual as something independent can the genuine striving and aspiration of nature be promoted, which consists of strengthening the good and noble and suppressing the bad and evil. Whoever believes that one must stop considering human action *sub specie necessitates* and consequently measures all humans by the same standard does not understand the voice of nature, does not recognise what nature is working towards with all its might, even if often with an inadequate selection and application of its means.

Bibliography

Feuerbach, Ludwig. 1874. "Noth meistert alle Gesetze und hebt sie auf." In: *Ludwig Feuerbach in seinem Briefwechsel und Nachlass sowie in seiner Philosophischen Charakterientwicklung*, vol. II. Edited by Karl Grün. Leipzig and Heidelberg: C. F. Winter.

Garbe, Richard, trans. 1905. *Die Bhagavadgîtâ*. Leipzig: H. Haessel.

Kant, Immanuel. 1998. *Critique of Pure Reason*. Translated and edited by Paul Guyer and Allen W. Wood. Cambridge: Cambridge University Press.

Kant, Immanuel. 2015. *Critique of Practical Reason*. Translated and edited by Mary Gregor. Cambridge: Cambridge University Press.

Rée, Paul. 1885. *Die Illusion der Willensfreiheit. Ihre Ursachen und ihre Folgen*. Berlin: Carl Duncker.

Schopenhauer, Arthur. 2009. "Prize Essay on the Freedom of the Will." In: *The Two Fundamental Problems of Ethics*. Translated and edited by Christopher Janaway. Cambridge et al.: Cambridge University Press.

Sivananda, Swami, trans. 2003. *The Bhagavad Gita*. Shivanandanagar: The Divine Life Society.

Spencer, Herbert. 1886. *Principles of Psychology*, 3rd ed. D. Appleton and Company.

Wetters, Kirk, trans. 2014. "Appendix: German Text and English Translation of Goethe's 'Urworte Orphisch' (with Commentary)." In: *Demonic History: From Goethe to the Present*. Evanston: Northwestern University Press.

Modern Attempts at a Replacement for Religion. A Philosophical Essay by Dr H. Druskowitz

1

{1} The premise of this writing is based on the observation, evident to any unbiased person, that Christianity is increasingly losing its power over people's minds among the first modern civilised nations and is inevitably heading towards its dissolution, albeit at different rates of acceleration among the various nations in question. We believe we do not need to explain to the readers, for whom this writing is primarily intended, why this process of weathering and mortification is necessary. This question has already been exhaustively answered elsewhere.

As important as the gradual detachment from a religion utterly incompatible with the modern spirit may be, mere liberation from it can never suffice. Religion, in its higher forms, is, after all, the expression of an ideal need of the human spirit, even if only a preliminary and imperfect one. Despite all the harmful elements it carries, it can give minds a certain uplift, allowing them to sense something higher, albeit in an illogical form. In contrast, mere atheism is one of the most unpleasant phenomena, as irreverence and lack of any seriousness are its necessary consequences. Therefore, one must not stop at the mere negation of religion, {2} and only those who, having shed superstition, seek a new and more reliable object of their highest trust and aspiration, one that satisfies both the mind and the understanding equally, have a full right to call themselves freethinkers. Something higher and more perfect must take the place of religion.

However, what will this higher and more perfect thing have to be like? Will there be various replacements or only one which fully deserves this designation? And if there is only one, will it be able to become an all-encompassing and unifying power like religion in the most advanced nations? Will it be able to unite the people and the educated?

In the eyes of most people in our—in the pejorative sense of the word—atheistic age, nothing could be more superfluous and untimely than to raise such questions and devote one's thoughts to them. The majority of those, however, who do not consider this inconvenience to be absolutely insignificant will certainly answer the above questions in such a way that the educated may need a replacement for religion but that it must be left to each individual to choose or create one for themselves. As far as the masses of the first civilised peoples themselves are concerned, however, they are more likely to fall victim to a new superstition than to transform into flesh and blood a doctrine based on a view of the world that accords with the facts.

Against the former remark, namely that it should be left to every educated person to choose or create a replacement for religion, it may be objected that religion in its highest manifestations expresses ideas {3} which can only be replaced more perfectly by very specific representations, but by no means by the first higher object that comes along. Neither art nor science, nor the cult of nature, nor philanthropic labour can replace the realm of religion, although, in a certain sense, they can become pillars and components of the new doctrine. The replacement for religion is a very definite group of thoughts and feelings which, in a vigorous combination, would satisfy the mind and the understanding to the same degree.

Furthermore, it is not at all clear to us why the only true replacement for religion, which would initially have to become a unifying bond among the educated, should not gradually embrace deeper strata (only within the first modern nations, of course). At least the possibility of a more general progress in this direction cannot be denied.

Human nature is generally considered too little capable of change and improvement, and one despairs before even an attempt has been made to guide it along new paths. It is self-evident that a higher, religion-replacing doctrine could not gain a firm root in peoples' minds by itself and establish its realm overnight. There is, however, the possibility that it could gradually, if raised to the status of an object of practice and instruction, nurtured by associations, and promoted by word and writing, become a spiritual guidance embracing all classes.

However, we have not yet identified the primary driving force that would need to come into play for the new doctrine to take effect. This [primary driving force] is the enthusiasm of the best for the new doctrine. Just as every religion required an enthusiastic band of followers {4} to be elevated to a power dominating the masses, the higher replacement for religion needs to be cultivated with enthusiastic devotion by a select minority to stir the lesser spirits as well.

Whoever now holds fast to the possibility that one day the modern nations gradually renouncing Christianity—and they are the best among them that, as far as we know, have ever populated this earth—could be animated by a new, more perfect world view and elevated to a higher life, will see the problem of a replacement for religion as one of the most significant, to which one cannot devote enough thought.

Since Comte and Feuerbach, a series of thinkers and writers have taken up the problem in question, and a wide range of views have been expressed about it. Only a few thinkers have focused on the general public; most have considered a replacement for religion only for the educated. It is the task of this book to present and criticise these attempts concisely, strictly avoiding lengthy and dragging explanations. We note at once that none of the thinkers and writers in question has treated the problem in a way that is satisfactory in every respect and taken all sides of it into account. However, almost all the significant elements of a replacement for religion are emphasised with varying degrees of energy and vigour in the various attempts. However, only that doctrine could be considered a true, more perfect replacement for religion, which would unite all those scattered components within itself and shape a powerful whole through a bold combination of them.

{5} Some of these attempts are based on the false premise that the replacement for religion must have the character of an atheistic religion. However, the relationship that humans have in the replacement for religion to the world as a whole on the one hand, and to the ideal on the other, is very different from that of the believer to their God and the law dictated to them by God, so that the retention of the word religion for the new relationship is completely inadmissible. Firmly connected with this point of view, which is to be overcome, the designation is to be dropped with the thing itself. Those who have achieved full, complete, and genuine freedom from supernatural religion instinctively avoid the word and seek to eradicate it completely from their usage.

2

To immediately establish a firm foundation for our critique of the various attempts at replacing religion, we want to determine which *legitimate* spiritual needs—for only these can be discussed here—religion satisfies in its highest manifestations and which, therefore, the replacement for religion must also satisfy, albeit in a more perfect way.

Religion, in its highest forms of development, offers a world view that is firstly an interpretation and explanation of the world that humans desire, by connecting all things and beings, and above all humans as their crown, with supreme power, with the deepest foundation of the world, designating them as *conditioned* by it. It furthermore awakens *trust* in the supreme perfection of the Universal Creator and the goal of the world process conditioned and determined by {6} him, and finally *reverence* for the supreme creative power, as something incomprehensible and mysterious. The replacement for religion will also have to account for moments of *conditionality*, *trust*, and *reverence*, providing them with a representational basis that is accessible to the understanding while discarding the unprovable hypothesis of a personal god. While in Christianity the moment of *trust* refers to a divine power and a future supernatural kingdom, with the earthly world appearing completely devalued, the replacement for religion will firstly place trust in the foundation of the world, whether we characterise it from a realistic standpoint or declare it to be unknowable and incomprehensible from an idealistic one, but then also in the world process (which is only partially unfolding before our eyes). Two thinkers, whose relevant attempts we will appreciate, have demonstrated in a compelling manner that such trust is objectively permissible and subjectively conditioned by the fundamental character of the better modern nations for whom a higher replacement for religion should be created. — However, religion also intervenes in life in a formative way, albeit in a thoroughly one-sided manner. Here, too, the replacement for religion must offer something more perfect in that it fills life with a higher content than religion was able to do, all the more so as it describes the earth as the only arena for humans. In its future perspective, the perfect replacement for religion will shatter the dreams of immortality that human vanity has created in its most naïve expression. However, instead, it will point to sublime possibilities that can be realised in the development of the human race.

{7} With this analysis of religion and the replacement for religion, which is unlikely to be contested, we have gained a firm yardstick against which we can now measure the various attempts to solve our problem.

However, one more preliminary remark: By emphasising the moment of *trust* in the foundation of things and the world process as a necessary component of the perfect replacement for religion, we have characterised our position towards pessimism. The replacement for religion must take a different turn from the misdirected trust of Christianity, thereby overcoming the pessimistic conception of reality. If it is to gain a firm foothold in people's minds, it must be appropriate to the innermost nature of modern civilised peoples—a point which it is mainly to Dühring's credit. Energetic, fresh and lively, and more nobly disposed of, as the best modern civilised peoples are, this pessimism is not a world view homogeneous to them. It can only intervene in modern life in the form of a temporary disease of the time. We will, therefore, leave aside any echoes of Buddhist longing for redemption, from which a religious surrogate could also be prepared, since we will only deal with modern attempts at a replacement for religion, i.e. those which, however unsound they may be in themselves, nevertheless correspond to the basic tendency of modern peoples. Similarly, we exclude all forms of more subtle theism, in which some believe they have found a replacement for religion, from our investigation, as they are based on fundamental ideas that the scientific, modern view of the world rejects as unprovable.

As long as Christianity still had a firm hold on the {8} masses, the idea of a replacement for religion could certainly not gain any power. Therefore, apart from the philosophical systems, which could only have the meaning of a replacement for religion for their authors and a small group of followers, we have searched in vain for a serious consideration of our problem until the last three decades. Only in our time, since faith has increasingly lost its authority, has the problem come to the fore.

In a French and a German thinker, the idea first emerged simultaneously that Christianity—against which the German thinker Ludwig Feuerbach struck such powerful blows, while the French philosopher Auguste Comte regarded it from the outset as a phase in the development of humankind that had been largely overcome—must be replaced by a replacement purified of all superstition. However, both erroneously conceived this as an atheistic religion. Both essentially emphasise that aspect of religion and its replacement, which determines the relationship between humans and society. However, as we shall see, Feuerbach happily emphasises another aspect, which arises from the position of humans towards nature, whereas Comte has not achieved anything satisfactory on this point. If, however, we have to construct Feuerbach's religion of love for ourselves from scattered remarks, Comte has elaborated his religion of humanity down to the smallest detail in a multi-volume, extremely voluminous work. As little as we can agree with the main ideas of his *Système de politique positive*, the work itself is nevertheless highly remarkable, indeed unique in its kind and the product of an extraordinary capacity for construction. Admittedly, the scheme of Catholicism served the new {9} founder of religion as a model in many ways.

After completing his *Cours de philosophie positive*,[1] Comte was not satisfied with the results of this work. What he had had in mind from his youth was a reform of society. He had initially only accomplished a reform of social theory as the science which, according to his "encyclopaedic formula," was the crown and summit of all other disciplines. He carried out this reform by applying the positivist method to social theory, which was still prevalent at that time, although theological and metaphysical methods also prevailed. At the same time, it had already found acceptance in other sciences. Comte, however, saw that there was something higher than understanding and knowledge, that the actual reform of society had to take place through the heart, through feeling, and that philosophy had to culminate in religion. The objective cursus could only be a preparation for subjective teaching. The unity that Comte renounced in the field of objective science,[2] he believed could be established in a religion of humanity, i. e. in a subjective way.

---

1 [corr. ex *Système de philosophie positive*]
2 Comte 1896, 17: "Because it is proposed to consolidate the whole of our acquired knowledge into one body of homogenous doctrine, it must not be supposed that we are going to study this vast variety as proceeding from a single principle, and as subjected to a single law. There is something so chimerical in attempts at universal explanation by a single law, that it may be as well to secure this work at once from any imputation of the kind, though its development will show how

However, it took a special occasion which, as he thought, enabled him to become a reformer of humanity {10}. He met Madame Clotilde de Vaux, who was separated from her criminal husband but unable to divorce him due to the indissolubility of marriage in France at the time. Captivated by the evidently exceptional qualities of her mind and heart, he developed a passionate affection for her. A blissful year united them in mutual, yet always chaste love until death swept Clotilde away. However, an enthusiastic memory of her remained. Comte never stopped celebrating her memory, praying to her, invoking her support and praising her as the author of the inner transformation that enabled him to complete his work of reform.³ The *Politique positive* is dedicated to her memory {11}; there is in words addressed to her something of the spirit that speaks to us from Dante's *Vita nuova* and Shelley's *Epipsychidion*.

As the reader will see from the quotations just given in the note, the self-confidence that filled our philosopher was no small one; indeed, it had become almost pathological in the elaboration of his new religion. Never did a mind feel more called to a high mission; never did anyone feel more entitled to pronounce a decisive and final word on all significant matters than Comte. By surrounding himself with the dignity of a high priest of the new religion, he had also immediately become an all-violating, infallible pontiff.

---

underserved such an imputation would be. Our intellectual resources are too narrow, and the universe is too complex, to leave any home that it will ever be within our power to carry scientific perfection to its last degree of simplicity."

3 Comte 1875a, xiv–xv: "My intellectual powers, wearied with their long objective toil, were inadequate to the construction of a new system from the subjective point of view, directed, as in earlier life, by a social rather than an intellectual purpose. A new birth of the whole moral nature was needed. And this was given me six years ago by the incomparable angel appointed in the course of human destiny to transmit to me the results of the gradual evolution of our moral nature."

Comte 1875a, xvi: "Thus the moral and mental value of this admirable nature can only be judged by its permanent consequences upon my own work. All those who have formed a sound judgment of the recent progress of Positivism may now judge, by comparing the past with the present, of the impulse that has been given to the full development of my philosophical task; consisting in the entire systematisation of human life on the basis of the preponderance of the hear over the intellect. It is as the result of these new services that this cherished name will become inseparable from mine in the most distant memories of grateful humanity. The loving duty which Dante so well fulfilled for Beatrice is more deeply incumbent on myself for obligations far more stringent."

Comte 1875a, xxxvii: "My warrant for claiming public sympathy in the performance of this sacred duty is that I saw in you not merely a noble friend and precious counsellor, but also a powerful fellow-worker in the immense work of regeneration called for in our time."

Of course, it would seem that no one could mean better by humanity than Comte. The happiness he enjoyed for a year in his love for Clotilde de Vaux fully strengthened in him the conviction he had already harboured earlier: that in altruism—*vivre pour autrui* [*to live for others*]—lay the most perfect guarantee for the common good, which is why it must be elevated to the highest principle of life. Only love of humanity could redeem humanity by making it the *primum mobile* of life, subordinating all other drives to it. A religion of humanity should replace supernatural religion.

Comte sees the essence of religion, on the one hand, in the harmonious formation of the individual and, on the other, in the harmony of individuals with each other.[4] This harmony {12} is essentially brought about by the fact that we come to recognise an essentially unchangeable world order and immutable laws of nature, to which we must humbly conform.[5] This is why the second clause of the formula that Comte placed at the head of his *Politique positive* is "Ordre pour base" [order as the foundation]. If the cult of the new religion corresponds to *vivre pour autrui*, then dogma corresponds to *ordre pour base*. The positive dogma is no easy matter; it requires from the adept of the new religion nothing less than the mastery of all the sciences of the "encyclopaedic formula," i.e. mathematics, astronomy, physics, chemistry, biology and sociology. In any case, it makes excessive demands on human understanding.

The world order, essentially immutable, nevertheless exhibits progress, which is why knowledge of the laws of nature leads a human individual to resignation on the one hand and to action on the other. This is why the third link in Comte's religious formula is *progrès pour but* [*progress as the goal*]. It is this sentence that highlights the importance of practical action and politics.

---

4 Comte 1851, 9 [our translation]: "This synthetic state thus consists, on the one hand, in regulating each personal existence, and, on the other, in uniting diverse individualities." *Cf.* Comte 1874, 42.

Comte 1875b, 8: "Throughout this treatise the term Religion will be used to express that state of complete harmony peculiar to human life, in its collective as well as in its individual form, when all the part of Life are ordered in their natural relations to each other."

5 Comte 1875b, 12: "In order then to regulate or to combine mankind, religion must be in the first instance place man under the influence of some external Power, possessed of superiority so irresistible as to leave no sort of uncertainty about it. This great principle of social science is at bottom merely the full development of that primary notion of sound Biology—the necessary subordination of every Organism to the Environment in which it is placed."

The new religion thus gives direction to thought, feeling and {13} action, a circumstance that Comte describes as one of its main advantages over the earlier religions,[6] which took too little account of action.

We can see from what has been said that Comte conceives of the relationship between human beings and the world as a whole quite externally, contrasting a human individual with nature as something alien, according to which no more profound feeling can be attached to this relationship for the human. We will revisit this major flaw in Comte's religious system later, but for now, we will take a closer look at his doctrine of altruism and its consequences for the various spheres of life and thought.

Altruism, which Comte places at the centre of the new doctrine, is intended to regenerate humanity and establish a realm of universal harmony. The new religion aims to nurture social feelings as much as possible and suppress personal feelings as much as possible. Now, as Comte admits, egoism cannot be eradicated entirely from human nature. However, it can be reduced to the mere instinct for self-preservation, which in turn forms the basis of all higher development. It seems that such a subordination of egoism to altruism, such a victory of altruism over egoism, is not within the realm of possibility. The philosopher argues, firstly, that through a happy arrangement of nature, competition also brings people closer together and unites them, and secondly, that {14} reflection and insight into the conditions of social welfare can influence people to work in its service. And this is the point where Comte's altruism differs from Feuerbach's love. While Feuerbach appeals to the natural love of humanity that flows freely from the heart, Comte calls on reflection to help overcome egoism. Comte also presupposes natural benevolence, but in his opinion, this requires the support of the intellect,[7] whose most outstanding merit again lies in this cooperation because, in the

---

[6] Comte 1875b, 7: "Religion, originally Spontaneous, then Inspired, and afterwards Revealed, has at length found its grounds in Demonstration. In its full maturity, it must satisfy at once the feelings, the imagination, and the reason, as each of these was, in turn, the source of one of its three earlier forms. But over and above this, it must govern directly the active powers of Man, powers which neither Fetichism, nor even Polytheism, nor least of all Monotheism, could adequately control."

[7] Comte 1875a, 12: "But the intellect may do much to confirm their influence. It may strengthen social feeling by diffusing juster views of the relations in which the various parts of society stand to each other, or it may guide its application by dwelling on the lessons which the past offers to the future. It is to this honourable service that the new philosophy would direct our intellectual powers. Here, the highest sanction is given to their operations, and an inexhaustable field is opened up for them, from which far deeper satisfaction may be gained than from the approbation of the learned societies or from the puerile specialities with which they are at present occupied."

new doctrine, the heart and feeling have the upper hand over the intellect. Even if the intellect can help the heart against egoism, it must nevertheless subordinate itself to the heart. If it was once salutary for the intellect to seize control so that the sciences could reach their present heights, the most important thing has been done in this respect, and the supremacy of the intellect, which has existed since the Middle Ages, must now be brought to an end by the heart taking over the further leadership of humanity. Comte characterises the difference between his first and second philosophical periods concerning the relationship between heart and mind in the dedication of his *Politique positive* with the words (Comte 1875a, xxxv): "After frankly devoting the first {15} half of my life to the development of the heart by the intellect, I saw its second half consecrated to the illumination of the intellect by the heart, so necessary to give the true character to great social truths."[8] — If, therefore, the spirit is not destined to rule but to serve because, as the ruler, it supports the individual and not the community, then it is only "the servant and not the slave" of the heart.

In this position of the "heart," science and speculation must necessarily be subordinated to morality. The guiding principle of all future research should be the common good. A study that does not promote this in some way is useless musing and can only lead astray. The heart should set the tasks, and the mind should solve them, but it should not set tasks itself. The general welfare—this is the point of view from which all human endeavour should be considered. However, Comte goes even further: he measures the right of animals and plants to exist solely according to their usefulness to humans and concludes that all animals and plants that do not fulfil this purpose should be exterminated.

Art is given greater importance than science in Positivism, as it appeals to emotions. Nevertheless, it is not given a leading position; all practical effectiveness is limited to political circles. If philosophers have no political power, artists have even less[9] Comte's demand {16} that all art should pursue a moral tendency can-

---

8 Comte 1875a, 12–13: "The intellect is intended for service, not for empire; when it imagines itself supreme, it is really only obeying the personal instead of the social instincts. It never acts independently of feeling, be that feeling good or bad."

9 Comte 1875a, 225: "In the normal state of human nature, Imagination is subordinated to Reason as Reason is to Feeling. Any prolonged inversion of this natural order is both morally and intellectually dangerous. The reign of Imagination would be still more disastrous than the reign of Reason, only that it is even more incompatible with the practical conditions of human life. Chimerical as it is, the mere pursuit of it may do much individual harm by substituting artificial excitement, and in too many cases, affection of feeling, for deep and spontaneous emotion. [All the more so, this vicious preponderance of imagination must alter public life when no social barrier any longer contains aesthetic ambitions.]" [The last sentence is not found in the English translation.]"

not come as a surprise to him. Since the purpose of art will only be fully understood in the positivist era, its highest flowering is to be expected in the future. Only then will art properly recognise its task and take on a milder character, giving expression mainly to gentle and benevolent feelings, which are far more aesthetic than those of hatred.[10] In Comte's opinion, art would also only be able to develop freely once the various historical epochs and phenomena could be viewed with an unbiased eye.[11] A key insight of Comte's is that artistic and speculative activity need not necessarily be separate but can be united in one and the same person. {17}

Since Comte presents the good of humanity as the purpose and goal of all activity, it is not surprising that he arrives at sublimating humanity to a *Grand-Être* [Great Being] to an *Être-Suprême* [Supreme Being]. In the *Supreme Being*, the individual disappears; indeed, it exists only in the mind of the metaphysician.[12] It only has value and meaning as part of the whole and not in itself (Comte 1851, 363 [in the French edition]). However, the *Supreme Being* by no means encompasses the entire human race, but only the useful members of society, past, present and future.[13] Comte also wants the useful domestic animals to be incorporated into the *Great Being*. This *Great Being* differs favourably from the old God in

---

[10] Comte 1875a, 241: "By teaching that the highest happiness is to aid in the happiness of others, Positivism invites the poet to his noblest function, the culture of generous sympathies; a subject far more poetic than the passions of hatred and oppression which hitherto have been his ordinary theme. A system which regards such culture as the highest object cannot fail to incorporate Poetry as one of its essential elements, and to give to it a far higher position than it has ever held before."

[11] Comte 1875a, 245: "Such examples, however, are but spontaneous and imperfect indications of the new career which Positivism now offers to aesthetic genius ; its scope ranging over the whole region of the Past and even of the Future. Until this vast domain had been conceived of as a whole by the philosopher, it would have been impossible to bring it within the compass of poetry. Now theological and metaphysical philosophers were prevented by the absolute spirit of their doctrines from understanding history in all its phases, and were totally incapable of idealising them as they deserved. Positivism, on the contrary, is always relative, and its principal feature is a theory of history which enables us to appreciate and become familiar with every mode in which human society has formed itself. No sincere Monotheist can understand and represent with fairness the life of Polytheists or Fetichists. But the Positivist poet, accustomed to look upon all past historical stages in their proper filiation, will be able so thoroughly to identify himself with all as to awaken our sympathies for them, and revive the traces which each individual may recognise of corresponding phases in his own history."

[12] Comte 1875a, 268: "Man indeed, as an individual, cannot properly be sad to exist, except in the too abstract brain of modern metaphysicians."

[13] Comte 1875a, 27: "The Great Being is the whole constituted by the beings, past, future, and present, which cooperate willingly in perfecting the order of the world."

that it is not an absolute being, but a being capable of development, to whose growth and perfection we can contribute,[14] by perfecting ourselves.[15] In this behaviour {18} towards the *Great Being* also lies a replacement for the fantastic illusion of personal immortality. Human existence is partly objective and real, partly subjective. However, only those whose objective existence has stood in the service of the *Great Being* can enter into subjective existence.

Apart from the philosophers, the proletarians who are not blinded by false metaphysical speculations and possess a lively social feeling are a mainstay of positivism.[16] Women occupy a very special position in the new doctrine. As the *sexe affectif* [affective gender], they are the highest representatives of the supreme principle of the new religion and play a significant role in the regeneration process, which can only be completed by drawing women into the movement. Comte arrived at a cult of the entire gender through his exalted love for a woman. He demands that every man should see a representative of humanity in his wife in order to prepare himself for the cult of humanity through the cult of woman. He says that women were only truly honoured in the Middle Ages. The new era should base republican morals on "chivalrous" feelings. As highly as our philosopher places the *affective gender*, he wants it to be strictly confined to the home, regarding it as inferior to the male gender in all activities of vigour, mental strength and strength of character. {19} Women are, therefore, only allowed to influence the public sphere indirectly through their husbands. In that, they cannot achieve any public activity, only in exceptional cases, as Comte admits. They are only assured a subjective existence if they gain influence over their husbands and train them to become worthy servants of the *Great Being*. This is one of

---

14 Comte 1875a, 268: "The Great Being whom we worship is not immutable any more than it is absolute. Its nature is relative and, as such, is eminently capable of growth. In a word, it is the most vital of all living beings known to us."
15 Comte 1875a, 264: "Positivists then may, more truly than theological believers of whatever creed, regard life as a continuous and intense act of worship; worship which will elevate and purify our feelings, enlarge and enlighten our thoughts, ennoble and invigorate our actions." [This diverges from the literal translation, which reads as: "This continuous worship of humanity will exalt and purify all our feelings ; it will expand and enlighten all our thoughts; it will ennoble and strengthen all our actions."]
16 Comte 1875a, 102: "The avowal of such a purpose is quite sufficient to prevent Positivism from gaining the sympathies of any one of the governing classes. The classes to which it must appeal are those who have been left untrained in the present worthless methods of instruction by words and entities, who are animated with strong social instincts, and who consequently have the largest stock of good sense and good feeling. In a word, it is among the working classes that the new philosophers will find their most energetic allies. The force necessary for social regeneration depends essentially on the combined action of those two extreme terms of the ultimate social order."

their most noble and sacred tasks, alongside the education of their children. They should be wholly excluded from earning a living; a *man must support a woman*.[17] The Frenchman betrays himself when Comte gives women an important role in the "positivist salon".

Comte treats the cult of the new religion in great detail. We shall only emphasise a few elements of it. It is divided into private and public worship. Its medium, as in the supernatural religions, is prayer, which here, however, is not intended to move a higher power to kindness or to thank it for what has been received but to express feelings of sympathy, love or veneration for worthy persons in a noble form.[18] Private worship should not take up less than two hours of the day, of which one hour is allotted to morning prayer alone. This is followed by a prayer during the day as a resting and gathering point amid business and one before going to sleep. The man addresses his prayer in the morning to his mother, at noon to his wife, and in the evening to his daughter—{20} as representatives of the past, present and future, while the woman, in turn, also prays to her mother, then to her husband and her son; in the absence of one of these persons, another worthy person takes her place. The new religion also contains nine sacraments: *la presentation* [Presentation], *la déstination* [Destination *or* Vocation], *l'initiation* [Initation], *l'admission* [Admission], *la maturité* [Maturity], *la retraite* [Retirement], *la transformation* [Transformation], *l'incorporation* [Incorporation].[19] The first sacrament signifies that the family presents the new citizen of the world to the priest. The second signifies the first entry of the future servant of humanity into public life when, at the age of fourteen, he passes from the hands of his mother into the school of priests to study the positivist dogma in a seven-year course. Through the third sacrament, the young citizen of the world receives the authorisation to serve humanity without determining his actual sphere of vocation. Entry into the sphere of vocation is only signified by the fourth sacrament, which, however, does not apply to women, who, according to Comte, have the sole vocation of becoming wives and mothers. The man, however, may find his own family only after he has received the fourth sacrament. For Comte, marriage is a particularly sacred institution. It is indissoluble, except in cases where one of the parties is guilty of a criminal offence. The average family consists of seven people: the husband and wife, the *couple's fundamental* unit, the husband's parents,

---

17 [Comte 1875a, 301: "The first principle is that Man should support Woman [...]."]
18 The prayer is divided into two parts: the commemoration and the effusion. Cf. Comte, 1874, 95 [our translation]: "When a fortunate combination of symbols and images sufficiently rekindles our feelings for the adored being, we express them with genuine fervour, which soon tends to amplify them further and thus brings us closer to the ultimate evocation."
19 [Druskowitz writes *nine* sacraments but lists only eight. Comte's ninth sacrament is Marriage.]

and three children. We can see how our philosopher endeavours to circle everything precisely.—The sixth sacrament signifies the entrance into that age when the citizen is no longer looked upon as neglecting his duties to humanity, when he should no longer shun *vivre au grand jour* [*to live in broad daylight*]. The seventh sacrament signifies a sensible withdrawal from public life and {21} the choice of a successor. The eighth indicates that the priest, uniting the regrets of society with the tears of the relatives, presents and examines the life of the deceased in a dignified manner. The ninth, which only comes into force seven years after death, indicates the judgement as to whether a person is worthy to be admitted to the *Great Being*.

The public cult takes place annually in 84 festivals, which are celebrated in temples by priests around whom the women are grouped. The temples face towards Paris; they are adjoined by the *bois sacré* [*sacred grove*], where the worthy servants of the *Great Being* are laid to rest, while criminals, duellists and suicides are buried outside.

The new religion has a numerous, strictly organised priesthood, headed by a *grand prêtre* [*Great Priest*] (who is of course based in Paris), because *aucune société ne peut se conserver et ne développer sans un sacerdoce quelconque*,[20] as our philosopher suggests. Priests are supposed to be perfect people in every respect. They play no political role, but even without one, their influence is substantial. They are the educators of the young; in their hands lies the cultivation of the arts and sciences, and the spiritual rape of the positivist era should go so far that the high priest determines the scientific subjects to be dealt with at any given time.

Politically, the populations of positivist countries—which Comte conceives to be of a moderate size—are divided into entrepreneurs and labourers. However, the relation between these two classes is supposed to be very different from that which actually exists, being based on the proposition: *dévouement des forts aux faibles, vénération* {22} *des faibles pour les forts*.[21] The favoured position that the patrician enjoys is, however, connected with far heavier obligations than that of the proletarian, whose position appears to be much improved in comparison with the present one.

For Comte, the highest political leaders of each country are the three richest bankers, in whose hands the highest worldly power lies and who have to choose their successors.

---

20 [*No society can sustain itself or develop without some form of priesthood.*]
21 [*Devotion of the strong to the weak, veneration of the weak for the strong.*]

So three powerful and completely uncontrolled bankers at the head of each country and, above all, a high priest who presumes to rule all intelligences—what a sophisticated system of tyranny! A. F. Lange rightly condemns Comte's hierarchical tendencies (1877, 507): "Are not the psychological laws which make every hierarchy, every priesthood exalted above the level of the people, domineering and arousing in it the jealousy of authority, immutably founded in human nature and independent of the content of faith? Indeed, we find this inevitable effect not only in the great typical forms of the Tibetan, the medieval Christian, and the ancient Egyptian hierarchy but, as recent ethnographic research shows, also in the smallest religious groups of the remotest peoples, in the most depraved Negro tribes and on the smallest islands of the world's oceans."

Comte's religious system, however, suffers from much more serious damage than hierarchy, a system of political violence and interference in the individual soul through norms such as the regulations on prayer.

Unsatisfactory, above all, as we pointed out above, {23} is the position in which a human individual is placed in relation to nature. Nature, following the first premises of Comte's philosophy, is conceived purely as a mechanism to which a human either submits without resistance or can master and modify to a certain extent. It is a barrier or medium for humans, nothing more. Comte thus sets humans opposite to nature in a completely external way instead of bringing them into a living connection , or perceiving nature as his foundation or as his mother, and thus all sensations that arise from the relationship so conceived must lack warmth and depth.[22] It is only with Feuerbach that the moment of human conditionality by nature is determined adequately, and a starting point for human endeavour is thereby gained.

Furthermore, the relationship of the individual to society, to humanity, as Comte conceives it, is impossible. Altruism, to the extent desired by our philosopher, would lead to the dissolution of the individual, to a state that would be no less intolerable than a generalised state of feud and war. No one would feel at home with oneself, no one would be allowed to go their own way to pursue their own goals, and a terrible monotony would hang over life. Herbert Spencer has excellently described in {24} his carefully considered way the absurdities to which altruism taken too far would necessarily lead (Spencer 1879, 204–208). Comte's *Great Being* is a vampire-like bogey, even worse than the old God. It

---

[22] In *Synthèse subjective*, Comte's last work, the connection between humans and nature is, of course, conceived differently. Here, the celestial bodies appear to be endowed with sentience as the universe cooperates in the advancement of humans. Nevertheless, this view of this relationship is just as far removed from a rational interpretation as the purely external juxtaposition of man and nature in *Politique positive*.

takes the whole person captive and demands the utmost sacrifice; the individual does not exist in relation to it at all.

Despite Comte's assurance that the flowering of art will only begin in the new era of religion, we fear that art would then, on the contrary, hardly flourish. It would be even worse for science. Neither art nor science, however, may be forced to fulfil any other purpose than that contained in their concept. If the creations of art or the discoveries of science result in a benefit for humankind, so much the better, but the benefit must not be intended from the outset. As long as there are genuine artists and researchers, the love of art or science will be the driving force in them, and consideration for the good of humanity will only be allowed to take second place.

Let us take a closer look at Comte's *Great Being*, to which the individual should give himself. Can it really be presented as a supreme idea to which the individual should sacrifice himself with all his powers? What J. St. Mill says about Comte's idea of humanity sounds very beautiful (Mill 1865, 135–136): "The power which may be acquired over the mind by the idea of the general interest of the human race, both as a source of emotion and as a motive to conduct, many have perceived; {25} but we know not if any one, before Mr. Comte, realised so fully as he has done, all the majesty of which that idea is susceptible. It ascends into the unknown recesses of the past, embraces the manifold present, and descends into the indefinite and unforeseeable future. Forming a collective Existence without assignable beginning or end, it appeals to that feeling of the Infinite, which is deeply rooted in human nature, and which seems necessary to the imposingness of all our highest conceptions. Of the vast unrolling web of human life, the part best known to us is irrevocably past; this we can no longer serve, but can still love: it comprises for most of us the far greater number of those who have loved us, or from whom we have received benefits, as well as the long series of those who, by their labours and sacrifices for humankind, have deserved to be held in everlasting and grateful remembrance. As Mr. Comte truly says, the highest minds, even now, live in thought with the great dead, far more than with the living; and, next to the dead, with those ideal human beings yet to come, whom they are never destined to see. If we honour as we ought those who have served mankind in the past, we shall feel that we are also working for those benefactors by serving that to which their lives were devoted. And when reflection, guided by history, has taught us the intimacy of the connexion of every age of humanity with every other, making us see in the earthly destiny of mankind the playing out of a great drama, or the action of a prolonged epic, all the generations of mankind become indissolubly united into {26} a single image, combining all the power over the mind of the idea of Posterity, with our best feelings towards the living world which surrounds us, and towards the predecessors who have made us what we are."

On closer inspection, however, there is much that is incorrect in these statements. To elevate the welfare of humanity to the object of the highest endeavour of the individual is to place humanity as the highest object of worship. But this is inadmissible for the simple reason that higher things than humanity are conceivable. The highest that exists for humans can only be the ideal of the good, the true and the beautiful, with the full realisation that this is not a fixed quantity and that it progresses with the progress of humans. Whoever is concerned only with the welfare of his fellow humans must not make the highest and most stringent demands either on himself or on others. Indeed, it may be said the other way around that the first thing should be the love of the ideal and the love of human beings should be second. For example, anyone who wants to inspire people with enthusiasm for a great truth will do so primarily out of love for the truth, and if this person is truly heroic, they will proclaim their conviction loudly, even if they foresee that they will divide humanity into fiercely opposing parties. It is not a superior point of view to regard the high manifestations of the human spirit merely as a means of evoking emotional states in humans. Should not the opposite view be the more correct and greater one, that nature uses a human being mainly as a means to make those high manifestations possible? Nature does not seem to be concerned with human happiness, but it does endeavour through humans to create an ideal order (morality), to attain more and more clarity about itself {27} ([scientific] research) and to perfect itself using the human spirit (art). On other celestial bodies it may be possible to bring about higher effects through higher beings, perhaps allowing humans to pass into a higher order.

Under no circumstances should humanity be understood as *the Great Being*, nor should the good of humanity be seen as the highest goal of an individual's striving.

We have thus pointed out the fundamental shortcomings of Comte's system of religion. It hardly corresponds to the idea of a more perfect replacement for religion in any sense. However, the *Système de politique positive* is, although a misguided work, a most remarkable one, which nowhere denies the genius of its author.

3

As can be seen from the quotation above, J. St. Mill also considered the religion of humankind to be a suitable replacement for supernatural religion. His essay *Util-*

*ity of Religion*²³ also provides evidence to support this view. Mill repeatedly attempted to analyse the content of the concept of religion. Thus, we read in the work on Comte (Mill 1865, 133)²⁴: "There must be a creed, or conviction, claiming authority over the whole of human life; a belief, or set {28} of beliefs, deliberately adopted, respecting human destiny and duty, to which the believer inwardly acknowledges that all his actions ought to be subordinate. Moreover, there must be a sentiment connected with this creed, or capable of being evoked by it, sufficiently powerful to give it, in fact, the authority over human conduct to which it lays claim in theory." When Mill further remarks in the already mentioned essay *Utility of Religion* (Mill 1874, 109): "The essence of religion is the strong and earnest direction of the emotions and desires towards an ideal object, recognised as of the highest excellence, and as rightfully paramount over all selfish objects of desire. This condition is fulfilled by the Religion of Humanity in as eminent a degree, and in as high a sense, as by the supernatural religions even in their best manifestations [...]." Thus, the reader will understand from this conception of the essence of religion why Mill did not go beyond Comte in the question of a higher replacement for supernatural religion.

After all, the English thinker corrected the French thinker on some points. Thus, Mill says very correctly about Comte's excessive altruism: "[We are obliged to charge Comte] with *fundamentally misconceiving the proper office of a rule of life*. He committed the error which is often falsely charged against the whole class of utilitarian moralists; he required that *the test of conduct should also be an exclusive motive to actdo*" (Mill 1865, 138).²⁵ Mill also rightly emphasises that altruistic action can only increase the {29} sum of human happiness if it is voluntary but that any compulsion in this respect contains an internal contradiction.²⁶ Mill is also quite correct in observing that to reduce the measure of personal enjoyment to what is necessary for the maintenance of existence is to diminish it too much. However, Mill also seems to us to go far too far in his restriction of personal pleasures when he says (Mill 1865, 145): "The moralisation of the personal enjoy-

---

23 [Druskowitz, most likely, used the following edition: Mill 1875. We are using the following edition: Mill 2009.]
24 [This quote was a part of the German edition of Mill's views on religion (Mill 1875), however, it does not come from any of the three essays: it is taken from Mill 1865.]
25 [The italics are Druskowitz's as well as the beginning of the sentence is different than in Mill's original text.]
26 Mill 1865, 143: "So long as they are in no way compelled to this conduct by any external pressure, there cannot be too much of it (making the good of others); but a necessary condition is its spontaneity; since the notion of a happiness for all, procured by the self-sacrifice of each, if the abnegation is really felt to be a sacrifice, is a contradiction."

ments we deem to consists, not in reducing them to the smallest possible amount, but in cultivating the habitual wish to share them with other, and with all others, and scorning to desire anything for oneself which is incapable of being so shared." What a thought! Then, the exquisite natures would have to scorn the pleasures accessible to them alone and suppress their high moods and sublime thoughts because the general public cannot share them. In contrast, the following passage in Mill differs very favourably from Comte's blind glorification of altruism (Mill 1874, 108): "A morality grounded on large and wise views of the good of the whole, neither sacrificing the individual to the aggregate nor the aggregate to the individual, but giving to duty on the one hand and to freedom and spontaneity on the other their proper province, would derive its power in the superior natures from {29} sympathy and benevolence and the passion for ideal excellence: in the inferior, from the same feelings cultivated up to the measure of their capacity, with the superadded force of shame."

In the essay *Utility of Religion*, Mill has quite obviously broken with all the components and delusions of a supernatural faith. To the objection that, given the limited nature of earthly life, no sublime feelings can be attached to it, he replies (Mill 1874, 106): "Let it be remembered that if individual life is short, the life of the human species is not short; its indefinite duration is practically equivalent to endlessness; and being combined with indefinite capability of improvement, it offers to the imagination and sympathies a large enough object to satisfy any reasonable demand for grandeur of aspiration. If such an object appears small to a mind accustomed to dream of infinite and eternal beatitudes, it will expand into far other dimensions when those baseless fancies shall have receded into the past." He also expresses the conviction that the more perfect a person's life is, the more content they will be with it, and the less they will long for immortality.[27]

{31} It is to be regretted that Mill has not always shown the same manly attitude towards the phantasm of immortality as he does in that treatise. In the essay *Theism*, the last of his essays on religion, he presents himself quite differently on the point in question. "The beneficial effect of such a hope is far from trifling. It makes life and human nature a far greater thing to the feelings and gives greater strength as well as a greater solemnity to all the sentiments which are awakened in us by our fellow creatures and by mankind at large. It allays the sense of that irony of Nature which is so painfully felt when we see the exertions and sacrifices

---

27 Mill 1874, 122: "It seems to me not only possible but probable, that in a higher, and, above all, a happier condition of human life, not annihilation but immortality may be the burdensome idea; and that human nature, though pleased with the present, and by no means impatient to quit it, would find comfort and not sadness in the thought that it is not chained through eternity to a conscious existence which it cannot be assured that it will always wish to preserve."

of a life culminating in the formation of a wise and noble mind, only to disappear from the world when the time has just arrived at which the world seems about to begin reaping the benefit of it" (Mill 1874, 249) and in another place Mill says that the religion of morality may secure a greater influence on the human mind by supernatural hopes,[28] statements which form a most unpleasant contrast to the attitude which Mill shows in the essay *Utility of Religion*, and which we must strongly regret.

4

{32} We have already noted that at the same time as the great French thinker was formulating his religion of humanity, the German, Ludwig Feuerbach, was teaching that true religion is to be sought in man's love for other people.

"Love, which is not a spiritual or spiritualistic phrase, not identical with the *actus purus*, the pure act of thought of the medieval and modern scholastics, and therefore only love of thought, but the real, true, human love is essentially pathological love, i. e. love seized by the material, real sufferings of humanity, and this love is the God who rules the world in truth" (Feuerbach 1866, 118 [our translation]). Furthermore, in the *Principles of the Philosophy of the Future* we read: "Being is a mystery of perception, of feeling, of love. Only in feeling, only in love does a 'This', this person, this thing, i. e. the individual, have absolute value, is the finite *infinite*, in this and only in this lies the infinite depth, divinity and truth of love. In love alone is the God who counts the hairs on our heads truth and reality" (Feuerbach 1846, 323 [our translation]).

We have already pointed out the difference between Comte's religion of humanity and Feuerbach's religion of love: with Comte, it is benevolence awakened and intensified by reflection, with Feuerbach it is the affect that comes directly from the heart. However, both thinkers harmonise in that both see the essence of religion in altruism.

There are also similarities in the views of both thinkers in other respects. For instance, simultaneously with {33} Comte, Feuerbach also emphasised the law of the three phases of the mind, at least for the individual, in the statement: "God was my first thought, reason my second, a human being my third and last thought." Just like Comte, the German thinker wants all things to be related to

---

28 [Druskowitz is referring to the last sentence of the essay "Theism", which reads: "But it appears to me that supernatural hopes, in the degree and kind in which what I have called rational scepticism does not refuse to sanction them, may still contribute not a little to give to this religion its due ascendancy over the human mind" (Mill 1874, 257).]

a human being; for him, too, there is nothing higher than humanity, and for him, too, only the social human being is a human being. Thus, we read in the *Principles of the Philosophy of the Future:* "The individual human being does not intrinsically have the essence of humanity in themselves, neither as a moral being nor as a thinking being; the essence of humanity is only contained in the community, in the unity of a human being with a human being—a unity that is based solely on the reality of the difference between 'I' and 'Thou'" (Feuerbach 1846, 344 [our translation]). "Solitude is finitude and limitation; community is freedom and infinity. The human being by themself is a human (in the ordinary sense); the human being with others, that is, the unity of 'I' and 'Thou', is God" (Feuerbach 1846, 344 [our translation]).

Given the numerous points of contact that exist between Feuerbach and Comte, it is surprising that E. N. Starcke, Feuerbach's appointed portrayer and interpreter, not only failed to draw a detailed parallel between the two thinkers in his recently published work but did not even mention Comte's name.

By seeing the essence of religion in love, Feuerbach comes to base all morality on the feeling of identity, on the natural love of one human being for another. The essence of morality does not lie in submission to the moral law, to the admonition of that voice which calls out to the human being "thou shalt", but in respect for one's fellow human being. Feuerbach's *love* is nothing else than Schopenhauer's compassion and differs {34} just as much from Comte's altruism. Both thinkers, Schopenhauer and Feuerbach, are in the same oppositional position to Kant here, and both are mistaken in their opposition.

Both start from the mistaken assumption that morality concerns only the relationship between human beings. In contrast, the relationship of a human being to their own personality, as well as to the idea of truth, designated by intellectual conscience, also comes into play. However, intellectual conscience may at times compel us to hardness, even cruelty, toward our fellow humans, and yet morality is still justified. Even when it comes to benefiting others or protecting them from harm, if our actions are to possess true moral value, the feelings of respect, sympathy, and love should always play a secondary role. At the same time, the primary driving force [*primum mobile*] must be something completely independent of those feelings. It is that inner voice, that consciousness, which asserts its power over us even when it involves acting against our will, subordinating our most fervent desires to the interests of others, promoting people to whom we are utterly indifferent, and administering justice to our enemies. It is that consciousness, given a priori and gradually awakening in humanity, of a higher, ideal order that a human being ought to implement; it is the gradually emerging sense of balance and harmony in human interests, a sense that is not only akin to but fundamentally identical with the aesthetic drive. It is more beautiful and more humane if we carry out our moral actions with sympathy for the {35} persons involved. However, sympathy must never become the determining motive if our actions are to have moral value.

We also cannot agree with Feuerbach's grounding of morality in the *need for the happiness of others*. We must reiterate what we have just stated: morality concerns not only the relationship between human beings but also the relationship to one's own self and truth, and intellectual conscience can lead us to actions that have little to do with the well-being of others. It is indeed indisputable that the intensification of moral feeling in human relations would bring an end to much suffering and misery, which is currently the result of brutality and license, particularly in the lower classes (we primarily think of the deplorable situation of women). However, one must also consider how much more serious, stricter, and more challenging life would become if everyone were to impose higher moral demands on themselves and others, if everyone monitored themselves strictly and were constantly at war with the tremendous power of egoism!

Thus, while a more perfect morality in one direction may be able to promote the happiness of society, in another it will tend to diminish it, from which it follows that happiness cannot be the aim and purpose of morality.

The advantage of Feuerbach's new doctrine over that of Comte lies in the fact that Feuerbach connects human beings closely with nature, while Comte confronts them as something foreign to nature, thereby providing {36} a stable representational substrate for the feeling of dependence expressed in religion. 'The new philosophy,' Feuerbach says, 'makes the human being, including nature as the basis of the human being, the sole, universal, highest object of philosophy.' This description of the relationship between nature and humans is, in fact, the starting point that a replacement for religion needs. Human beings are not something isolated from nature but must be viewed in intimate connection with it. Whether we adopt a materialistic or idealistic standpoint, we must understand the human being as the highest link in a long series of development. Therefore, one does not necessarily have to share Feuerbach's materialistic standpoint in order to endorse his firm integration of human beings with nature. Even if, like Kant, we regard all processes and things, including human beings, as appearances, we must nevertheless admit that certain appearances had to precede others so that the appearance of a 'human being,' for example, presupposes an incalculable number of other appearances, so that, in the relationship of appearances to one another, a law is expressed which is entirely independent of us, but on which we are entirely dependent.

For Feuerbach, various things are tools of nature with which it pursues different goals; the human being, in terms of their highest faculties, is nature's highest tool. However, this can only apply to the arena and sphere of the perception of humanity. Possible higher organisations could be imagined on other celestial bodies, and the human beings themselves may possibly transition into a higher order. By presenting the human being as {37} the highest type, Feuerbach falls into the same error as Comte. However, as has been remarked, the human being is the highest tool of nature on their own stage. There is a powerful impulse and incentive in the thought that nature itself has set humanity the sacred task of developing those faculties and powers which, as far as they can observe, they alone possess, and that they can only understand the voice of nature and fulfil its will when they bring their own human nature to expression.

Feuerbach, however, has grounded only that kind of feeling of *dependence* which humans experience in religion toward the universal, in a manner equally satisfying to both understanding and mind, and thereby has given morality as well as every striving for perfection a firm point of attachment. He emphasizes neither the feeling of *reverence* before the world-whole that transcends the individual, nor the trust in the ultimate world-powers—whether one conceives them as dispositions in the formlessly conceived primordial matter or as something unknowable reigning behind appearances.

D. Fr. Strauß does this, albeit in an imperfect and heartless manner, in his last work (Strauß 1872, 139–141 [our translation]). Nevertheless, one will always have to take the following passage into account, whatever one may think of the book. We reproduce the passage in full: "We perceive in nature tremendous contrasts, terrible struggles, but we find that through them the existence and harmony of the whole is not disturbed; on the contrary, it is preserved. We continue to perceive a gradual process, an emergence of the higher from the lower, the fine from the coarse, the mild from the raw. Therefore the more we succeed in subjecting the arbitrarily {38} changing to the rule, in developing the higher from the lower, the tender from the coarse, the more we find ourselves promoted in our personal as well as in our social life. When we encounter such things in the circle of human life, we take them sensibly and well. We cannot fail to call what we perceive in the world around us the same. Since we feel ourselves to be absolutely dependent on this world and can only derive our existence and the organisation of our being from it, we must also regard it, in its full concept or as a universe, as the original source of all that is reasonable and good. The old religion concluded from the fact that what is reasonable and good in the human world emanates from consciousness and will and that what is found in the world on a large scale must also emanate from a conscious and willing author. We have abandoned this way of concluding; we no longer regard the world as the work of an absolutely rational and good personality but as the workshop of the rational and good. It is no longer created for us by a supreme reason, but it is created for a supreme reason. Of course, what lies in the effect must also lie in the cause; what comes out must also have been in. It is only the limitation of our human representation that we differentiate in this way; the universe is cause and effect, external and internal at the same time. It is, therefore, that on which we feel ourselves to be dependent, by no means a brute superiority to which we bow with mute resignation, but at the same time order and law, reason and goodness, to which we surrender with loving trust. And still more: since we perceive in ourselves the disposition to the reasonable and the good, which we believe we recognise in the world, and find it recognised by the beings by whom it is to be felt, {39} in whom it is to become personal, we feel ourselves at the same time intimately related to that on which we find ourselves dependent, and we find ourselves at the same time free in our dependence—in our feeling for the universe pride mingles with humility, joy with submission."

However, the main ideas expressed at this point were only further elaborated and substantiated by Julius Duboc on the one hand and E. Dühring on the other.

5

We will now consider various experiments that belong here, to which we must be quite negative.

Let us at least mention Dr. Löwenthal and Dr. E. Reich as writers who have dealt with our problem. However, neither is a phenomenon significant enough for us to deal with in detail. It is noteworthy that Dr. Reich is strongly influenced by Comte, although not in a higher sense. His "Church of Humanity"[29] is rather one of the most banal ideas ever conceived.

We must now take a closer look at F. A. Lange's view that Christianity should be maintained, but understood *sensu allegorico* instead of *sensu proprio*. "There are only two paths," says Lange about the future of religion (Lange 1877, 546 [our translation]), "which can be seriously considered in the long run after it has been shown that mere enlightenment runs into the sand of shallowness without ever becoming free of untenable dogmas. One path is the complete {40} abolition of all religion and the transfer of its tasks to the state, science and art; the other is to go to the core of religion and overcome all fanaticism and superstition through the conscious elevation above reality and the definitive renunciation of the falsification of reality by myth, which cannot serve the purpose of cognition. The first of these paths entails the danger of spiritual impoverishment; the second concerns the great question of whether the core of religion is not now undergoing

---

29 [Druskowitz is referring to Reich 1872.]

a transformation that makes it difficult to grasp with certainty. The second concern is the lesser one because it is precisely the principle of spiritualisation that must make every transition caused by the cultural needs of the advancing age easier and more peaceful."

"As long as the core of religion was sought in certain doctrines about God, the human soul, creation and its order, it was inevitable that any criticism that began by separating the wheat from the chaff according to logical principles would end in complete negation. One sifted until there was nothing left. — If, on the other hand, one sees the core of religion in the elevation of the realms above the real and in the creation of a home for the spirits, then the purified forms can still evoke essentially the same psychic processes as the charcoal-burning faith of the crowd. One will never arrive at zero with all the philosophical refinement of ideas. We, therefore, accustom ourselves to attaching a higher value to the principle of the creative idea as such, without agreement with historical and scientific cognition, but also without falsifying it; we accustom ourselves to regarding the world of ideas as equally indispensable {41} to all human progress as the cognition of the understanding, by attributing the greater or lesser importance of every idea to ethical or aesthetic foundations." — There are many a sentence in this passage that one can readily subscribe to. Above all, however, the assertion that there are only two paths to the future of religion is completely erroneous: the abolition of religion and, as a result, its spiritual impoverishment or the retention of its representations and forms with the full awareness that they can only be grasped symbolically. Lange opts for the latter, but we consider it to be just as misguided as the former, which Lange also rejects.

The πρῶτον ψεῦδος [fundamental error] of that view is precisely the assertion that the essence of religion consists in the elevation of the spirit above reality. Although it must be conceded that this psychic process plays a significant role in religion, it must not be made the essence of religion if one does not want to identify religion with a one-sided conception of poetry. This equation is, however, completely inadmissible. The fact that every religious confessor believes himself to have the only true revelation is the most evident proof of what religion is all about. It is not exaltation above reality—although, as we have already remarked, this is of great importance in religion—but the most profound conviction, rock-solid faith, unshakeable trust in representations which are the highest in the eyes of the believer, that form the essence of religion. Every religion is an imperfect attempt to interpret and construe the world, a provisional answer to the questions of the origin of things, the meaning of reality and the final destiny {42} of humans. The answers that religion gives to these questions form believers' view of the world to which they cling, the truth of which fills them even if they are incapable of comprehending it. Now, if trust in these representations ceases, if believers realise that they are to be taken only *sensu allegorico*, how will they then relate to them? Will they really still have a significance that cuts into their life?

Before we answer this question, however, let us examine the examples Lange gives to prove that the educated have always had a conception of religion similar to his and that the people have at least dimly sensed this state of affairs.

First example: "If this fact had not been clearly in the consciousness of the wise and, at least in intuition, also in the consciousness of the people, how else could poets and sculptors in Greece and Rome have dared to keep the myth alive, to give the ideal of the deity new forms?" [Lange 1877, 549, our translation].

To this, it must be replied that the Greeks did indeed begin to regard their gods as figments of the imagination at an early stage. Their unbelief was in no way to blame for their early ruin, a circumstance that constitutes striking proof against the correctness of our philosopher's view that religion can still offer support if it is only conceived as allegorical or symbolic poetry. A people for whom their gods can no longer be an object of devout veneration needs to replace religion with more trustworthy representations and ideals.

Second example: "Hence the value that truly pious minds have always regarded inner experience and realisation as proof of faith. Many of these {43} believers, who owe their peace of mind to a fervent struggle in prayer and have spiritual contact with Christ as a person, know quite well in theory that the same emotional processes can also be found with the same success and with the same proof in completely different doctrines, indeed, among the followers of completely foreign religions... Does it not become clear that the essence of the matter lies in the form of the spiritual process and not in the logical-historical content of the individual views and doctrines? This predominance of form in faith is also betrayed by the curious fact that believers of different even mutually hostile denominations agree more with each other and show more sympathy with their most ardent opponents than with those who are indifferent to religious questions" [Lange 1877, 550, our translation].

It can be objected, however, that when adherents of one religion show sympathy for those of another religion, this sympathy is always accompanied by the feeling that the others are in error. Even when they respect the religious devotion of those of another faith, they simultaneously pity them for worshipping a false god. Furthermore, if believers feel more sympathy for those of another religion than for non-believers, it is because they consider the former as seekers and strivers who only need to be made to understand the *true* faith in order to convert to it. The fact that adherents of religion seek to *convert* others to their faith is the most evident proof that, for believers, it is not only the elevation of the spirit that matters but also the object to which it is elevated.

Finally, our philosopher refers to those humans of outstanding talent and solid education who, in contrast to mocking flatheads, cling to religion "because they have led a rich life of the mind {44} from their youth and cling to the familiar ground with a thousand roots of imagination, the memory of consecrated beautiful hours" [Lange 1877, 485, our translation]. However, we can see in this attachment of enlightened humans to religion nothing other than a sign that a human being indeed needs firm confidence. This desire makes enlightened humans envy the believers all the more, the less they have succeeded in creating a perfect replacement for religion. If, however, one were to expect human beings, as Lange thinks of them, to occupy themselves seriously with Christian representations, viewed symbolically, they would declare themselves incapable of doing so. The reason is that religious representations, as soon as they are no longer accepted with faith, very soon lose all weight.

For, if we are to adhere to old symbolical representations, they must, first, contain a more profound meaning and, secondly, be expressed in a truly poetical form. The truth is, however, that no religion, apart from a few ethical precepts, offers tenable ideas and that most of its representations, if one goes to the bottom of them, prove to be unpoetic and crude.

And how would it be possible to maintain religion in the form Lange thinks of it? A religious feeling cannot be produced at all through the presentation of symbols, however honourable they may be, or it would very soon either lose all its support or merge into "literal faith". As Lange himself admits: "In any case, ideology is all too easily tainted by the poison of literalism; the symbol involuntarily and gradually becomes a rigid dogma like the image of a saint becomes an idol" [Lange 1877, 555, our translation].

If Lange's conception of religion, which he identifies with poetry, is erroneous, his view {45} of the nature of poetry itself, when he describes it as an elevation above reality, is one-sided. It is no wonder that with this conception of poetry, Schiller's poetry seems to be Lange's highest ideal, while it is not an ultimate model. After all, the most profound and most lasting effect can only be produced by poetry in which "realism" and idealism are in balance.

Lange's noble compassion, with which he takes up the cause of the poor and miserable, is sympathetically touching. He emphasises two important moments, even if he does not propose a perfect remedy, when he says: "If a new thing is to emerge from the old, two great things must unite, a world-inflaming *ethical idea* and a *social achievement* that is mightily small to lift the oppressed classes a great step" [Lange 1877, 556–557, our translation].[30]

---

30 [Druskowitz paraphrases the beginning of the sentence which reads as follows in the original

6

Friedrich Nietzsche's original book *Thus Spoke Zarathustra* is one of the remarkable endeavours to solve the problem that concerns us.[31] There can be no doubt that the author, who in many respects occupies an exceptional position among the writers of our day, believes he has created a new gospel with this work. He even endeavours to reproduce the form and tone of the holy books, which he, the master of the form, succeeds in doing admirably.

Nietzsche's numerous works have, to date, remained largely unnoticed by the public and critics. Nietzsche is actually only known {46} and highly respected in educated, musical circles, both due to a long-standing intimate friendship with Richard Wagner and through his treatise *The Birth of Tragedy from the Spirit of Music*, which, according to experts, contains the most ingenious representation of the spirit of Wagner's music, and through the brilliant commemorative publication *Richard Wagner in Bayreuth*, which was also translated into French. Incidentally, Nietzsche's name is often mentioned and recognised as a great one, without one always knowing on what this fame is based. We, therefore, take the liberty of making a few general remarks about this writer, as well as a brief characterisation and criticism of his main ideas set down in his earlier works, before we go into his main work in question here—a criticism which will, of course, be essentially negative.

Nietzsche is, above all, an artistic spirit, a poet in terms of sensitivity, subtlety, visualisation, and the harmonious beauty of his speech. As a stylist, he has few equals. He also possesses a way of thinking that is far removed from all stereotypes, an astonishing wealth of ideas, a magnificent overview of various areas of life, art, and science, and a very definite, even sovereign judgment.

However, Nietzsche was hardly satisfied with this recognition. He has certainly considered himself a philosopher, at least since the publication of his work *Human, All Too Human* (1878). Is he entitled to do so? Are his works philosophical works? In any case, they contain a large number of philosophical thoughts in his collections of longer or shorter reflections and aphorisms, which he published under the sometimes {47} paradoxical titles *Human, All Too Human*, *The Wanderer and His Shadow*, *Dawn*, and *The Gay Science*, and in which he touches on almost all the more important questions, stringing together thoughts of the most varied weight and values, usually in a completely unmethodical way. There is indeed

---

text: "[...] wenn ein Neues werden und das Alte vergehen soll, müssen sich zwei grosse Dinge vereinigen [...]."

31 [Druskowitz uses the first edition of Part 1 and Part 2 from 1883 and Part 3 from 1884.]

an extraordinary amount of spirit in these works. However, what is the particular value of the philosophical thoughts that the author offers us in them? Above all, it should be noted that Nietzsche has hardly dealt with any problem in depth. Where others have laboured, he is pleased to indulge in winks and allusions and witty images; he is generally more pleased in the role of a scientific task setter than a scientific worker. Is he entitled to do so? In our opinion, his strength seems to be based mainly on his ingenious reproductive capacity. He possesses the superiority of expression and form. In fact, he has shown the results of research and speculation in a new light through many an apt word, through many a new designation, through many a happy picture, which, of course, often leads him to take a position towards the actual authors of these thoughts that lacks modesty.

It cannot be denied, however, that there is no lack of original thoughts, psychological analyses and flashes of genius in his works. In general, it may be said of his philosophical reflections that the treatment of the problems does not harmonise with their importance, that utterances of genuine wisdom alternate with useless quibbles and questionable sophistries, samples of genuine sagacity with paradoxes and sometimes quite regrettable blunders, and that the author contradicts himself on almost every {48} point. Nevertheless, we must especially admire his unusual reproductive capacity in the philosophical field. The limits of his philosophical talent become apparent as soon as he attempts to determine ultimate tasks and goals based on his insight. Immediately, a striking lack of a healthy sense of reality, as well as the inability to strike the right balance, becomes apparent.

Although Nietzsche is influenced by certain modern currents of thought, he is conversely completely distant from the practical questions of life and is an extreme idealist if being an idealist really means not taking reality into account. Ancient ideals and states of mind that have no application to our time float before his mind, while he is coldly opposed to many of the best and noblest contemporary endeavours. No wonder the public is also cold towards him.

He immediately demonstrated his remarkable lack of capacity for a just and correct appreciation of life and humans in his first philosophical text, *Schopenhauer as Educator*[32] (1874), where society is given the task of *producing genius*. And it is not a future, ideal society, in which people have learnt to preserve their human dignity, in which they have generally achieved greater spiritual maturity and education, that is given this task, but rather the imperative of our time: "You should bring forth and promote genius". Admittedly, this imperative would appear to any society as a strange demand for the simple reason that it is not

---

[32] The treatise forms the third part of the *Untimely Mediations*.

within its power to fulfil it through reflection. Nietzsche {49} is, of course, convinced of the opposite. Using the example of Schopenhauer, with whom he was caught up in an almost unpleasant way at the time he wrote the work in question, he wants to show what society has to learn in order to facilitate the rebirth of the genius, especially of Schopenhauer, whom Nietzsche is primarily concerned with here, or of the philosophical genius since the same reasons must prevent the emergence of the genius that impede its *effectiveness.*

What was essentially to blame, asks Nietzsche, that Schopenhauer had to wait so long until the day finally came when he exclaimed in an admittedly painfully touching triumph: *legor et legar* [*I am read and I will be read*]? The lack of simplicity and naturalness of his contemporaries is the answer. For this reason, Nietzsche thought, Schopenhauer's friends and admirers had to be gathered together in order to create a current flowing through them that would facilitate the rebirth of the philosophical genius.

A highly misguided cult of heroism, a complete inversion of the actual state of affairs, of the actual relationship between genius and society!

The genius opens up a new spiritual domain for society by either developing in opposition to the prevailing trends of the times or by giving expression to what contemporaries can only dimly perceive. Society often only learns to take possession of this domain gradually, but it cannot know it before the genius appears in order to prepare itself for its appearance, so to speak. The mere naturalness of thought and feeling is certainly not enough. Society needs a certain spiritual maturity to understand the genius, but this can only be given to society again by the genius. Thus, we see that Nietzsche completely misconceives the relationship between genius {50} and society, indeed completely reverses the actual state of affairs. Finally, how Nietzsche envisions the promotion of genius rebirth by society is quite incomprehensible to us. Until now, Nietzsche has always clung to the idea that nature is only concerned with the "heroic human being".

When Nietzsche wrote the essay on Schopenhauer, he did not yet consider himself a philosopher, nor did he believe he would ever become one, as he openly admitted[33]; at the time, he was merely an enthusiastic follower of Schopenhauer.

Soon afterwards, he completely detached himself from his old master. Nietzsche had grown tired of unconditional worship, and his sense of self had matured. There is no doubt that in *Human, All Too Human*, he believed he had expressed a significant, independent thought. Nietzsche had come to the painful

---

33 Put the following passages in context: p. 92: "A scholar can never become a philosopher" and p. 97: "But even Kant was, as we scholars tend to be, considerate and submissive." [Our translation.]

conviction that we are determined by motives in all our actions and, as is usually the case, he drew the fundamentally false conclusion that there is no difference between good and evil, that there are neither moral nor immoral actions, that virtue deserves no admiration, that it is a logical error to be angry at vice and to punish the criminal. However, Nietzsche could not calm himself with this realisation until a comforting thought came to his aid. "But there is one consolation," we read at the end of the chapter *On the History of Moral* {51} *Sensations* (Nietzsche 2005, 58–59),[34] "[...] such pains are birth pangs. The butterfly wants to get out of its cocoon, it tears at it, it breaks it open: then it is blinded and confused by the unfamiliar light, the realm of freedom. It is in such men as are capable of that suffering—how few they will be!—that the first attempt will be made to see whether mankind could transform itself from a moral to a knowing mankind. [...] Even if the inherited habit of erroneous evaluation, loving, hating does continue to rule in us, under the influence of increasing knowledge, it will grow weaker: a new habit, that of comprehending, not-loving, not-hating, surveying is gradually implanting itself in us in the same soil and will in thousands of years' time perhaps be strong enough to bestow on mankind the power of bringing forth the wise, innocent (conscious of innocence) man as regularly as it now brings forth —not his antithesis but necessary preliminary—the unwise, unjust, guilt-conscious man."

The possibility of a wise humanity is an idea that no one had previously considered. Spinoza considered a community of thinkers possible in which nobody would offend. He would have shaken his head at the idea of a "wise humanity". Should the intellect really ever have the power to become master over the more primal powers of the emotions? Moreover, if it should be able to become such a magician, would not the aesthetic feelings also disappear with the ethical feelings, and finally, apart from an unerring intellect, only the lowest feelings {52} remain? When Herbert Spencer dreams of a future state of society in which personal and general interests will be in perfect harmony, this is a beautiful dream, and there are moments when one can believe in its realisation. In contrast, Nietzsche's utopia presents a bleak picture of the future. It is all the less understandable that this thought should reassure Nietzsche since shortly beforehand, he had expressed himself as follows (Nietzsche 2005, 28): "Only very naive people are capable of believing that the nature of man could be transformed into a purely logical one; but if there should be degrees of approximation to this objective, what would *not have to be lost if this course were taken!*" Incidentally, we cannot declare ourselves in agreement with this debate either since we must reject the underlying view that

---

34 [This text is included as a second essay in vol. I of *Human, All Too Human.*]

our moral judgements are based only on errors of the intellect. However, we do not consider it our task to develop our own view on this point at this point.

When Nietzsche expresses the idea in one passage of *Dawn* (1881) that people should be given back their confidence in their actions, which have been decried as selfish, because this would remove the appearance of evil from life, and people would cease to be evil if they no longer considered themselves evil, this is a very daring assertion.

Furthermore, Nietzsche's attitude towards pity is downright disconcerting. He sees in it only a manifestation of the feeling of power, a "pleasant impulse of the instinct of appropriation" [Nietzsche 2011, bk. 3, fr. 118] the most pleasant feeling in {53} those who have little pride and can make few other conquests. For him, it is nothing but a moral fashion, and the compassionate person is only a special kind of egoist.

Nietzsche is right a thousand times over when he censures the intellectual frivolity with which "good deeds" are usually performed and, concerning Comte's teaching, warns of the dangers of altruism taken too far. However, Nietzsche does not distinguish between the clumsy, insulting behaviour of those who have not attained a higher culture of feeling and follow their impulses and the noble forms of genuine compassion. True compassion, of which only the truly moral, imaginative and intelligent person is capable, does not want to use violence and cannot offend. As in almost every point, Nietzsche contradicts himself in this instance as well. In *The Gay Science*, it says: (Fr. 74) "What is the most human thing? To spare someone shame." Is not sparing someone shame also a form of compassion? The deepest reason why Nietzsche treats compassion so disdainfully is the awareness that there are cases where the good of one's neighbour must be sacrificed for a higher purpose. Thus, in the section "Even ignoring your neighbour" in *Dawn* (Nietzsche 2011, 111–112, fr. 146), it says: "The essence of what is genuinely moral is supposed to lie in our keeping our eye attuned to the most immediate and direct consequences actions have for others and in our making decisions accordingly? This may even be a morality, but only a narrow and petty bourgeois morality: it seems to me, however, to be a higher and freer manner of thought that *looks beyond* these most immediate consequences for others and to furthermore distant aims, under some circumstances *even at the expense of the suffering of others—* for {54} example, to further knowledge despite the insight that our free thinking will at first plunge others directly into doubt, dire distress, and even worse." We must be grateful to Nietzsche for strongly emphasising this point of view. However, because in some instances there are higher considerations than the welfare of fellow human beings, these are only exceptional cases, and how impoverished life would be if compassion were to disappear from it!

What touches us most sympathetically in Nietzsche is his emphasis on *shared joy*, the existence of which some philosophers, e.g. Hobbes, denied; on intellectual conscience, which in fact only asserts itself in the very fewest, and his courageous, joyful affirmation of life with a proud view into the distance, doubly pleasant in a former disciple of Schopenhauer. In *Thus Spoke Zarathustra*, Nietzsche's last work, to which we shall pass immediately, this has received the most intense but admittedly misguided expression. Finally, Nietzsche's strong individualism is also sympathetic, except that Nietzsche also goes too far in this respect, as he contradicts his contempt for the average person by considering everyone to be unique and denying the justification of generally binding laws.

What does Nietzsche ultimately want to teach in *Thus Spoke Zarathustra*? We have already mentioned that Nietzsche believed he had created a new gospel with this work and that he himself reproduced the form of holy books in it without our being able to approve of this. Even if the old language has the advantage of greater force and power, it is not capable of reproducing our modern, refined feelings and thoughts. Whoever, therefore, uses this language will not be able to avoid a coarsening repercussion to his thoughts, {55} as is only too clearly shown in Nietzsche's work. W. M. Salter, in the book which we shall soon discuss, has struck a far more appropriate tone for how a doctrine must be presented today in order to inflame hearts.

The thought on which *Zarathustra* is based is a consequence of Darwinism and had already been expressed repeatedly before Nietzsche. However, Nietzsche must be given the credit for having grasped it more affectionately than anyone else. Of course, as is so often the case, Nietzsche is tempted by affect to overshoot the mark by far.

We quote the central passage from Zarathustra's first speech, which he addresses to the assembled crowd, in order that the reader may gather from the hero's words the main conceptions of the book and form an opinion of how the author has Zarathustra speak (Nietzsche 2006, 5–8):

"I teach you the overman. Human being is something that must be overcome. What have you done to overcome him?"

"All creatures so far created something beyond themselves; and you want to be the ebb of this great flood and would even rather go back to animals than overcome humans?"

"What is the ape to a human? A laughing stock or a painful embarrassment. And that is precisely what the human shall be to the overman: a laughing stock or a painful embarrassment."

"You have made your way from worm to human, and much in you is still worm. Once you were apes, and even now a human is still more ape than any ape."

{56} "But whoever is wisest among you is also just a conflict and a cross between plant and ghost. But do I implore you to become ghosts or plants?"

"Behold, I teach you the overman!"

"The overman is the meaning of the earth. Let your will say: the overman *shall be* the meaning of the earth!"

"I beseech you, my brothers, remain *faithful* to the earth and do not believe those who speak to you of extraterrestrial hopes! They are mixers of poisons whether they know it or not."

"They are despisers of life, dying off and self-poisoned, of whom the earth is weary: so let them fade away!"

"Once the sacrilege against God was the greatest sacrilege, but God died, and then all these desecrators died. Now to desecrate the earth is the most terrible thing, and to esteem the bowels of the unfathomable higher than the meaning of the earth!" [...]

"What is the greatest thing that you can experience? It is the hour of your great contempt. The hour in which even your happiness turns to nausea and likewise your reason and your virtue." [...]

"The hour in which you say: 'What matters my reason? Does it crave knowledge like the lion its food? It is poverty and filth and a pitiful contentment!'"

"The hour in which you say: 'What matters my virtue? It has not yet made me rage. How weary I am of my good and my evil! That is all poverty and filth and a pitiful contentment!'"

{57} "The hour in which you say: 'What matters my justice? I do not see that I am ember and coal. But the just person is ember and coal!'"

"The hour in which you say: 'What matters my pity? Is pity not the cross on which he is nailed who loves humans? But my pity is no crucifixion.'"

"Have you yet spoken thus? Have you yet cried out thus? Oh, that I might have heard you cry out thus! Not your sin – your modesty cries out to high heaven, your stinginess even in sinning cries out to high heaven!"

"Where is the lightning that would lick you with its tongue? Where is the madness with which you should be inoculated?"

Behold, I teach you the overman: he is this lightning, he is this madness!" [...]

"Mankind is a rope fastened between animal and overman—a rope over an abyss."

"A dangerous crossing, a dangerous on-the-way, a dangerous looking back, a dangerous shuddering and standing still."

"What is great about human beings is that they are a bridge and not a purpose: what is lovable about human beings is that they are a *crossing over* and a *going under*."³⁵

{58} First, it should be noted that the position assigned to humanity by Zarathustra is not at all a favourable one. Even if humanity is to progress to a higher order, it is an ugly and unworthy idea to think of it in a relationship to this order similar to that of an ape to a human being. What an imposition that humans should strive to produce a higher type, to which they will only be "a laughingstock and a painful shame"! And what can be said about the assertion that, up to now, humanity alone has created nothing beyond itself while all other living beings have done so? It is regrettable to find such a misguided idea in a writer like Nietzsche.

Furthermore, it can only be posited as a possibility that humanity will one day advance to a higher order, but not as a certainty. Extraordinary perfection of humanity is conceivable without the ideal beings of the future having already surpassed the human type. The qualities Nietzsche highlights as characteristic of the *overman* have, in fact, been embodied in human geniuses; yet, as the *overman* would evidently have to surpass even the genius, Nietzsche ultimately provides us with no real clues as to how we should imagine him. Since the *overman* is not a certainty, he cannot, for this reason alone, be set forth as the goal of human striving. This would not be possible even if such a transition were definitively guaranteed because we do not know the conditions for the emergence of a new type and because the ideal of human striving cannot tolerate any specific embodiment. It grows with humanity's growth; the higher humanity rises, the higher its ideal. The *overman* would also be merely the realisation of a particular {59} stage of development of the ideal and thus cannot be posited as the ultimate goal.

Therefore, the fundamental idea of *Zarathustra* proves to be erroneous in every respect. Nevertheless, considered as a whole, the work belongs to the most peculiar phenomena of paradoxical literature.

---

35 We see that the thought of this *crossing over* and *going under* of man has suddenly awakened in Nietzsche from the following passage in *Dawn*, where Nietzsche expresses the opposite view: "Formerly one tried to get a feel for the majesty of human beings by pointing backwards toward their divine descent: this has now become a forbidden path, because before its gate stands the ape along with other heinous beasts [...]. So, one has a go of it now from the opposite direction: the path humanity pursues shall serve as proof of its majesty and kinship to God. Alas, this, too, leads nowhere! [...] However high humanity may have evolved—and perhaps at the end it will be standing even lower than at the beginning! There is in store for humanity no more a transformation into a higher order than for the ant and the earwigs, which, at the end of their 'earthly days,' will not ascend to kinship with God and eternal life." [Translation of the fragment 49 is taken from Nietzsche 2011, 38–39.]

7

We now have to speak of three thinkers, each of whom has emphasised an element of a higher replacement for religion in a more or less effective way, but without any of them having completely solved the problem. We mean Julius Duboc in his work *Optimism as a World View in its Religious-Ethical Significance for the Present* (1881); furthermore, E. Dühring in *Replacement of Religion by Something More Perfect and Elimination of All Judaism from the Modern Spirit of Nations* (1883) and finally William Mackintire Salter in *Religion of Morality* (1885).

Duboc distinguishes between two spheres regarding man's relationship to god in religion: the practical and the aesthetic. "As long as someone, in the religious sphere of representation, especially in its most popular form, that is in the belief in god and immortality, considers the *helping, counselling, consoling G*od, the supreme ruler and lawgiver, as far as they approach him as such spiritually in representation or mentally with desire and a feeling of gratitude, they move and remain in the practical sphere. [...] However, next to it or {60} above it, another sphere stretches out like a brilliant rainbow. It is as if illuminated by a mysterious light from beyond, as if resounding with a mysterious sound from beyond. Indeed, in its relation to man's inner being, it is nothing but the effect on imagination and mind, which is added to the impression that in all these religious moments, in the existence of a supreme ruler who judges righteously, in the continuity beyond the grave and death, etc., which cancels out our visible, sensible transitoriness, a *high and sublime relationship of being* is woven and exists around humans *which cannot be grasped by intellect*. In so far as the effect of this impression reaches into humans, in so far as it sustains, animates and fills them, in so far as their religious nature is built up peculiarly on this basis, the same is to be attributed exclusively to the aesthetic side" [Duboc 1881, 2–3, our translation].

By opposing the "this-worldliness" of our time, i.e. the preoccupation with purely human interests or, in other words, the "decline of religious consciousness" in the present day, Duboc wants to present this impression of a "high and sublime relationship of being which cannot be grasped by intellect" as one that is justified independently of any positive religious norm and to justify it by the facts. Even without a belief in a god, we should recognise that a mystery hovers around us and grasp it with a religious, reverent feeling. However, every cautious thinker will have to admit the existence of a world mystery. For Duboc, the mystery of the world consists in the infinity and unmanageability of the world process, or he simply wants to be aware of this moment of mystery.

Duboc, however, defines the mental impression in question {61} as follows (Duboc 1881, 88 [our translation]): "The most general mental impression (namely of a high and sublime relationship of being which cannot be grasped by reason), if we detach it from all other moments that embrace it but do not emerge from it, is to be described as a certain *aesthetic being captivated* by contemplation and elevation. Before every mystery that does not inspire us with terror and horror—therefore, it must be a *noble* mystery, which in this direction denotes the extreme opposite of everything terrible—which furthermore stands *so great* and *towering* that it is not merely seized by *curiosity* as a suitable object of investigation, and so *serious* that *curiosity* falls silent before it, before every such mystery there is such a being-captivated for the receptive human being."

This is the character of the mystery as it appears in religion, but it also exists outside it; the need to rise to the idea of it, or instead to embrace it with feeling, has been lost to modern man. While *infinity* rolls above our heads in billions of stars, while the cosmic process of development takes place in *incalculable* processes and forms, while a mystery exists that surpasses our conceptual sphere, all this is only an example of calculation, a curiosity for us, the highest things are just good enough to satisfy our curiosity and thirst for knowledge. The religious person harbours a certain reverence for *god's* mystery and would consider it an insult to his personal god to approach it merely as an object of investigation. However, for unbelieving {62} people, this obstacle falls away. Duboc admits that this 'aesthetic captivation with contemplation and elevation' depends on individual capability, mood, and level of education, but the motives for it are objectively given.

For us to understand the mystery of the world as a *sublime* one, which inspires us with awe rather than fear, we must, above all, recognise that there is meaning in the world process, whereas pessimism sees only *senselessness* in it. Duboc seeks to prove the sense in the cosmic process by first presenting the meaning of human endeavour and, from this, concluding the world process. The sense of human striving, however, consists in the fact that all striving is a striving for improvement, for an advantageous change. "But the improvement also contains at the same time, even if unconsciously, the betterment, the progress to a higher, in truth *transfigured* level of existence, for in recognising lies, together with the *explanation*, also the *clarification*" (Duboc 1881, 88 [our translation]). Moving on to answer the question of the relationship to the world process, Duboc says: "If I have acquired the right to express what is stated as the sense of being from the place where a striving active in the vicinity of consciousness takes place, that is, in humans and other living creatures, then this gives results, on the one hand in the right to take the expression in the cosmic sense, to transfer it from the world process, and on the other hand, to the meaning in which this is to be taken. If in all striving [...] lies the content of feeling, only in an altered form, if feeling is the fundamental fact of mental life, the fundamental fact of the life-process in general, which {63} finds expression in it and conditions it, then the progressive living development as the content of striving, as the sense of being, is also the sense of the world-process, that is, the *essential nature* of it, the *centre of gravity* in the direction of its execution, its *necessary* and therefore also *certain form of movement*" [Duboc 1881, 62–63, our translation]. Admittedly, the labelling of the mystery of the world as a *sublime* one seems to be contradicted by the fact that the *individual is at the mercy of the world process,* as it can be destined at any moment to "fall under the wheels of doom and be irreparably damaged or crushed" (Duboc 1881, 230 [our translation]). Duboc is the last to deny the evil of the world; he recognises it in all its terrible power, but at the same time, he astutely demonstrates that the evil of the world, the suffering of the world, has the same necessity as the necessity of becoming. "No matter whether we lend it a metaphysical or physical background, the *necessity of the existence* of becoming—it applies to both points of view—conditions an emergence from lowest beginnings, an elevation to which a sinking, an attraction to which a repulsion of other parts, in short, a process to which countless victims fall, goes side by side. What an immense amount of suffering is not able to be overcome by *insight*, what an immense amount of world suffering is thus only set by the fact that insight must first become, that it must first work its way through to brightness from instinctive impulses, dark drives, must swell from the slightest stock in the course of generations to a sum through which world suffering, as far as it was dependent on this, can be spared for the next generations" [Duboc 1881, 278, our translation]. Viewed as a whole, the world process therefore, despite the price paid by the individual, nevertheless {64} represents nothing other than a "working out of light out of darkness, of order out of chaos, as an overcoming of hardship and bondage in order to rise to freedom, to well-being. It is a *process of shaping light* in which *all* are involved, from which no one can escape, no matter how he chooses his position (insofar as there can be any question of choice), except that the individual's part in the process can be active or passive. The destiny of humanity presents itself under the image of a human being who, under adversity and tribulation of all kinds, but for the overcoming of which their strength is sufficient, works towards that—light, freedom, beauty—to which all his pulses beat. And in this fate of a victorious struggle and overcoming, there is nothing in itself that is capable of cancelling out the character of the sublime" [Duboc 1881, 270, our translation].

Nevertheless, it is not enough to *know* this; it must also be *felt*. By emotionally grasping the idea of world progress, by devoting ourselves to it, a concentration that we succeed in achieving at least for a few moments, we simultaneously rise above the earth, rise above our individuality and its relationship to us, thus also above compassion, indeed, as far as this is possible, above our own suffering and pain. By trusting in progress in the world process or optimism in the scientific sense of the word, we overcome the danger "of losing the noble character of the mystery of the world and thus religiousness, the aesthetic-religious feeling, through the effect of earthly suffering on our feelings" [Duboc 1881, 273, our translation]. The author has thus built a bridge from the mere *understanding* of the world's evil as a moment in a developmental process, in the sense of optimism, to the aesthetic and emotional aspects of humanity. Through liberation, through detachment from individuality and through elevation to a higher sphere, humans are {65} filled with a peace and a joy that is the "pure reflex of the sublime". At the same time, however, this aesthetic self-emptying is a worthy preliminary exercise for death as the complete extinction of individual consciousness. Duboc does not view the practical and aesthetic spheres as being in hostile opposition to each other, as is often the case in Christianity, for example. "It cannot be emphasised strongly enough [...]," are the concluding sentences of this interesting book, which at the same time summarise the significance of optimism for the moral behaviour of man, "that in this religious conception, there is no kind of hostile opposition to the sphere of the individual and the purposes and aspirations that arise in it. With the strongest *legitimate* bonds of sensuality, sympathy, and need, we know ourselves to be bound to the same in every phase of life! It is true that in religious exaltation, we must abandon the individual and lose ourselves as such if the cry of pain of our sensual nature is to fade away and the sublime mystery of the world, which we have grasped in our consciousness, is also to come to us as harmony in the emotional sphere. We can only do this if our life's work is directed in this direction. The honourable only exists by becoming, but it also only exists for the one through whom it becomes, and it only becomes by emerging from the hand of humanity. By approaching adversity, the world's evil, as a distortion of the world view, the optimistic point of view generates from itself, from its ethical-aesthetic basic idea, what has always been the best aspect of all religion, its comprehensive work of redemption" [Duboc 1881, 378–379, our translation].

{66} Duboc must be credited with having brought forth many a cogent argument against pessimism and with having strongly supported the idea of progress in the world process. We will not deny that both—refutation of pessimism and substantiation of world progress—can be done in a much more energetic way. The justification of optimism, however, only forms the necessary prerequisite for the feeling of reverent emotion through the grasping of the world process insofar as it is known on the one hand and a mystery on the other. It is a further merit of our philosopher to have first grasped this moment in an affective way separate from any religious norm.

The primary deficiency in Duboc's works is the one-sided definition of the concept of the world's mystery. Duboc thinks only of the immeasurability and indeterminability of the world process in the sequence of time, or he describes only this side of the great mystery as the object of religious exaltation. But even more than the mystery of becoming is that of the most profound essence and the primal grounds of all being, a mystery to which Duboc certainly alludes, but without giving it the place it deserves.[36]

Furthermore, however, the aspect into which the receptive mind is moved by the comprehension of the world process and the mystery of the world is not defined by Duboc in the sense of a truly enlightened world view. As the title of his book already indicates, Duboc does not {67} distinguish sufficiently between the emotions of the religious on the one hand and the pious confessor of the new doctrine on the other. The reverence that befits the modern, enlightened person before the world as a whole, as well as before the world's mystery, will still have to differ from that of the believer before their God. If we wisely refrain from searching for the ultimate reasons for being, this should not happen out of holy shyness but because we realise that we cannot know anything beyond a certain limit. As a result of the changed basis of representation, the feelings with which we grasp the world as a whole in the new doctrine must necessarily take on a different colour than in religion. In contrast, Duboc would like to attribute a religious character to them erroneously, for it is not, as Duboc thinks, an atheistic religion but a higher replacement for religion.

Despite this misjudgement of what is actually important, Duboc has rendered essential services to the new doctrine.

8

Our problem received a decisive boost from Eugen Dühring's work, *Replacement of Religion by Something More Perfect and Elimination of All Judaism from the Modern Spirit of Nations*.

Of all the thinkers mentioned so far, Dühring is the one who has broken most thoroughly with religion, who has freed himself most completely from all religious echoes, admittedly not without having lost with religion the feeling for humans' relationship to the world as a whole, which exists objectively and {68} should therefore also be felt subjectively. In this, as in many other respects, he stands in sharp contrast to Duboc.

We will pass over the polemical part of the book, which is directed against Semitism and demonstrates its complete incompatibility with the modern spirit

---

36 Gaëtano Negri (1878) seeks a replacement for religion in the awareness that a mystery surrounds us, that there is an ultimate, impersonal cause, and that alone.—The significance of the book lies in its incisive polemic against Christianity.

of the people. We are only interested here in the idea with which Dühring believes he has offered a more perfect replacement for Christianity.

Dühring firmly believes that, as Christianity and its underlying world view originated from a nation relatively low on the scale of nations, the world view that replaces religion must be based on the good tribal characteristics of modern peoples, in which Dühring sees the best human development to date. "A spiritual leadership that is not to be discarded," says Dühring, "must be rooted in the physiological character of the peoples concerned" [Dühring 1883, 125, our translation].

But to what extent should the modern spirit of nations in its best features be thought of as the starting point of a new doctrine? By taking it as the principle of a characterisation of the primal ground of things. If Duboc essentially has the characterisation of the world process in mind, then Dühring goes back to the foundation of the world. We will first disregard how he conceives it. Both thinkers complement each other, for the foundation of the world and the world process must be considered with equal intensity in the replacement of religion.

The first era of humanity, the Asian one, where relatively inferior but older peoples left their mark on the younger ones, is to be followed by the European, in which the modern civilised peoples, {69} especially the Germanic peoples, having eradicated Asianism from themselves like a pernicious infection and immersed themselves in their nature, create for themselves a new world view and spiritual guidance that naturally results from their better racial character.

The nature of an individual or a nation will undoubtedly be reflected in their behaviour towards the general and their conception of this. The lowly humans, the lowly nation, will not be able to avoid betraying their own limitations and the deficiencies of their intellectual and affective life in their conception of nature, whereas the higher humans, the higher nation, must naturally have a better conception of the primal causes of all being, or at least be capable of a higher representation of them. The basic relationship of the higher human to nature is entirely different from that of the lowly. They stand freely before it; they do not throw themselves in the dust before it. However, Dühring goes too far in emphasising the free position of humans towards nature, as he allows no place for feelings of being conditioned by it and reverence for the overarching whole of the world. Dühring's human is excessively proud. They consider themselves, as it were, their own creators, whereas they are only free children of nature; they recognise no secret before which they must fall silent; there is no self-forgetful absorption in the world process for them.

Dühring lays a correct foundation for justifying the *trusting* view of the core character of things by nobler humans based on the fact of their existence. "The nobler character always remains an instance that bears witness to the existence of the good amid manifold corruption. They who are good themselves can, therefore, never {70} completely and permanently lose their belief in the good. They will at least have an example at hand in themselves that not everything is bad. Now, it would be a strangely contradictory thought to accept such examples of the good and to deny a tendency towards the good based on all beings. If this trait had not existed, how could the truly good have come into existence? So it takes despair of the good in one's self not to find it in the basis of all being" (Dühring 1883, 139 [our translation]).

Accordingly, the reason for things may well be conceived as character itself, namely as good character, and only by doing so is a moral world view possible and morality given a firm foundation. If morality is not understood absolutely, it ceases to exist. "The firmest morality must ultimately be ground to dust for the masses of people if the overall character of things is continually passed off as contradictory to it" (Dühring 1883, 163 [our translation]).

If Duboc wanted to prove that evil is only a necessary moment in the world's process of becoming, then Dühring wanted to prove that evil, whose existence, of course, cannot be denied, is something that is not actually intended at the bottom of things. Thus, both thinkers complement each other here as well (Dühring 1883, 166 [our translation]): "Evil is only indirectly, thus not actually itself, but only its possibility is included in the world's organisation, and it is only *included in the course of things* with the *addition of a reaction directed against it.* If we consider it artificially for itself and disregard that {71} reaction by which it is principally rejected as a fact, the false appearance arises as if it ruled absolutely in all its glory. But what is supposed to be and cannot but be is, as it were, only the open door to all possible paths and deviations. If the way out is not only characterised as such, but also always leads, as it were, to an impenetrable wall, then these barriers are sufficient to do justice enough."

Dühring is well aware that his principle of basing the characterisation of being on the content of human character types can easily be countered with spurious arguments. "One need only brazenly assert that all such labelling of being and nature according to human characteristics is subjective and grossly anthropomorphic" (Dühring 1883, 144 [our translation]). Dühring rightly objects to this accusation: "Anthropomorphism, understood in a certain sense, also has its right. A human being has nothing other than the content of the human being to characterise the epitome of things. They do not have to dispense with the core of their being but only with the contingencies in their characterisation. They have the eyes in order to see the world, but not in order to harbour the foolish conceit that the world or God on which it is based is an eye" (Dühring 1883, 145 [our translation]).

Dühring now takes a materialistic view of the primal ground of things. Yet, one need not share this point of view to agree with his principle of proceeding from the modern spirit of nations to the characterisation of the ultimate grounds – however one conceives of them. There is only an apparent limitation in the idea of starting from national merits to characterise {72} the deepest ground of nature. These national advantages in question are precisely the highest manifestations of national morality to date. The laws of morality, however, have their roots in the deepest ground of things. The nobler people, the nobler nation, therefore, have the right to think of themselves with their moral qualities in the most intimate connection with the core character of things, a world view which, for its part, cannot fail to really fulfil better humans, since it has emerged from their nature, and which must enliven them with a new joy in the good.

If it is initially a need of the nobler intellect, the better mind, to characterise the foundation of the world according to its own constitution, then these premises can be confirmed by research. "Thus, Copernicus initially believed that the system of nature must be simple and harmonious, not convoluted and distorted, as the learned astronomers portray it" [Dühring 1883, 175–176, our translation]. In this way of looking at things, humans are no longer alien to the world as a whole, like mere mechanisms, a play of physical forces. "For it is also the effects that lead to humans and satisfy them, that is all the well-organised relationships between the empathiser and the sensitive. It is not merely understanding, but it is also participation for the mind of sentient beings in the organisation of the world, and this truth reaches further than the Greeks ever penetrated. The newer nations enter here with their nobler minds, and see the ground of the world in the light of their own nobler instincts" [Dühring 1883, 178, our translation].

Dühring very rightly emphasises that the nobler spirit can only feel related to the good of this world {73} and by no means indiscriminately to everything and everyone. The feeling of community, however, requires another closer definition. Although we have risen from the foundation of all things, we must not consider ourselves identical with them. "Just as every true sympathy for the joy and pain of others has nothing to do with one's own interest and fate, and must not arise by thinking oneself in the place of the other, instead of, as it were, thinking the other, uninterested in oneself,—just as here the natural cause of sympathy acts by detaching humans from self-interest, so also for the core character or the good in the universal sense, sympathetic understanding and feeling is only possible by the fact that its qualities, but not our affairs, excite us. The good and the harmonious in being, as well as the true conceptions of it, must excite us entirely as something situated outside our ego ; otherwise, we fall into self-deception" [Dühring 1883, 182, our translation]. We are connected with the core character of things ideally through our sense of community, but also materially, firstly on the side of those roots that reach into the primordial past and secondly by the life stimuli "that come to us through the forces of nature and from the rest of human existence" [Dühring 1883, 182–183, our translation].

The world view that we have outlined here, often letting the philosopher speak for himself, is not only suitable for providing salutary impulses to the *striving* person but also for offering comfort to the *dying person* by teaching them to think confidently about the reason for things and the continuation of the good.

In the direction of the conduct of life, Dühring sets the better modern nations the task of manifesting their nobler tribal traits {74}. This can only be achieved by making these traits the object of special practice. "This modern national character, with its striving for freedom and its proportionate capacity for a higher degree of justice, trust and loyalty, must be made the direct object of cultivation in public teaching and public life. All institutions, from the family to the state, that is, up to the general form of social community life, are to be understood and developed based on the principles flowing from this character. These principles must be publicly recognised and explicitly referred to as the foundations of all sustainable institutions. The modern state needs a flag that is more than mere morality in the usual, limited, and often vague sense of the word. Morality is usually presented in a falsely one-sided way as if it were the first cause of better behaviour and as if character arose from it. On the contrary, character is the cause of morality. Even in individual life, it can be observed how essentially good behaviour arises from good character. Character, better by nature and by practice, is the source of better principles and behaviour" (Dühring 1883, 197 [our translation]). And later, we read: "The replacement for cult must therefore consist not only in a doctrine but also in the *systematic formation of fixed habits of thought, feeling and behaviour*. Of course, we are talking here about thoughts, feelings, and actions only insofar as they relate to the view of the world and life. The formation of a moral conception of the whole world {75} in the minds and hearts is the main issue here, for not the ordinary concept of morality, but only that of a view of the world and of being which agrees with the better national morality, and in which this morality finds a universal confirmation and itself a support, is sufficient here" [Dühring 1883, 205, our translation].

A main means of communication, more than writing, will be oral communication, be it through dialogue or lectures, the latter of which, however, must not have the character of sermons. Dühring considers the formation of associations and communities to be proper. Although he is far from proposing bodies to replace priests for the new teaching, he does consider notable bearers and interpreters of the new spiritual guidance to be necessary for the transitional period.

The new world view also includes the cultivation of science, but not of science in general, but of that "through which trust in the order of the world and being and a sense of the justice perceptible in the natural order is formed" (Dühring 1883, 204 [our translation]).

Like life, art will also receive a changed character through the new doctrine in that it will be its task to express the tribal characteristics of the newer peoples more intensively and thus to become truly and in the highest sense national. "In order to illustrate the matter in a very special way and, as it were, in a domestic example, German art should, above all, bring the ideal German in all directions of his nature to a plastic and painterly representation through creative immersion in the components of his character."[37] Many remarks could be made on these and other statements {76} about the art of the future, but since we are only concerned with the main ideas of the work, we will refrain from doing so. — Morality takes on a higher meaning in the new doctrine in that, in contrast to Palestinian-Christian morality, which is "often a mixture of inapplicable paradoxes, even absurdities" [Dühring 1883, 210, our translation], which contains not a grain of freedom and dignity and in many points is virtually a servant morality—a criticism of which we subscribe to every word—it refers to all virtues and processes arising from the better nature of nations.

In the final chapter of his substantial and, in many respects, epoch-making work, the philosopher explains how the new doctrine, which he also calls spiritual leadership, should be realised in the state and society.

Dühring recognises that, like religion, the new doctrine has significance above all for the individual; however, just as religion has also unmistakably influenced the leading institutions of state and society, although these institutions are by no means based on it, so the replacement for religion must also have an effect on state and society. If religion were merely an addition to the foundations of state and society, which originated from other sources, then this addition would be completed in the religious replacement. In order for spiritual guidance to take effect in the state, the latter must, above all, free itself more and more from religious elements, while the church, for its part, must by no means detach itself from the state but must be subject to its control. However, eradicating the religious elements is only half the work; a more perfect one must fill in each of the gaps created. Thus, for example, the replacement of the religious oath will consist in the return of the oath to {77} its original and true form, and this is "the pure appeal to the powers of conscience and the natural bonds of honest intercourse, that is, the appeal to holiness, to the salvation and inviolability of fidelity" [(Dühring 1883, 241, our translation)].[38] For, as Dühring reminds us, the oath

---

37 [This quote cannot be found in Dühring's book; our translation.]
38 [Druskowitz slightly changes the text.]

was not invented by a public authority, and even the religious cloak is not the essential thing about it (Dühring 1883, 238–240 [our translation]). Through the abolition of "otherworldliness," many forces will be able to exert themselves in the right direction, the value of life and its most important institutions will grow, the family will receive a higher consecration, tribe and nation will become the object of increased participation. For the state, therefore, the elimination of the "otherworldliness" can only be desirable since it benefits from "everything that is gained for reality through the elimination of phantasms" (Dühring 1883, 248 [our translation]). The state is, therefore, only acting in its own best interests if it accelerates the eradication of religious elements as much as possible. If the state wants to be truly modern and win the sympathy of modern people, it must mould itself more and more in the spirit of these people. Christianity, however, is an irreconcilable contradiction to this. If, for example, the state wants the right kind of marriage, it cannot be Christian since Christianity, as Dühring rightly points out, especially given the Apostle Paul's view of this institution, was on tense terms with marriage from the outset. Dühring never forgets to emphasise that the replacement for religion is not a matter for the state, however, and that the actual bearer of spiritual guidance is society. Dühring sharply emphasises that the minorities of the most characterful and {78} gifted individuals will always be the starting point from which the raising of the general level will be achieved and that governments, therefore, will not be able to do anything decisive in the matter in question until the change has begun in society (Dühring 1883, 262). Only when the new doctrine has found an echo in broader strata, following the example of the best, will it be possible for the state to take action.

There are no signs that a world-dominating new religion could thwart spiritual leadership. New religious founders may still emerge and gain a following among people at lower cultural levels. In contrast, it is not foreseeable "how, under modern conditions, a new superstition, which is not a mere transformation of the old one, should come to dominate the leading cultural nations" (Dühring 1883, 263 [our translation]). But what makes the difference between the founders of religion and the representatives of the new spiritual leadership is that the founders spoke in the name of a fictitious authority, while the representatives of the new authority "have to speak and act in the name of the modern spirit of the people."

There is no doubt in Dühring's mind that the downfall of the Christian religion must necessarily follow. It is not an external resistance, as our philosopher rightly remarks, that will hold out the longest against the substitution of religion, but the false habituation of the mind, especially the artificially excited hope in death and in hardships that lead people to despair of life" (Dühring 1883, 265 [our translation]). We have already pointed out what turn the thoughts must take here with the replacement of religion.

{79} Although we agree with the author of *Replacing Religion with Something More Perfect* on most points, we cannot help but consider his attempt insufficient in some respects, even apart from the materialistic world view on which it is based. We have already emphasised that concerning humankind's position in relation to nature, Dühring takes no account of the moments when we are conditioned by nature and awestruck by being captivated by the world and the world process. This awakening is also compatible with Dühring's philosophical standpoint. Concerning the practical conduct of life, it is a shortcoming of Dühring's work that it emphasises moral perfection only. In contrast, the spiritualisation, embellishment and general idealisation of life should also be emphasised. Religion also pointed to moral perfection; the replacement for religion must overcome this one-sidedness by simultaneously initiating a higher, more spiritual, more ideal conception of things, an all-around higher culture of feeling. —Dühring emphasised other aspects, but without sufficient intensity, without the right fire. Thus, he concedes that there can be no ultimate ideal for man, but without grasping this idea in its full significance and without giving it a vivid expression.[39] As we have seen, Dühring also correctly emphasises that the new doctrine would first be grasped by the best individuals of the highest character and communicated through them to the lesser ones. But how must it {80} be grasped by the authoritative minority in order that a new movement may reach the broader strata? In *an enthusiastic, passionate* way, obviously, which for the time being would not even exclude some exuberance. Dühring's work itself is not capable of having an enthusiastic effect.

William Mackintire Salter's book *The Religion of Morality* exudes an entirely different power. The very title of this work indicates that, in terms of its thought content, it corresponds much less to the idea of a replacement for religion than Dühring's attempt. However, Salter has expressed the idea that mainly concerns him in a brilliant form. Salter knows that the new doctrine will not be able to gain power over the minds by employing mere *raisonements* but that it requires enthusiastic feeling and inspiring language.

---

[39] Dühring (1833) says only p. 256 [our translation]: "There will always be something left for the initiative of the few. For otherwise, the type of creation which, according to all previous phenomena, is conceivable in nature alone, would obviously cease."

9

The *Religion of Morality* seems to be making progress in America.[40] There is a society for ethical culture in New York under the leadership of Felix Adler, the author of the poem "In the City of the Light," in which he sketches a picture of a future social order in which perfect justice prevails, much like Shelley's visions of the future. W. M. Salter is the founder of a special congregation in Chicago.

Salter is not a superior but a noble, pure, bold and enthusiastic spirit. To him, morality is a principle, a higher law, the only object which can excite sacred awe and reverence, the only law {81} which can exist among humans, which a human being does not create but finds, which exists even when humans do not submit to it, since it does not act irresistibly, like the law of gravitation, and which is a form of the general law according to which things become what they ought to become. Something is captivating in the ardour with which Salter advocates the idea of universal justice—even if, as we shall see shortly, he places too bold a trust in human nature—and his noble enthusiasm is matched by the effective beauty of his speech, which springs from the heart.

We cannot proceed from chapter to chapter with the author but will instead delve into some of the main points of the work in more detail.[41]

Salter's philosophical standpoint is not uniform, but Kant most inspires him, as his first remarks on the subject immediately reveal. Thus, he says on p. 23: "The moral nature is that by which we transcend ourselves and enter into an ideal region. Science, with its methods of observation and experiment, is limited to the world as it is. Ethics is essentially the {82} thought of what ought to be. It is not an account of man as he is, nor is it a transcript and summary abstract of the facts of society; it declares the law according to which man should act, and in obedience to which society should be constituted." And later: "Morality is ideal in nature. It is not what humans do, but what they ought to do; nor is it what they wish,

---

40 [Druskowitz refers to Salter 1885. This book is the German translation of Salter's lectures, which precedes the English book published by Salter under the title *Ethical Religion* (1889). Salter's English book was published *after* Druskowitz's *Modern Attempts*. We use Salter's English version unless Gizycki's translation, used by Druskowitz, diverges from the later publication, in which case we note the discrepancy.]

41 The headings of the ten chapters are as follows: 1) The Religion of Morality, 2) The Ideal Element in Morality, 3) Wendell Philipps, an Example of Ideal Morality, 4) What is a Moral Act? 5) Is There a Higher Law? 6) Is There Anything Absolute about Morality? 7) The Moral Teaching of Jesus, 8) Does the Moral Teaching of Jesus Satisfy the Needs of Our Time? 9) The Success and Failure of Protestantism, 10) Why Unitarianism does not Satisfy Us, 11) The Social Ideal, 12) The Problem of Poverty, 13) The Basis of the Ethical Movement, 14) Speech on the First Anniversary of the Society for Moral Culture, 15) Consideration of Objections to the Ethical Movement.

but what they ought to wish."[42] However, these sentences, as they stand, contain an overly pessimistic characterisation of the current state of society, and they require restrictive additions. Salter would only have had the right to say that the *majority* of people neither practised nor desired morality, whereas it cannot be denied that it is both desired and practised by many. If Salter underestimates the present measure of morality, he nevertheless considers humans capable of the highest moral perfection. Thus, we read: "If thou wilt ever see the *perfect*, thou must *create* it; till that time, thou rangest over the earth or through the heavens in vain! The only idea of perfection is in us; the perfect itself is *to be*" (Salter 1889, 10). "Nothing is closed to the spirit. The most divinely perfect things are but thoughts of what can be."[43] "We are to become *divine:* we are to make this world *a scene of justice*" (Salter 1889, 12), assuming that we can do so. Perhaps these sentences are all too trusting. It is absolutely impossible for us to set a fixed goal for humans and to form a definite picture of his capacity for perfection. {83} The moral teacher can do nothing but spur humans on and make them hope that they are capable of perfection when they delve into themselves. A certain lack of healthy realism, of a just appreciation of reality and of the realisation that the possible is not already a certainty, characterises the otherwise so excellent and uplifting work of the moral teacher from Chicago. Salter sees the goal of morality in general happiness, a view that we have already rejected as erroneous.—Again, Salter is a Kantian in that he holds to the freedom of the will, by which he evidently understands only intelligible freedom.

Salter provides an excellent analysis of moral action by emphasising the following points: a moral action must be our own; it must be intended to produce good results; it must be performed voluntarily; it must not be motivated by self-interest; and it must be done out of principle. Summarising the result of his analysis, he says (Salter 1889, 56–57): "[I]t is far from being a light or trifling or petty thing to perform a genuinely moral action. The dignity of man lies in his capacity for such action; for such action means that man need not follow the crowd, that his thoughts can determine him, that he can freely will the good, that he can be absolutely unselfish in so doing, that he can take captive his wandering desires and impulses, and reflect the pure heaven of principle in his life. And this were, it seems to me, to be a man; this were to be lifted above anxieties, to be no longer the slave of fears or hopes. The only hope could be to be {84} more truly this; the only fear to fall from such a thought and such an aim, and become

---

42 [The quote cannot be found in Salter's *Ethical Religion*.]
43 [The quote cannot be found in Salter's *Ethical Religion*.]

caught and entangled in any of the lower concerns that are so easy, so natural, and tempting to men."

Furthermore, in the same chapter, he says very beautifully: "For a moral action is not most truly any outward deed, or any single partial act of the will within; all so called moral actions are after all parts of one action, and that is the total purpose of the soul, the action of life. Notwithstanding all trifling variations, we are moving in one direction or another. No single good thing we do counts save as it is part of a purpose which sweeps on beyond it; and no purpose is adequate which does not cover, in thought at least, the whole life and all its possible future" [Salter 1889, 58].

The consolation that the religion of morality offers to the dying person can be seen in the following passage: "I would suggest the thought of deathless principles to the dying man. I would have him think that justice does not die because he dies; that love does not cease to urge its claims because his own heart's love seems about to cease. I would have him think that though justice and love had failed in all the past to get an entrance into human hearts, they ought to have had an entrance, for they belong there, — their meaning was there, — and that they are the unalterable pattern after which the life of men must be shaped {85} in the future. These laws, also, are stable; they seem to give something of their own firmness to those who contemplate them; they are witness that within, as well as without, man is connected with an eternal order of things" (Salter 1889, 101).

The chapter: "Is there anything absolute about morality?" is recommended to all those for whom morality is merely a matter of opinion and fashion.

Salter generally seems to overestimate the value of Jesus's teaching in the section "The moral teaching of Jesus," while in the next chapter, "Does the moral teaching of Jesus satisfy the needs of our time?," he concludes that it is only a "partial proclamation" of the moral principles that our time needs, and that it does not satisfy certain modern needs. Thus, the need for *intellectual conscientiousness* and *honesty*, furthermore the need *for higher political concepts* and *higher political morality*, and thirdly, the need for a new explanation of the *purpose of human existence*. Salter does not, however, address other shortcomings in Jesus' moral teaching.

The chapter on the problem of poverty is very nice. The author has a keen eye for social harm, as well as a deep sympathy for the countless people who are cruelly denied their human rights, while many do not even recognise poverty as a problem. "The chief and deepest cause of poverty," says Salter eloquently,[44]

---

44 [We could not find this text in the English edition. In the German edition, it is on p. 287.]

"the main cause is that the wealth which the poor help to create returns to them but in small measure. They work, and their {86} labour counts and lasts, but they get nothing for it except what is just necessary to keep them able to work. They have no advantage from their labour; they have, strictly speaking, no reward for it since they have only what is necessary to enable them to do it. This is immoral, but how easily the perception of right in man is obscured is shown by the fact that few, and seldom even the labourers themselves, consider it immoral." Salter, therefore, turns to employers as the ones who can remedy the situation, and the section concludes with the warm but straightforward words: "Better to restrict ourselves, better even to suffer, than to inflict or support injustice on others. And then, as far as we ourselves are direct employers, we can be an example in our own behaviour towards our workers of the ideal method of treating labour. I am not above speaking openly. If we want to improve others, let us first improve ourselves."[45]

---

[45] Some of Ralph Waldo Emerson's sayings on our topic are interesting. Thus, it says in *Conduct of Life:* "You say., there is no religion now. 'This like saying in rainy weather, there is no sun, when at that moment we are witnessing one of his superlative effects. The religion of the cultivated class now, to be sure, consists in an avoidance of acts and engagements which it was once their religion to assume. This this avoidance will yield spontaneous forms in their due hour" [1876, 168]. And (Emerson 1876, 188–189): "The religion which is to guide and fulfil the present and coming ages, whatever else it be, must be intellectual. The scientific mind must have a faith which is science. 'There are two things,' said Mahomet, 'which I abhor, the learned in his infidelities, and the fool in his devotions.' Our times are impatient of both, and especially of the last. Let us have nothing now which is not its own evidence. There is surely enough for the heart and imagination {87} in the region itself. Let us not be pestered with assertions and half-truths, with emotions and snuffle. There will be a new church founded on moral science, at first cold and naked, a babe in a manger again, the algebra and mathematics of ethical law, the church of men to come, without shawms, or psaltery, or sackbut; but it will have heaven and earth for its beams and rafters; science for symbol and illustration; it will fast enough gather beauty, music, picture, poetry. Was never stoicism so stern and exigent as this shall be. It shall send man home to his central solitude, shame these social, supplicating manners, and make him know that much of the time he must have himself to his friend. He shall expect no co-operation, he shall walk with no companion. The nameless Thought, the nameless Power, the super-personal Heart, — he shall repose alone on that. He needs only his own verdict. No good fame can help, no bad fame can hurt him. The Laws are his consolers, the good Laws themselves are alive, they know if we have kept them, they animate him with the leading of great duty, and an endless horizon. Honor and fortune exist to him who always recognises the neighbourhood of the great, always feels himself in the presence of high causes." [It is noteworthy that, in Druskowitz's text, the last part of the last sentence is written in cursive and slightly differs in translation: "Happiness and honour exist only for those who always feel close to the great, *always in a strict relationship to the primal reasons for existence.*"]

10

{88} Our investigation has shown that Feuerbach, Dühring, Duboc and Salter have most satisfactorily presented the elements which a higher replacement for religion must contain, however without any of the thinkers mentioned having considered these elements together. They did not connect them organically with one another or sufficiently emphasise all the elements which a replacement for religion should contain.

We see that a perfect replacement for religion must first define man's relationship to the world as a whole more precisely and, furthermore, establish an ideal for the striving and acting human being. The relation of humans to the universal is not sufficiently determined either by the consciousness of conditionality, or by that of trust in the ultimate world powers and the world process, or finally by reverence for the formative forces of the universe and the recognition that a mystery surrounds us, however deeply we have penetrated phenomena—if we consider each of these relations by itself. Instead, these are only different sides of that relationship, which only, when taken together, fully express what humans should feel towards the general. The thinker and the work that would do justice to the doctrine in all directions, which alone could replace religion more perfectly, would therefore have to represent all those relations effectively. Furthermore, the ideal {89} according to which the more perfected replacement for religion instructs humanity to aspire ought to be conceived more perfectly and more multidimensionally than it has ordinarily been depicted for the ideal is conceived primarily as a moral one. Although Comte could not repeat often enough that he had taken into account all aspects of man's higher nature, the intellectual and aesthetic perfection in his account seems too dominated by the demands of morality. For the majority of the other thinkers whose ideas we have honoured, the concept of a replacement for religion with the striving and acting human being merges into that of morality. However, as we have already mentioned, it is not only a matter of moralisation but also the spiritualisation of life. A new enthusiasm for all higher factors—that would be the more perfect replacement for religion in the direction of the conduct of life. An ideal conception of things, a spiritualisation of even the least activity, a more courageous and trusting, a more joyful and higher view of life—that is what we need. Human self-esteem must become a different, more correct one. However, supreme power is not concerned with their every thought and their most insignificant deed, and the hope of personal immortality is probably the dream of all dreams. In all humans, only the consciousness should be awakened that the germ of a higher development lies within them and that even the lesser nature is capable of rising to an ideal sphere. The thought that nature itself calls upon humans to unfold their higher faculties, which alone are characteristic of them, and that humans, when they live up to their own nature, cooperate harmoniously with the deepest foundation of things must be a powerful incentive to them. A definite goal of these endeavours cannot be set. {90} One can only call out to humans: Strive high so that you can strive still higher, and in your striving, feel yourself, to repeat Emmerson's words, "in strict relation to the primal grounds of existence"!

We by no means fail to recognise that a more perfect doctrine, substituting religion, would have no sooner prospect of gaining a foothold among the lower classes of the people in the first modern cultural nations than the existing social conditions would make way for a more just order. As long as large classes of people spend their lives in the servitude of labour, which must be performed without joy and with excessive burdens, without more than their physical existence being made possible, a general spiritual upswing, a higher conception of life cannot be expected. First of all, significant social progress must be made, and modern culture must be given a different material basis. However, the need and ability to rise above religion to higher perspectives will become increasingly more common!

Bibliography

Comte, Auguste. 1851. *Système de politique positive. Traité de sociologie instituant la religion de l'humanité*. Paris: La librairie scientifique-industrielle de L. Mathias.
Comte, Auguste. 1874. *Catéchisme positiviste*. Paris: Ernest Leroux.
Comte, Auguste. 1875a. *System of Positive Polity or Treatise on Sociology*, vol. I. Translated by John Henry Bridges. London: Longmans, Green, and Co.
Comte, Auguste. 1875b. *System of Positive Polity or Treatise on Sociology*, vol. II. Translated by Federic Harrison. London: Longmans, Green, and Co.
Comte, Auguste. 1896. *The Positive Philosophy*. Freely translated and condensed Harriet Martineau, with an introduction by Federic Harrison. I–III. London: George Bell & Sons.
Duboc, Julius. 1881. *Der Optimismus als Weltanschauung in seiner religiös-ethischen Bedeutung für die Gegenwart*. Bonn: Emil Strauß.
Dühring, Eugen. 1883. *Der Ersatz der Religion durch Vollkommeneres und die Ausscheidung alles Judenthums durch den modernen Völkergeist*. Karlsruhe and Leipzig: Reuther.
Emerson, Ralph Waldo. 1876. *The Conduct of Life*. Boston: J. R. Osgood.
Feuerbach, Ludwig. 1846. "Grundsätze der Philosophie der Zukunft." In: Ludwig Feuerbach, *Sämmtliche Werke*, vol. II. Leipzig: Otto Wigand.
Feuerbach, Ludwig. 1866. "Ueber Spiritualismus und Materialismus." In: Ludwig Feuerbach, *Sämmtliche Werke*, vol. X. Leipzig: Otto Wigand.
Lange, Friedrich Albert. 1877. *Geschichte des Materialismus und Kritik seiner Bedeutung in der Gegenwart. Zweites Buch: Geschichte des Materialismus seit Kant*. 3rd edition. Iserlohn: J. Baedeker.
Mill, John Stuart. 1865. *Auguste Comte and Positivism*. London: N. Trübner.
Mill, John Stuart. 1874. *Three Essays on Religion*. London: Longmans, Green, Reader, and Dyer.

Mill, John Stuart. 1875. *Ueber Religion. Natur – Die Nützlichkeit der Religion – Theismus*. Translated by Alfred Lehman. Berlin: Franz Duncker.
Negri, Gaëtano. 1878. *Die religiöse Krisis*. Translated by M. G. Conrad. Breslau: Schottlaender.
Nietzsche, Friedrich. 2005. *Human, All Too Human*. Translated by R. J. Hollingdtle. Cambridge *et al.*: Cambridge University Press.
Nietzsche, Friedrich. 2006. *Thus Spoke Zarathustra: A Book for All and None*. Translated by Adrian del Caro. Cambridge *et al.:* Cambridge University Press.
Nietzsche, Friedrich. 2011. *Dawn: Thoughts on the Presumptions of Morality*. Translated by Brittain Smith. Stanford: Stanford University Press.
Reich, Eduard. 1872. *Die Kirche der Menschheit*. Neuwied: J. H. Heuser.
Salter, William Mackintire. 1885. *Die Religion der Moral*. Translated by Georg von Gizycki. Leipzig: Wilhelm Friedrich.
Salter, William Mackintire. 1889. *Ethical Religion*. Boston: Robert Brothers.
Spencer, Herbert. 1879. *Die Thatsachen der Ethik*. Translated by Berhard Vetter. Stuttgart: E. Schweizerbart (E. Koch).
Strauß, David Friedrich. 1872. *Der alte und der neue Glaube: ein Bekenntniß*. Leipzig: Verlag von S. Hirzel.

Towards a New Doctrine.
Observations by Dr H. Druskowitz

1

{1} By new doctrine, we would like to understand a world view which—assuming its possibility—puts a more reliable and perfect content in place of the belief in a god and immortality. The doctrine would deserve to be called new in contrast to religion as the old doctrine, in that its content will be based on certain supreme results of modern philosophy and natural science.

So far, no philosopher has utilised these results in such a way that a universally valid and complete new doctrine has been created. Instead, there are only a few more or less imperfect attempts to establish such a doctrine. May the content of these pages also be regarded as merely a contribution to the new doctrine, which, as of now, remains an ideal and will only crystallise very gradually from the intellectual efforts of many. The author is fully aware that she is only expressing her personal views on the solution of one of the most important problems, in the hope, however, that they may resonate with others. {2} Certainly, a new doctrine or world view is by no means a general need.

First, there is the great mass of those for whom Christianity, or even the mere belief in God, is an object of affective need. They are still in the mythological phase of the mind. Their mental constitution requires them to think of the foundation of the world—to emphasise only the most important feature of every religion—as a personal power in whose objective existence they believe. Religion is quite obviously the outflow and expression of a specific primitive mental disposition and, therefore, an inner potency that has not yet been overcome. Since, however, a critical philosophy teaches us that a more precise determination of the world's foundation is not attainable for our mental organisation, we can regard religion as a deception of an ideal need of the human imagination, namely the need to rise above the given world. All higher mental activity indeed rests upon a striving to go beyond the actual world, no matter in what form it may occur. The deception, however, which lies at the root of religion, consists precisely of mistaking a mere product of the imagination for an actual truth. In reality, even among the most advanced nations, the majority of people—although relatively few of them are deeply devout—are still psychologically unable to rise above this error, whether due to an excess of imagination over reflection or because reflection {3} has never played a role for them in this area, and their religious instincts have never been shaken. If one were to expect such organised people to go beyond the religious point of view, the certain consequence would be that they would sink even deeper below it and lose all and every foothold.

It is precisely because religion, in reality, forms a view of the world that is homogeneous with the great mass of people that it continues to exist and will likely persist for a long time to come. As soon, however, as the need for imagination and faith, which religion satisfies, should fade from humanity, religion will cease and cannot be sustained by any force. It is, therefore, a quite senseless expression to assert, as is so often done, that religion must continue to exist. This is no different from saying that art must continue, yet here, everyone sees that one should speak only of a possibility, not a necessity. But just as art will only endure as long as the creative and aesthetic drive within humanity remains active, so too can religion only be maintained as long as people find inner support in it and believe in its objective truth.[1]

---

1 The reasons usually used to support this assertion are just as untenable as the claim that religion must continue to exist. Religion is supposed to form the basis of morality above all. It is, however, so little that the necessity of introducing moral instruction in elementary schools is increasingly recognised, and France deserves credit for having already taken this important innovation seriously. Among German philosophers, it is B. Carneri who, in his work *Development and Bliss* [1886, 415 ff.], advocated the teaching of morals in schools. A noble morality will not be produced by religion as long as fear of the punishment of hell or the prospect of heavenly reward acts as impulses. But what about the moral influence of religion when faith is on the wane? Faith, however, cannot be artificially fixed in the mind; it arises from the individual disposition of man, and therefore, religion never forms a firm foundation of morality. Those who defend religion because of its poetic content—which, moreover, is vastly overrated—are obviously not sincere friends of truth. M. Guyau, *The Irreligion of the Future* [1886], remarks very correctly on this point. Préface (1886, xix): "Today, when people are increasingly beginning to doubt the intrinsic value of religion, religion has found sceptical defenders who support it sometimes in the name of the poetry and aesthetic beauty of its legends, sometimes in the name of its practical utility. At times, in modern minds, a resurgence of fiction over reality occurs. The human spirit grows weary of being the too passively clear mirror in which things are reflected; it then takes pleasure in fogging its glass to obscure and distort images... For our part, we are far from rejecting poetry, and we believe it to be exceedingly beneficial to humanity, provided its own symbols do not deceive it and do not elevate its intuitions to the level of dogma... Poetry is often more philosophical not only than history but also abstract philosophy; only this is on the condition that it is sincere and presents itself for what it is.—But, proponents of 'beneficial errors' will tell us, why insist so much on dispelling poetic illusion, on calling things by their names? Are there not, for people, for humankind, for children, useful errors and permissible illusions? Surely, one may view a great many errors as having been necessary in the history of humanity, but does progress not consist precisely in reducing the number of these useful errors for humanity?"

The attempt to maintain religion as a conscious illusion will be discussed later.—Finally, those who argue for the continued existence of religion in favour of the "poor and wretched" are guilty of an ugly perfidy. According to these philanthropists, freedom from religion is a privilege

{4} Even if every freethinker, every follower of the doctrine of the capacity for progress and perfection of human nature hopes and assumes that the modern civilised peoples, as the highest representatives of humanity, will one day emerge from the religious phase in their entirety, it is by no means possible to determine whether this significant transformation will take place in the foreseeable future or only in the distant future.

In any case, it must be acknowledged that the power of Christianity, however great it may still be, is nevertheless in a marked decline, with the number of its adherents clearly diminishing. No objective observer of modern life will be able to deny {5} that not only a large proportion of the educated but also a good part of the masses no longer find a foothold in it. The cause of this phenomenon may generally be said to be the diminution of the corresponding need for imagination, while only in a few causes is it the result of the influence of genuine philosophy and actual science and a predominance of reflection over imagination.

Do the enlightened now need a new doctrine, that is, a world view that replaces religion with a higher content? Such a doctrine should indeed be their need, but it is evident that the vast majority are completely satisfied with mere freedom from religion. What is actually {6} given is enough for them. Their interest does not extend beyond what is given. They do not know or do not wish to know that there are other relations than those offered by experience. For them, there is no world problem, no higher outlook, and therefore, the higher point of view for life and the conduct of life is lacking.

For this reason, only those freethinkers will long for a different doctrine or world view, who, unlike those shallow people, are never content with mere faithlessness. This is why they are still more likely to sympathise with the believers than with the mere atheists, for at least the believers are aware of connections beyond the given world and see something higher than themselves. In contrast, atheists do not raise their gaze beyond reality and lack any reverence for anything that transcends the given.

{7} Even if religion is only a naïve and illusory view of the world, it is nevertheless a view of the world through which all things are seen in a higher context. Therefore, the elimination of religion is not the end of the matter. When religion is recognised as an error, the questions to which it provided a preliminary answer

---

of the well-to-do. At the same time, the "lower people," who are weighed down by the double burden of work and hardship, must be kept in religious delusion so that they do not lose their last comfort and support and, especially, their patience. Instead of keeping the masses down through the illusions of religion, thought must be given to reforming their situation; these philanthropists are not disturbed by this consideration.

only become all the more urgent for the deeper mind, and the demand for a perspective arises, which instead of being founded on dreams and illusions, is based on knowledge, cognition, and truth—or at least on a far greater probability than that offered by the religious interpretation and explanation of the world. If our life is to attain a higher meaning, we must connect it with something greater than ourselves. If we are to be filled with a powerful striving for self-perfection, then we must have a supreme goal in mind, the idea of which forms, as it were, the central fire of our mind.[2]

{8} Religion inspires in humans lofty and noble feelings by elevating them above reality and connecting them, on the one hand, with the world's foundation conceived as a personal entity and, on the other hand, pointing them towards an ideal future. Therefore, the fundamental question of our problem is this: Is it possible, from a higher world view—as created by knowledge, in contrast to belief—to gain exalted and inspiring feelings that surpass those of the religious world view in value, just as the world view from which they arise surpasses the religious world view in value, thus conferring a higher consecration upon life and opening up a grander perspective for our aspirations?

It is self-evident that mere atheists deny this possibility—both the subjective and the objective. However, the fact that a considerable number of attempts to establish such a world view and philosophy of life have been recorded and that each of these perspectives was composed at least with a sense of genuine conviction by its authors and satisfied them is probably the best evidence that for certain natures, not only does the need for a new doctrine exist {9}, but also the possibility of such a doctrine. It is only claimed that for certain natures who have reached spiritual freedom, both of these exist. It is to them that anyone concerned with our problem must turn their thoughts; it is to them that they must direct their attention.

The question now arises as to where we will see the new, the more perfect, where we will find fulfilment. For us personally, the attempts known to us to establish a new world view are not entirely sufficient. For us, therefore, this ques-

---

2 Rightly remarks W. M. Salter, the noble moral preacher of Chicago, regarding the mere atheists in one of his recent speeches, entitled: *The Duty Liberals Owe their Children* (A Lecture before the Society for Ethical Culture of Chicago, 1886). We quote from p. 4 of the separate print available to us [our translation]: "The liberal spirit in the world is simply a possibility. The vainest and emptiest person is one who thinks that with the rejection of the old creeds, he has reached the end-all and be-all of wisdom. If he has not something else to give colour and tone and substance and purpose to his life, such a liberal is apt to be as thin and flat in his mental and moral life, as juiceless as any a man you can well find. Liberalism in religion simply means that the old order is breaking up, but it is not itself the soil that the plough has ripped up, but in which the seed of a new harvest is yet to be sown." However, Salter is speaking from a one-sided moral perspective, but his words are entirely accurate in this case.

tion still awaits an answer, which we must seek to find and justify ourselves, hoping thereby to inspire others.

2

{10} As indicated by the above, the intellectual ideal of the new doctrine will consist of a harmony of thought and feeling. In contrast to this monistic ideal stands the viewpoint of that group of atheists who maintain that the freethinker should not refrain from religious representations and emotions but should continue to indulge in them, albeit with full awareness that they are purely subjective constructs without any claim to objective significance. As is well known, this view is primarily linked to the name of A. F. Lange. According to him, metaphysics, art and religion are an outflow of the synthetic poetic drive in humans and form a supplement to what is given in experience. Just as little as the poetic creations correspond to reality, so little do religion and metaphysics possess real value, so that basically both merge into the concept of synthetic poetic drive, a view with which everyone who is neither a believer nor a metaphysician will agree. However, when Lange suggests that even if we no longer attribute any real value {11} to religious and metaphysical representations, we should still find upliftment in them, an impartial observer will always object that such an approach lacks any higher justification. Now, we must certainly add that Lange wanted to see religious representations understood allegorically as poetic symbols of ethical truths. Upon closer examination, however, the poetic value of such symbolism is only slight, and as for the truths that religion is supposed to contain, the matter is rather peculiar, and true ideas can likely be drawn more effectively from another source.[3]

---

3 Recently, J. J. Borelius, professor at the University of Lund, in his treatise "Views on the Current State of Philosophy in Germany etc." (translated into German as "Blicke auf den gegenwärtigen Standpunkt der Philosophie in Deutschland etc.", 1886, 22–24) criticises Lange's view of religion, albeit from a different standpoint, saying: "A religion, which is expressly declared to be illusory, (is) no religion; even if a serious striving for the ideal can exist alongside the insight that all our attempts to grasp and comprehend the ideal are imperfect, the conviction is nevertheless presupposed that this ideal is not mere fiction, but something substantial and real in itself. A recognition of this view does indeed lie in Lange's assumption of the ideal as a pictorial representative of the full truth, but since he nevertheless refers to the ideal exclusively to poetry, he overlooks the fact that the archetype itself is only an image insofar as it contains correspondence with the depicted. But if the ideal is recognised as pure illusion, one can no longer believe in it; it cannot then even be regarded as an image of a higher truth, but only as fiction, as conscious self-deception." And now a turn against Vaihinger: "This is also how Lange 's declared follower Vaihinger understood his view, which he summarises briefly as follows: 'A religion without the

{12} Even more unsympathetic than Lange's justification of the maintenance of religion recognised as illusory is the one presented in the anonymously published and postumous work *Philosophy of Religion Based on Modern Science*[4]. While for Lange, religious representations possess the value of profound symbols, for the author of this work, they are merely illusions that should not be suppressed, as they are benevolent and correspond to a need for fantasy. Even genuine scientific enlightenment should not prevent someone who possesses a lively imagination from nevertheless indulging in religious representations that he has recognised as illusions.

{13} For, according to our author, humans are "predominantly neither sensual nor rational beings, but, according to scientific expression, fantasising ones, i. e. they form representations on the occasion of sensations, but these usually relate to them like illusion and hallucination, if one looks closely. They possess reason only in the formal sense in that it posits ultimate principles, but they mostly conceive of these in the manner of imagination; they do not align with precise perception, nor can they be formally derived from it. This imaginative conception appears entirely instinctive; it is evidently a predominant expression of the physiological-psychological constitution of humans."

As a result of this mental organisation, it is a human tendency to conceive of causes removed from sensory perception in a mythological manner as personal beings. This tendency was not present only once in humanity; on the contrary, we are all still more or less vividly under its influence, "except that what once appeared in us as evidence of divine power, or as revelations and signs of such power, still appears similarly, but is immediately paralysed by the representations which a long development of exact science has produced" [Lange 1886, 19, our translation]. At this point, it is particularly striking that the author seems to believe that among the educated, there are no longer any believers who regard religion as objectively true; rather, all educated people have recognised it as an illu-

---

foundation of faith, a metaphysics without the claim to knowledge, these are ideas, seemingly paradoxical and yet in fact the only ones that are scientifically tenable!' It is doubtful for several reasons that Lange himself, had he still been alive, would have been satisfied with this formulation of his view, but at any rate, it expresses the logical result of his view. However, this result is, in truth, a *deductio in absurdum*. In certain forms of insanity, it happens that the sick person, without having lost the consciousness of his personal ego, at the same time imagines himself to be quite another. It is difficult to find a more apt picture of a person who would realise Vaihinger's philosophical point of view in all seriousness."

4 With the preface by Julius Baumann (Leipzig, 1886). [We couldn't identify the author of the book *Religionsphilosophie auf modern-wissenschaftlicher Grundlage*. Borelius, in the Preface, claims that the author was a religious Protestant, and suggests that he or she might have some connection with India.]

sion, yet—{14} at least most of them—nevertheless continue to move within its representational circles because it pleases their imagination. However, we consider this view to be quite wrong. Firstly, even among the educated, faith has by no means died out. Secondly, among the enlightened, only a very few are likely to give in to religious thoughts out of a need for fantasy because this need for fantasy plays a significantly smaller role in the people of our time than the anonymous author assumes. If the author believes that a person for whom the religious perspective is natural, due to their entire mental constitution, would be completely ruined physiologically and psychologically if they attempted to replace it with the scientific one, then we must add that such a person organised in this way will not be made for knowledge at all. Still, for faith – this, however, will probably not address the author's intent, who expresses his guiding thought in the most diverse variations in the work incidentally, composed in a highly amateurish manner. Just as the lark would perish or at least lose its joyfulness if it wanted to suppress its urge to sing, so too would a person be spiritually ruined if they attempted to suppress their religious representations, for the scientific view must not want to abolish religious representations in their directly psychological nature, just as we must not attempt not to see colours, not to hear sounds, etc. However, we are convinced that colours, sounds, etc., do not {15} exist. "Just as one would ruin oneself mentally, and quite uselessly if one wanted to *see* the world bodies in a Copernican rather than Ptolemaic manner, so one ruins oneself mentally if one wanted to suppress the next representations about ever-recurring immediate ideas about these intellectual phenomena and replace them with scientific ones.—Imagination, as the essential trait of humanity, must not be disturbed; within it, one's immediate life must unfold and take shape. In imagination, one's innate spiritual nature is expressed, stirred inwardly by sensations, and, from there, moved to aspirations and outward actions. [...]

Humans should not believe that they can endure with mere knowledge and strict adherence to precise experience; they must have a vast domain where they are free to idealise without such self-restraint, and thus they need either art in whatever form suits them individually or poetry, or superstition, or religion.—If someone feels particularly stimulated to activity or thought by the blue colour of their room, they should give in to this stimulation; if someone feels particularly comforted and strengthened by the idea that a guardian spirit or a god watches over them, they should not shy away from it, and so on."[5]

---

[5] The author goes so far as to suggest a new cult that should emerge from this "faith" (sic!). The following remarks will edify you: "A primary need of the mind is temporary liberation from the pressures of earthliness; it is precisely this that drives forth the idea of a supramundane God and blissful immortality, and the cult that arises from this belief. I can imagine that one would devote

{16} Obviously, the representations and ideals of mental perfection are very different. For our part, we regard the anonymous author's advocacy in favour of a sharp dualism between intellectual and imaginative life—whereby intellect denies what imagination affirms, and vice versa—his advocacy in favour of the separation of the various spiritual realms, in favour of intellectual consciencelessness and conscious illusionism, as utterly reprehensible and see in it nothing other than mental Epicureanism of the worst kind. The believer should hear with astonishment, indeed, with distaste, {17} of a preoccupation with religious representations without the seriousness of inner conviction, simply because they are found to be pleasing and beautiful; but with no less revulsion will the one holding the opposite viewpoint—the true freethinker, for whom knowledge has become second nature—turn away from this theory. For it is not a matter of mere knowledge; rather, it is about the fact that the one who possesses knowledge must also show oneself to be inwardly imbued with the cognition one has gained and that the entire thought process must bear witness to it. The freethinker who truly deserves this noble name will, instead of allowing their imagination to wander into the realm of religious illusions, strive to find in knowledge itself a foundation for elevated feelings, and in this way seek to bring thoughts and emotions, intellect and mind, into harmony. Thus, we are not speaking of a characterless {18} union of enlightenment and superstition but of a vitalisation of knowledge through feeling. To bring about this reconciliation between knowledge and feeling is, as we have already emphasised, the task of a new world view.

---

oneself to such a religion in the same way as one devotes oneself to the contemplation of works of art, the noble enjoyment of nature, and poetry. The places of worship would have to be of such a nature that they support the representations of a blissful spiritual life; that is, everything that inhibits the spirit would have to recede. Everything that awakens and inspires it would have to come to the fore, namely the spirit as hope and fantasy. From Protestantism, we should take song, prayer, and enthusiastic yet soothing speech; from Catholicism, art, both in terms of construction and decoration. Decorative art should depict the great phenomena of nature and history, which have an uplifting or morally awakening power. The keynote of worship should be: In life, you are endowed with good and evil; the more you learn to overcome evil with good, the more the hope awakens in you to live eternally on this Earth in a higher and purer spiritual state held together by a great spirit of peace. Gather together in this hope, and it is strengthening peace and enjoy a foretaste of what you hope for in the religious association. The words of all religious founders and great men from all nations and times should be a treasure for sermons, prayers and songs. In short, the divine service should give a world view and, at the same time, keep man in the world and fill him with hope beyond it, but not by contrast, as in the great religions up to now (the world is a valley of misery, heaven salvation), but from the beginnings of a satisfying spiritual existence on Earth, faith and hope of a blessed existence with a spiritual centre should grow" [Lange 1886, 213–214, our translation]—But enough.

3

{19} Before we approach our problem, we must refute the view that the new world view or doctrine is the establishment of a new, more perfect religion.

What is the source of this erroneous view? Quite obviously, it is an arbitrary conception of religion that contradicts its very essence. If we recall the known forms of religion, they are all based not only on the feeling of dependence—which Schleiermacher describes without further definition as the basic feeling of religion[6]—but also on the feeling of human dependence on an animistic and personally conceived world power. Whether the supreme world power is endowed with coarser or finer human attributes {20}, it will always be conceived in the form of such. Does it not follow that a world view which abstains from any characterisation of ultimate things, because true philosophy denies the determinability of the same, goes beyond religion and must, therefore, be called supra-religious? Nevertheless, August Comte calls his new doctrine, in which the concept of God has no place and which replaces the cult of God with the cult of humanity, religion. Herbert Spencer quite obviously confuses religion with philosophy (as Schiller already did in the well-known distich) by describing every attempt to characterise the foundation of the world as irreligious but also as religious, the recognition that an unfathomable mystery surrounds us.[7] The {21} consequence of this strange view, however, is that all historical forms of religion are not religions at all since they all undertake a characterisation of the foundations of the

---

[6] And after Schleiermacher, among others, D. Fr. Strauss in *The Old and the New Faith* [*Der alte und der neue Glaube*, 1872, 138, our translation], where he says: "Religion is no longer for us what it was for our fathers, but it does not follow that it has died out in us. In any case, the basic component of all religion, the feeling of unconditional dependence, has remained with us." To this description of the basic feature of religion must be added a more precise definition of the power on which humans feel themselves dependent.

[7] We reproduce here the most characteristic passage for this view from *First Principles*: "Everyone has heard of the king who wished he had been present at the creation of the world, that he might have given good advice. He was humble, however, compared with those who profess to understand not only the relation of the Creating to the created but also how the Creating is constituted. And yet this transcendent audacity, which thinks to penetrate the secrets of the Power manifested through all existence—nay, even to stand behind that Power and note the conditions to its action—this is which passes currently as piety! May we not affirm that a sincere recognition of the truth that our own and all other existence is a mystery absolutely beyond our comprehension contains more of true religion than all the dogmatic theology ever written?" [Spencer 1887, 112. Druskowitz is quoting from the German translation of Herbert Spencer's "First Principles", the first volume of his 10-volume work *A System of Synthetic Philosophy*, titled in German "authorised" translation as *Die Grundlagen der Philosophie* (Spencer 1875, 111 – Druskowitz gives an erroneous pagination).]

world, a venture which Spencer regards as irreligious. Spencer's effort to reconcile science and religion, which is based on erroneous premises, goes hand in hand with this false conception of the nature of religion. Spencer rightly points out that science originally contributed in many ways to the clarification, purification and expansion of religious concepts. But he overlooks the fact that science is a deceptive comrade of religion in that it ultimately destroys and annihilates it with the same weapons with which it has contributed to its purification and clarification.[8] If {22} Spencer confuses religion with philosophy, W. M. Salter, the American moral teacher, who is also becoming more and more recognised in Germany, confuses religion with morality by speaking of the "religion of morality". Here, too, the word "religion" is retained for a supra-religious point of view, and thus, many an unjustified transfer of this word to a sphere which extends far beyond that which it denoted initially could be emphasised.[9]

Among all those who have addressed the question of a higher replacement for religion, Eugen Dühring deserves credit for keeping the spheres of religion and a world view based on knowledge strictly divided. Even if we are not able to describe Dühring's attempt to solve the problem in question as a satisfactory one, we must all the more agree with his sharp distinction of what must be separated.[10]

{23} Whoever therefore still calls the supra-religious point of view religion proves only that they either have not sufficiently overcome the old doctrine, or that they do not sufficiently distinguish between the different spiritual realms,

---

[8] Spencer's idea of reconciliation between science and religion is reflected in the work of the American preacher M. J. Savage, also published in German translation: *Religion in the Light of Darwin's Theory* [*Die Religion im Lichte der Darwin'schen Lehre*] (1886). The book is the translation of Minot Judson Savage, *The Religion of Evolution* (1876)]. According to Savage, the world is a gradual development of God; his doctrine is, therefore, best described as panentheism. The doctrine of evolution is said to "go back to the pure word of Jesus and fill it powerfully with all the knowledge and power of modern science. By conceiving every law of nature, of the spirit and religion only as an outflow of the living, loving and just God, it identifies morality and religion completely, or rather makes morality a branch of religion, which is greater and more comprehensive." The book is full of naïve marvels, as when the author, when asked how long it will take for the world to reach its climax, replies: "Thousands of years, for God, is in no hurry; he has eternity for his work," etc. But the author's confidence that a great future lies ahead for mankind has a beneficial effect.

[9] Thus, Wundt in *Ethik* (1886, 41) also defines the term religion too broadly when he understands it to mean "those representations and feelings which refer to an ideal existence which corresponds perfectly to desires and demands" [our translation].

[10] We have already pointed out the necessity of a precise differentiation and delimitation of the areas of religion and a higher world view in our essay *Moderne Versuche eines Religionsersatzes* (1886).

or that they finally, guided by false considerations, strive to combine the new with the old, without such a combination being possible.

4

{24} The new doctrine or world view, as we have already emphasised, must be directed towards an effective grasp of the world problem and the highest goal, as critical philosophy and true science teach us to consider them. From this understanding, duties and motivations for acting human beings will naturally arise.

From this determination, it follows that the new doctrine cannot be subsumed under the concept of morality, which many view as equivalent to religion. In contrast, we consider it an enhancement and perfection of morality rather than one of the effects that the new world view must bring about.

For others, Goethe's well-known verses, according to which he who possesses science and art has no need of religion, and he who does not possess these two must have religion, have something captivating about them.[11] According to this famous saying then, the pursuit of art or science is, in its generality, a full equivalent of religion. A deeper consideration, however, shows that neither of these two spheres in their generality can accomplish this {25} feat. As far as science is concerned, only those of its results that relate to the highest questions of the world come into consideration for our problem, while art, and especially poetry, play a role here only insofar as they give ideal expression to those highest thoughts. The concept of art, in its generality, contains only a formal definition, while the nature of the content remains completely undecided; our problem, however, requires a very definite, highest content of thought.

There is now no lack of attempts to replace religion with a new view of the world and life, attempts that are mainly linked to the names Comte, Feuerbach,

---

11 [This is taken from Goethe's collection published under the title *Zahme Xenien* [1827]. Goethe's text reads:
"Wer Wissenschaft und Kunst besitzt,
Hat auch Religion;
Wer jene beiden nicht besitzt,
Der habe Religion."
(He who possesses art and science
has also religion;
he who does not possess them,
needs religion.)

Pace Druskowitz, Goethe does not say that who possesses art and science does not need religion, but that he *also* possesses religion, along with art and science.]

Dühring, Duboc, Nietzsche and Salter, the latter of whom is, however, primarily an ethicist, and one of the most excellent ethicists we know. We have critically appraised the statements of these philosophers in our paper *Modern attempts to replace religion*. However much we found in those thinkers that was significant and worthy of consideration, we could not give our complete approval to any of them. We would emphasise the negative side of the result obtained in that work even more sharply today than we did then because we had to subject our own position on the problem to correction in many respects. However, it is not our intention to revise our critique of those attempts here. This will come of itself through a more detailed exposition of our {26} own views on the content of what we would like to call a new doctrine in contrast to religion. We repeat, however, that we are by no means of the opinion that we are saying anything absolutely correct or universally valid; we merely express our personal view, hoping to strike a chord in others.

How, then, can we, guided by knowledge—whether positive or negative—arrive at an idea of the foundation of the world and a supreme goal which, by connecting our life and striving with something superior to us, can serve as the basis of uplifting and inspiring feelings? These feelings will be none other than those of the most profound reverence for the foundation of the world, of the highest hope for a world or even human goal.

By what knowledge, then, does the foundation of the world first become the object of our most profound reverence? Only by the recognition that characterisation of it or the last and highest things eludes our judgment that the world is an insoluble riddle, an unfathomable mystery for our intellectual organisation.

According to critical philosophy and natural science, which confirm its doctrine, our experience does not exhaust the content of the world. Our representations do not align with real beings; the poverty and limitation of our senses, the inadequacy of our understanding, can only offer us a completely subjective and imperfect {27} picture of the world. Every conclusion drawn from our world of representation to real existence proves to be deceptive, for, as we are constituted, it is not in our power to break through the barriers that separate us from the knowledge of the world.—Just as little as the outside world do we recognise ourselves, for psychic phenomena are also only phenomena. But what is their deepest essence? What are they? We cannot find an answer. The world is an enigma; we are an enigma, life is an enigma, and death is an enigma. Let rash metaphysicians persist in the belief that they have found the world formula and drawn the ultimate conclusion of wisdom. Let our own ultimate conclusion of wisdom be that the last things are unfathomable to us, that we live surrounded by enigmas amid a mystery—we ourselves, a mystery. By this insight, however, we demonstrate a more profound reverence toward the highest questions, not only more than the metaphysicians but also more than the religious, who regard the foundations of the world as something known to them.

Now, we do not deny that the consciousness that we are denied an understanding of the world can also awaken a feeling in us which excludes true reverence, namely that of a dull pain, a feeling as if we were banished to a dungeon from which we long in vain for the light, against whose iron walls all our attempts to come closer to the truth fail. This feeling is also justified, and in some minds, it may be the predominant one. {28}. Others, however, will only be fleetingly touched by it, while the nobler sensation of reverent understanding of the world's mystery is more homogeneous to them. Only a few, especially in our day, may be capable of this deepening; our time is lacking reverent people and Goethe's beautiful self-confession: "My disposition was by nature inclined toward reverence, and it required a great upheaval to make my faith in anything venerable waver" [Goethe 2024, 65, our translation] can probably only be grasped in its depth by a few. Individuals, however, will nevertheless be able to immerse themselves reverently in the world problem, and the truly philosophical mind, which at the same time possesses the power of imagination to absorb the results of thought into a living feeling, will be seized by this feeling again and again. For the desire will always arise in them to elevate themselves from the given, in which common sense remains trapped, to the thought of the mystery, or to consider things in connection with it, whereby their significance gains a wonderful deepening. In moments of highest intensification, however, this affect of reverence will appear in the form of an inner trembling, as the spirit, leaving the given world of appearances, dives into the riddles of existence. And this affect has a cathartic effect, for it means turning away from the inadequacy, limitation and transience of the given world, from the dissonances and dualistic disruption of life, as {29} far as we recognise and comprehend it. If we focus our eyes exclusively on the given, we easily arrive at a pessimistic condemnation of existence in general. The only thing that can protect us from this is the awareness that the deepest meaning of existence and its actual significance is closed to us and that we are not entitled to any judgment of it.

We are opposed to confusing the idea of worshipping the world as a mystery with the idea of immersing ourselves in the immensity of the universe and the immensity of the world process. In doing so, we remain within the world of phenomena while we rise above phenomenality by grasping the foundation of the world as an impenetrable mystery. Furthermore, suppose we remain within the world of appearances. In that case, the totality of things, despite its incomprehensibility, is no more wonderful than an apparently vanishing individual thing, the cosmic harmony no more wonderful than the harmony of the parts of a work of art. It is always a sign of a coarser sense to allow ourselves to be dazzled by mere quantitative relationships.

It is fitting for humans, according to their intellectual organisation, to grasp the world mystery reverently, but it would be a more perfect state if knowledge of the last things were attainable for them, if their thinking could align with being, their understanding could grasp the content of the world, and the power to comprehend the force {30} that reveals itself in both the intellectual and material world.

But would it be inconceivable that latent powers lie dormant in humanity, whose awakening and gradual development—if not for the people of the present or the near future, then for those of a more distant future—would be able to raise them to that higher level? Shouldn't humanity have the ability to one day emerge from its state of imperfection, of half-life, from the dualism in which even its noblest spirits remain imprisoned? Should it not be within the realm of possibility that not only the ideal powers that humanity has shown so far would be capable of a tremendous increase but also that new, unknown potencies would one day come to light, which would finally bring about a transformation of the world view and with this most probably the elimination of a thousand imperfections of nature, which the human will would never be able to overcome, but which in the end are only due to our deficient subjective way of representation? For it is precisely through the richer and more perfect formation of the world picture in the more highly organised representative mind that knowledge of the content of the world would be conveyed. Does science now provide any support for the assumption that humanity might be destined, first along the path of conscious perfection, but later through the awakening of new spiritual powers, to move toward a goal—under which no millennium, no {31} future paradise, nor other childish daydreams are to be conceived—a goal that signifies victory: the victory of nature's higher aspect over its lower, indeed a breakthrough of the barriers in which human cognition is still bound, through the development of higher spiritual organs, even if this goal in itself were not the ultimate one?

There are faint-hearted natures for whom the idea of progress, even if they do not view it sceptically, holds nothing stimulating or warming. There are others again who cling to it vividly but would be content with specific improvements in human society, especially with the moralisation of it. Finally, however, we can also represent such spirits who would only attach value to humanity and its development if there were some indication that it would lead to victory, to the highest knowledge, i.e. to the transition to the world of the future. i.e. to the transition to a higher order—an accomplishment of which we can form no representation. And is not the thought of a goal, of a conclusion, even if only a provisional one, a need of the human spirit? Is it not a need of the same to see a goal above itself that reaches beyond all that is given? As long as we consider humans as beings who will never reveal higher forces than those they have shown so far, there is indeed no goal for them; such a goal only appears when we consider the possibility of humanity {32} elevating to a higher level of organisation, even if this goal in itself is not yet the ultimate and highest. For humans, however, it must be an object of the highest hope, the highest trust.

Does science offer any support for the idea that humans should give themselves to this hope?

Indeed, Darwin's theory of evolution seems to provide support for this. This doctrine is not a certainty but rather a hypothesis of the highest probability, which has become indispensable in various fields of science. Only few who have penetrated it would not have been converted by it, so great is the power of conviction that emanates from it. According to it, the higher has developed from the lower. Humans have progressed from the lower animal stage through gradual development. At the same time, a turning point in the organic life of the Earth has occurred with them, for their appearance marked the possibility of an immense increase in consciousness and intellectual progress while maintaining the same physical form of life. Therefore, it can be rightly assumed that any progress beyond humans could only take place through intellectual perfection, through the awakening and development of hitherto unknown or barely hinted at psychic organs, that an intellectual increase in organisation could occur independently of a physical one. Darwin and the majority of his followers stop at humans, {33} in their current highest development, as if with them, the climax of the organic progress of the Earth had been reached. But does not the human tremendous capacity for progress, their tremendous struggle and striving, indicate that they want to go beyond themselves? Does the law of progress no longer correspond to the assumption that humankind is called to flow into a higher type, in which its ideal will would be transformed into a sublime ability, and that the ascending organic development will only culminate in beings in which thinking and being coincide and reason has become the ruler?

In Germany, the idea of a biological increase in organisation beyond the human being has its most eloquent representative in Carl du Prel. In his major work, *The Philosophy of Mysticism* (1885), the insightful researcher points out the imperfection with which the theory of development views humans by drawing only one of its conclusions about them. However, if each higher link in organic development has two aspects to consider—first, one that points to the biological past, and second, another that prophetically hints at future development—then humans must also be viewed from this dual perspective. "Now, if we would not treat the evolution theory one-sidedly, if we would be logical," says {34} the author, "we must consider man also from the double point of view. Darwinism has cast a retrospective glance upon the history of the development of earthly life but is at no trouble to discover in human nature those indications that are prophetic and which must be as present in the *existing* final member of evolution as in every earlier one. As to every product of nature, the indications of future development, no less than the rudiments of the past are attached, so must man also have his Janus-aspect" [1889, 119].[12] The beginnings of a higher psychic development of humans—since, as previously noted, higher development will occur only in the psychic realm—would themselves be a product of development and evidently a later one than the other mental faculties of humans. Does it not follow from this that those beginnings and germs of a higher stage of organisation need by no means make themselves felt in humans at present but will possibly only announce themselves in the future? Du Prel, however, as can be seen from these sentences, regards it as self-evident that these symptoms must already be noticeable at present. That is why he investigates the life of the human soul. Now, it is certainly a correct thought that those symptoms could only be found in abnormal mental states. Such are the phenomena of somnambulism, of dreams, of double {35} vision, of mind-reading, etc., which we may call visionary phenomena in general. These, however, deserve serious consideration even if one is entirely opposed to spiritualism and attaches no real significance to it. The peculiarity of all these phenomena consists in the fact that perceptions are made or effects achieved, as it were, through organs other than the normal ones, transcending time and space. The relations between subject and object appear sometimes more immediate, sometimes more manifold than in the normal state. It cannot be denied that these abnormal states are those of mental elevation and confer advantages on the subject as well as, under certain circumstances, on the object. Nor do we wish to deny that it is very tempting to regard these phenomena as symptoms of a biological increase in organisation. There is, however, no certainty, all the less so because in those phenomena, only a more spiritual kind of connection, as it were, is created between subject and object, but not either perceptions are made or effects achieved that could not likewise be brought about within the subjective forms of perception. Even less than seeing prophetic signs with certainty in those phenomena, which are nevertheless conspicuous, are we entitled to see in them more than at most the beginnings of a higher development. Although du Prel

---

12 [This quote is from du Prel 1885, 380–381. The English translation is taken from Carl du Prel, *The Philosophy of Mysticism* (1889). It is interesting to notice that the German phrase "Wenn wir die Entwickelungslehre nicht als den Mohr betrachten wollen, der seine Schuldigkeit gethan, nachdem er uns bis zum Menschen geführt [...]"—literally translated as "If we do not want to consider the theory of evolution as the Moor, who has done his duty after leading us to humans [...]"—is replaced by the expression "one-sidedly" in the English translation.]

himself admits that in these abnormal states, we have only to see, as it were, a "sheet lightning," {36} he does not hesitate, on the other hand, to draw the highest conclusions from these observations, and to see in them the key to the solution of the most difficult questions. From the circumstance that in those visionary states a second, higher consciousness, as it were, awakens in us, it immediately follows for du Prel that a human being is a double being, consisting of the empirical person, which manifests itself in normal consciousness, and a transcendental subject, which emerges from time to time in those abnormal phenomena. Furthermore, our philosopher concludes from the knowledge that somnambulists reveal in their salvific decrees about the human body and the laws of inner life that the transcendental subject is the organising principle and the creator of the empirical person. Accordingly, the earthly embodiment is a free act of the transcendental subject, a voluntary incarnation for the purpose of purification and perfection. Now, there is no further step to the idea of palingenesis, which, however, comes to life in du Prel in the form of a metaphysical Darwinism, in that the various stages of biological development appear as voluntary embodiments of the transcendental subject in an ascending line; finally, the biological ascent, which leads beyond the human being, signifies the liberation of the transcendental subject from its last sensual form of disguise, in that the purpose of our individual development is the preparation of the future type of planetary man.—It would require special writing to unravel the web of errors {37}, fallacies and ambiguities contained in this conceptual poetry, which by believing that it removes difficulties, only creates them. The whole structure of thought floats in the air since its apparent foundation: the conclusion that a transcendental subject reveals itself in somnambulistic and related states is the worst fallacy metaphysics has been guilty o, and which only proves anew how impotent the human mind in its present condition is in its ability to fathom ultimate things.

While du Prel thus derives a whole theory from the fact that abnormal states exist, we regard it only as a possibility that those abnormal functions are already the beginnings of higher psychic forms.[13] While for our philosopher, the solution

---

[13] The interpretation usually given to visionary phenomena, however, is often considered superstition. The simple fact that the appearance of these phenomena seems to be particularly favoured by certain climatic and terrestrial influences—one thinks of the special inclination of the Scots, Westphalians and Esthlanders to the "second sight"—proves what an error those are in who see transcendental revelations in them. The existence of certain abnormal phenomena, however, seems to be as certain as that of normal phenomena themselves. But it does not follow from the acceptance of such phenomena that the possibility of spiritualistic phenomena is also confirmed. What matters here is not the individual phenomena but the existence of such phe-

to the most difficult problems arises from {38} those phenomena, we do not consider it impossible that from those very phenomena, the psychic powers may develop which will enable the future humans, or the higher level of being to which humankind will ascend, to comprehend the nature of these phenomena. Only then would it be possible to recognise what underlies all phenomena, including the personality.[14]

The essential reasons, however, why we need a confident dedication to the idea that humanity is destined to progress to victory through increased organisation, i.e. to the highest knowledge, to the overcoming of the dualism in which it is now caught, to a not only truer but also richer and more perfect {39} world view—regardless of whether the beginnings of this higher state already exist or not—are the law, emphasised by Darwinism, of the development of the higher from the lower and human undeniably powerful urge for perfection, their profound dissatisfaction with all that has been achieved, their sublime longing for a higher state of existence.

A great part of the progress to be accomplished could, however, only take place through processes in the intellectual organisation of man which fall entirely outside the sphere of his conscious effort, just as the thought which lights up in the genius and when proclaimed brings about a general increase of consciousness rising freely from the depths of the mind. However, before those higher forces in humans come into effect, before they could possibly come into effect, the greatest conscious efforts, both intellectual and moral, must precede, which would then evidently benefit the higher state of existence so that this is not only a goal of hope but also, in a certain sense, a goal of striving. It can be assumed that the proven forces of humans must first be exhausted before new forces can emerge in them. These will be a richer perception and enhanced capacity to conceive encompassing the content of the world, while our aesthetic and ethical consciousness will not be lost for future humans.

---

nomena in general. Since this field of phenomena is often misused as a playground for dizzying activities, it will often be difficult to distinguish between truth and fraud.

14 Let us not identify biological progress beyond the present organisation of man, as we think of it, with Friedrich Nietzsche's doctrine of the "over-human," which he expressed in the strange book *Thus Spoke Zarathustra*. Even the name Nietzsche chooses for his ideal seems to us to be a misnomer. The ideal itself, however, which is presented to us in this thought poem, is simply the genius above which the higher type, as we think of it, would rise since even the genius remains caught up in human half-life and in the lack of higher cognition, which is to be overcome. In the vivid grasp of the idea of a higher type, the reader will recognise the most essential progress of this writing beyond *Modern Attempts*, etc., since this idea was hinted at but not grasped more deeply, not emotionally, and therefore, the possibility of an ultimate goal for man was also denied.

{40} The idea of humans transitioning into a higher order may seem fantastic and strange to most, although it is fundamentally, as we have previously noted, only the expression of a deep need in the human spirit to strive beyond all that is given. However, this is mainly because one brings that goal too close to our current level of development and does not consider that this would be mediated through an immense chain of progressive increases and expansions of consciousness, through a constant increase in the relationships between spirit and world, through an ever more sovereign mastery of nature using ever more perfect inventions, through a growing liberation of human forces, through a progressive refinement of our will, a spiritualisation of life, an infinite enrichment of our knowledge, an ever more perfect development of their specific moral and intellectual virtues by modern civilised peoples, and finally through the emergence of new forces in humans. This progress can only take the form of a slow, laborious process,[15] but progress itself is undeniable. Philipp Mainländer remarks very beautifully, albeit from the standpoint of the dogmatic {41} pessimist, for whom a voluntary demise of humanity in the future through a slackening of the forces of life is a certainty: "Just as stars stand still, indeed, seem to be receding, so too, to the mind immersed in the individual, humanity soon seems to stand still, soon to recede. The philosopher, however, sees only resultant movement everywhere, a constant forward movement of humanity" (Mainländer 1876, 291).

In our era, not only has the idea of progress emerged more powerfully through the theory of evolution than at any other time, but progress itself—despite the claims of those who focus on details and diminish our time—has become noticeably intense in various fields, no matter how imperfect the existing state may still be.

First of all, there is progress in the sphere of morality. However deficient our morals may still be, it cannot be denied that today, there is greater respect for human beings, that people think more of one another, and that the idea of a just social order occupies the minds to a greater extent than in earlier times. Our moral ideal has become a higher one, and W. M. Salter[16] shows that the moral teaching of Jesus can no longer satisfy our demands {42}. But the fact that our moral ideal has become a more perfect one is proof that our morality it-

---

15 Goethe rightly says: "The world should not reach its goal as quickly as we think and wish. There are always the retarding demons that intervene and oppose us everywhere so that although progress is made on the whole, it is very slow" [1896, 159, our translation]. And Jean Paul says: "Through a red sea of blood and war we wade towards the promised land and our desert is long."
16 [Druskowitz refers to Salter 1885. This book is the German translation of Salter's lectures, which precedes the English book published by Salter under the title *Ethical Religion* (1889). Salter's English book was published *after* Druskowitz's *Towards a New Doctrine*.]

self has become more perfect. For its part, the dissemination of the theory of development can only contribute to the elevation of morality "for the realisation of the fact that mental and physical qualities are inherited, if not by children then by children's children, inheritance whose sphere of action we can never determine in individual cases—must work towards an increase in the feeling of responsibility, since we thus realise that the consequences of good and bad actions extend even further than we had previously suspected" (Gizycki 1885, 264).[17] The welcome appearance of ethical culture societies in North America, whose numbers are growing, must also be welcomed as a sign of the times.

We scarcely need to recall the powerful advances made by the sciences in recent decades, the flourishing of new branches of knowledge and new methods of research, or the enormous progress in the technical mastery and utilisation of natural forces as evidence for the assertion we made above. {43} Even if Dühring's statement that the greatness of our century is to be sought solely in its polytechnical achievements is a one-sided one, it nevertheless points to an area in which the greatest progress has indeed been made. And yet, we seem to be on the eve of new discoveries and inventions, and certain technical additions to our imperfect physical organisation can already be predicted.[18]

The deniers of progress are probably most easily refuted by the fact of the growing historical overview, which must certainly be regarded as a form of progress. Through the flourishing of numerous new sciences, the historical overview has been significantly expanded, especially in recent times, and our consciousness has been immensely enriched as a result. Not only our thoughts but also our emotions have been enriched, for example, by the mediation of the poetry of ancient or foreign peoples, thereby conquering new subject areas for our modern poetry. The most important result of the growing overview of history, however, may be that we learn to know humans more and more precisely, to perceive more and more clearly the causes that have promoted the progress of people and those that have hindered it, whereby we again become more clearly aware of the paths {44} that peoples must take in the future in order to progress more securely and rapidly and not to be repeatedly misled and held back by the "retarding demons". However, there is no need to consider the possibility of the collapse of

---

17 See W. M. Salter's treatise "Darwinism in Ethics," which appeared in the third issue of the newly founded American journal *The Open Court* in Chicago.—G. von Gizycki is one of the most intellectual representatives of a doctrine, namely utilitarianism, to which we personally have a thoroughly negative attitude.

18 Cf. du Prel's interesting and instructive book *Die Planetenbewohner und die Nebularhypothese* (1880). [Druskowitz indicates the year of publication as 1887. We could not find this edition; it is most likely an error.]

modern civilisation, like that of ancient civilisation, due to the attack of barbarian or semi-barbarian peoples because today, conversely, it is the culture-bearing races that are increasingly threatening the existence of the primitive peoples. Culture cannot be lost, even if some of the less vigorous cultural peoples should one day disappear from the scene.

The arts, on superficial consideration, seem to be in a state of decline, but one should not overlook the fact that our time has produced an epoch-making musical genius of the highest order, that some branches of art have experienced an upswing such as they never had in any earlier epoch, that the technique of some arts has been perfected, that the range of materials has been immensely extended and that some nations, which until recently were considered artistically unproductive, have at one stroke produced several important poets and artists who, drawing on the fullness, have enriched art with new types and forms.

Nevertheless, it must be admitted that imagination today celebrates far greater triumphs in the sciences and technical fields than in the arts. But there are signs that art, once the leading {45} nations have emerged from their current state of social revolution and society has taken on firmer forms, and once the results of natural science and the enormous expansion of the horizon it has created have more powerfully gripped the imagination, will only flourish all the more powerfully on a new foundation.

One of the most important advances of modern civilised nations at present is the growing renunciation of religion; one of the most important advances of the future will be that among those nations which are called to lead humanity and which will perhaps one day form the epitome of humanity, a new doctrine will be established, by virtue of which all life and striving will receive a higher significance. That the theory of evolution, which opens us to vast perspectives when correctly understood, will play a significant role in this regard—by effectively grasping the law of progress, it will itself accelerate progress—seems to us to be beyond doubt. Individuality will always have a wide latitude in the way that doctrine is utilised. The idea of progress, if grasped with imagination, has something exciting and inspiring, even if the goal of progress is left completely undefined. It must seize the mind all the more powerfully when it is associated with the idea of a supreme goal into which all human achievements, like the rivers in the ocean of the world, shall one day flow. This transition will be accomplished by those peoples {46} or nations which have proved themselves most vigorous and capable of progress and have thus become the natural masters of the Earth.

So, would our worldview be decidedly optimistic? Certainly, as the doctrine of evolution itself is, but only in the sense that the human race is trusted with an immeasurable power of progress and a great future is expected of it. But the fact that perfection is only expected of the future, that our hope is directed towards it, is proof that we do not consider an optimistic view of the present and the past to be justified, despite all our admiration for individual outstanding achievements. We do not wish here to repeat the judgment of the great philosophers and poets of pessimism about the given world, who, however, were mistaken in that, firstly, they confused the world as we know it with real existence, and secondly, from the gloomy past and gloomy present they prematurely inferred the necessity of a gloomy future—a view which contradicts the theory of evolution and the immense striving for progress of humans. The pessimistic view of the state of affairs, however, is itself a lever of progress, for progress is only born of deep dissatisfaction with the actual state of affairs. Only by being constantly accompanied by the feeling of our imperfection do we perfect ourselves. The same is true of life in general as well as of individual life, and the awareness that suffering is the most powerful originator of all progress, that the elimination {47} of suffering would be the end of all striving and all forward movement, can protect us from unmeasured lamentations and prevent us from a prematurely condemning judgment of the content of life. The merely pessimistic view of the state of affairs must lead to dull resignation and despondency if we are not inspired by the confidence that human nature can be improved by unceasingly striving forward, which causes suffering, and that a high goal beckons to humanity.

However, the goal that signifies victory is not a certainty. Humanity may only be capable of a certain degree of perfection without being able to exceed this limit. It is possible that humans, in a somewhat higher state of perfection than they currently exhibit, nevertheless represent the pinnacle of the Earth's organic development. In this case, the development so far would have been aimless and deceptive; the striving and struggling of humanity would have been in vain since insurmountable and ineradicable defects and infirmities would forever prevent it from attaining perfection and bliss as it is.

How should we imagine the future of humanity in such a case? Mainländer's prophecy would probably come true. According to it, civilisation and education would initially penetrate ever-wider circles until, after the indomitable enemies of culture had worn themselves out in the struggle with the culture bearers, they would have encompassed all humankind. Gradually, {48} however, a decline and finally a standstill of the creative forces would become noticeable. Humanity would no longer progress. But as the original power of the passions would be tempered by culture, the state of stagnation would soon pass over to one of general fatigue and exhaustion, with the longing for death overcoming the drive for life, not through a general suicide, but through a natural cessation of humanity.

The goal promised by the theory of evolution has far greater probability than this, but since even this goal is not a complete certainty, it follows that the value of life, of our life, cannot at present be determined with certainty—in the sense of whether existence is to be preferred to non-existence or vice versa—and that the philosophers who have nevertheless undertaken it—and the majority of them have undertaken it—have judged prematurely, for as long as we cannot judge the course and goal of life with certainty, we are also unable to estimate its value with certainty.

According to this, however, we would have only one certainty: namely, that humanity is approaching its redemption in any case, whether through victory and the redemption from imperfection or through a voluntary downfall and the redemption from an aimless life. But even in the latter case, people would not have the right to value non-being more highly than being in general, but only higher than the specific being {49} that was allotted to humanity. If, however, an earthly catastrophe were to sweep humanity away before it had reached certainty about its destiny, then this would only be proof that the conditions that would have enabled humanity to progress towards a higher goal were lacking from the outset.

But even if only the redemption of humankind in itself, whether in one form or another, and not the redemption through victory, is a complete certainty, the latter form of its redemption is nevertheless incomparably more probable, and the greater degree of probability is what matters here as everywhere else. No definite prophecy can be made about the development and destiny of humanity. However, the greater the probability of a goal, the more it will determine our hopes and aspirations. Therefore, given the doctrine of evolution and its consequences, it behoves us to raise our guiding star to the thought of humankind's immeasurable progress, the emergence of new, unknown powers, and an approach to a sublime goal.

Now, there will be no shortage of voices to object that, however lofty the goal that future humanity may attain, this thought cannot provide any elevation to present-day human beings since they themselves will not personally experience those achievements, nor will any share in them be granted to them. On the other hand, however, it must be emphasised that {50} it is no less inadmissible to deny immortality absolutely than to assert it, even though there seem to be far more reasons against than in favour of assuming it. For those who find the hope of a personal higher state of existence is an irrefutable need, this hope need not be abandoned entirely, although it would be more dignified to be content with the thought that the good deeds accomplished will always continue to have an effect than to be immortal.

Braver, stronger and more selfless spirits, unconcerned about their personal fate, will find an elevation and encouragement for personal advancement in the idea of an immeasurable capacity for the progress of humanity and a great goal, a victorious conclusion of the ascending planetary development. As humans strive for that lofty goal, they feel one with the light-creating force of nature itself, and what they seek and love will be, like that force, great and perfect. Those imbued with this idea will not fall victim to the *doctrine of utility*, which finds so much favour today, for it will be clear to them that it is never about the emotional states of individuals but about their work and their achievements. Utilitarianism regards "the greatest happiness of the greatest number" or the "maximisation of happiness" as the supreme principle of morality; however, the assumption that increasing morality generally enhances human happiness is simply an illusion. While we reserve a {51} more detailed justification of this assertion for another occasion, we shall, at this point, only emphasise the following as evidence. First of all, concerning those who are acted upon, it can only be said that, on the one hand, the perfection of morality does indeed eliminate many sufferings. However, it is by no means possible to determine to what extent positive happiness is also created since justice, consideration, and compassion are by no means always perceived as happiness by fellow human beings. There are significant differences in how people perceive and experience the same things.

On the other hand, injustice and oppression are not always perceived as suffering, and someone can be just as well helped as harmed by an injustice that has befallen him. Concerning those who act, however, it can be said with certainty that the more people follow the voice of duty instead of the call of their selfish inclinations, the more persistently they will stick to their positions, the more they force themselves to do justice, the more strictly they will monitor themselves, the more sensitive their conscience becomes, the more severe, more serious and more arduous life will be. To reiterate: just as humanity, as it is constituted, is not called to perfection, so too is it not called to happiness, for all cultural progress consists in an intensification of humanity's severity toward itself. Utilitarianism mistakenly regards human beings {52} as an end in itself, whereas it is only a transitional type and, in all likelihood, aspires toward a higher order of being, to which all its achievements will one day accrue. Therefore, in the moral sphere as well, the concern is not with the emotional states of individuals but with the consolidation, fortification, and strengthening of the human community as the necessary precondition and foundation of all higher culture. Hence, in the establishment of the highest principles, the question is not what a person feels but what they affect—what they are likely to affect for the benefit of a higher order, as whose precursor they are to be regarded.

Humans should recognise something about themselves. Since they do not represent perfection, they should venerate it and dedicate their services to it. The perfection should not only be an object of veneration for us but should guide our entire striving. Every ideal exertion of strength signifies progress, and the greater the context in which it is viewed, the more joyfully the attainable must be striven for. By looking towards a sublime goal, however, our assessment of what is given and what can be achieved by humans in their present form is corrected at the same time. Accordingly, we will be able to appreciate the individual achievements without, however, regarding them as something final or ultimate. It will also become clear to us that, as humans are currently constituted, harmonious development and all-round perfection cannot be expected of them, that a person will only {53} be able to achieve something significant in particular directions, and that it is enough if each person exercises and develops the power they possess.

But if someone should object that the goal towards which humanity is likely to move, if all signs do not deceive, is too remote to act as an impetus for our actions, then it must be replied to this faint-hearted person that in every ideal thought, in every noble and creative deed, a ray of the future sun is already shining, a note of future harmony is already resounding, which will prepare the transition to a higher state.

In the reverent immersion in the mystery of the world and the prospect of a sublime goal, the probability of which is supported by such weighty reasons, but which humanity will be able to attain partly by consciously striving forward, partly by the awakening of higher spiritual potencies within it, there does indeed seem to us to be a world view that is superior to religion not only in truth but also in ethical value, the latter, however, in that it is not personal egoism that finds satisfaction in that goal.

Bibliography

Borelius, Johan Jakob. 1886. *Blicke auf den gegenwärtigen Standpunkt der Philosophie in Deutschland.* Translated by Emil Jonas. Berlin: Fischer (H. Hornfeld).

von Carneri, Bartholomäus. 1886. *Entwicklung und Glückseligkeit. Ethische Essays.* Stuttgart: Schweizerbart.

von Gizycki, Georg. 1885. "Darwinismus und Ethik." *Deutsche Rundschau*, vol. 4, 261–281.

Goethe, Johann Wolfgang. 1827. "Zahme Xenien IX" In: *Gedichte. Ausgabe letzter Hand.* Stuttgart and Tübingen: Cotta.

Goethe, Johann Wolfgang. 1896. *Gespräche*, vol 10. Edited by Woldemar Freiherr von Biedermann. Leipzig: J. W. von Biedermann.

Goethe, Johann Wolfgang. 2024. *Dichtung und Wahrheit.* Düsseldorf: Null Papier Verlag.

Guyau, Jean-Marie. 1886. *L'irréligion de l'avenir: étude sociologique.* Paris: Félix Alcan.

Lange, Friedrich Albert. 1886. *Religionsphilosophie auf modern-wissenschaftlicher Grundlage.* Edited by Julius Baumann. Leipzig: Veit.

Mainländer, Philipp. 1876. *Philosophie der Erlösung. Erster Band.* Berlin: Theobald Grieben.

du Prel, Carl. 1880. *Die Planetenbewohner und die Nebularhypothese.* Leipzig: Ernst Günther.

du Prel, Carl. 1885. *Die Philosophie der Mystik.* Leipzig: Ernst Günther.

du Prel, Carl. 1889. *The Philosophy of Mysticism*, vol. II. Translated by Charles Carleton Massey. London: George Redway.

Savage, Minot Judson. 1876. *The Religion of Evolution.* Boston: Lockwood, Brooks, & Company.
Savage, Minot Judson. 1886. *Die Religion im Liechte der Sarwin'schen Lehre.* Translated by Richard Schramm. Leipzig: Otto Wigand.
Spencer, Herbert. 1875. *Die Grundlagen der Philosophie.* Translated by Berhard Vetter. Stuttgart: E. Schweizerbart (E. Koch).
Spencer, Herbert. 1887. *A System: Synthetic Philosophy vol. I: First Principles.* London: Williams and Norgate.
Strauß, David Friedrich. 1872. *Der alte und der neue Glaube.* Leipzig: Hirzel.
Wundt, Wilhelm. 1886. *Ethik: Eine Untersuchung der Thatsachen und Gesetze des sittlichen Lebens.* Stuttgart: Ferdinand Enke.

Pessimistic Cardinal Propositions.
A Manual for the Freest Spirits by Erna
(Dr Helene von Druskowitz)

{3} Bring a 99-year-old man to court, and you will experience something like reading this text.

This work is to be read and appreciated with equal reverence, just as the Chamonix Valley and Rhône Glacier are admired.

1 No God in the Ordinary Sense

1. {7} There is such a thing as an Over-Sphere, a higher principle, as the next chapter will show. There can be no substrate for the general representation of God. What we logically represent as the higher principle or being is in no way comparable to the delusion of general theism, which is a delusion about what is credible.
2. The primary reason for the contradictions and dishonesty in the standard representation of God is the anthropomorphic configuration of God as a male figure. This explains why, in any representation of God, one always begins with a great and powerful God and ends with something wretched and timid. One cannot speak of true wisdom and real goodness, which his worshippers profess the Lord God possesses—it is, of course, only a hypothesis... His lack of providence and incapability to well configure his so-called creation, and his backwardness, that he created something far *below himself*, compared to any artists or artisans, who look beyond themselves in order to create something *larger than themselves*, {8} must provoke shuddering and consternation. The world we know is governed by fundamental evil; it is nothing but a patchwork. It is rotten to the core, and this rot spreads through painful laws of development until it reaches the highest field, the one of human consciousness. This is so wrongly arranged that the more beautiful, purer and milder gender remains subservient to the craving and concupiscence of the other gender, which is prone to ugly and raw follies as much as it is driven by greed and salaciousness. If we add to this the representation of the so-called punishments, which are to be expected in an imaginary afterlife, there comes a picture of a god as an evil Shockheaded Peter, who himself deserves hell a millionfold and the suffering to which he subjects his followers.

After having identified God as a fool and a fraud, we can hardly imagine that he could be a metaphysical being or that he could ever be thought of as such. It is even more absurd to suppose that a so-called metaphysical being could have created a material entity such as the world—a metaphysical being, no less, that *does not even recognize* its own creation.

3. God's collected work is a miserable, male concoction, replete with perniciousness, especially for womankind, whose development it has always unduly inhibited.
4. No worse is the issue of philosophical monism with an intellectual basis, {9} because it conjoins all good and evil in one. When the errors of the entire world structure are enumerated, one can point out even the most shameful cases; it only makes an old, wise face.

    With an incomprehensible peace of mind, monism lets evil emerge from good. In its optimistic delusion, it feels no need to set an end to the criminal tragicomedy of existence. The corrupting saying—what is well suited for one is harmful to another—may be a powerful critique of the monists by the altruists, the mildest thinkers, but a much sharper critique by psychological thinkers.
5. Theism is equally unedifying in its presuppositions as in its consequences. It leads to war, inhibits peoples and states in their natural development, is an enemy and oppressor of the female gender, promotes lies, slander and vulgar delusion, promotes any lack of virtue, produces the crassest illusions and favours the worst castes and institutions, as is proven by the behaviour of the so-called high clergy in its pride, its exclusive banquets as well as of the spiritless and vulgar nobility that is devoted to all pleasures, carnal games and all material joys with devilish lust.
6. {10} The normal mind is atheistic. It explains all processes by reference to earlier ones and so *ad infinitum.* In its ethical actions, it allows itself to be guided partly by innermost feelings and partly by a moral consciousness that has gradually become consolidated.[1] The atheist is a genuine philosopher. He possesses the key to that wisdom and freedom; he can think it through to the utmost consequences and can proclaim a definite statement in a broader judgment on life and death. He can be holy only through himself and without any

---

1 [Druskowitz uses the unusual term *konkreszieren*, which may be an allusion to Nietzsche's text in *Human, All Too Human* (2005, I, sec. 2, paragraph 39). There Nietzsche mentions *Konkreszieren* (from the Latin *concrescere: to grow together, to consolidate*) which symbolizes his "hermeneutics" of philosophy: something that has "grown together" as a consequence of historical changes has been transformed into something new.]

ceremony simply because he keeps the raw and childish representation of a "god" entirely apart from himself.
7. The atheist, if consistent, must oppose the believer on every important point. For example, he has to conceive of matter ironically and sceptically; moreover, he has to be inimical to the blind and idiotic population growth and marriages.

2 The High Principle, Only to Be Platonically Comprehended

1. {11} There is a High Principle. The existence of such a thing follows from the perception of a law that rules within the complete representation and conceptual world. As light and shadow exclude each other, so are all things dominated by opposition. That perception expresses the highest opposition to the supreme, philosophically rendered Sphere, namely the opposition to matter and the pure spirit.
2. Therefore, we may refer to the original spiritual world as an *Over-Sphere* because it is free from the errors of material nature; we may also refer to it as a *Substance* because it essentially encompasses everything that the everyday world lacks.
3. The High Principle takes over all the attributes which matter does not possess. It is unique, uniform, harmonious, and beyond participation in common alteration and change!
4. This sublime Sphere must not be expected to have created the clump of matter despite its [clump's] relative capacity for development. {12} However, we may acknowledge a form of spontaneous magic which exerts its influence upon matter. For, through the first category—namely, that of Being—which is connected to matter, it [the High Principle] might, as the abundant, exorbitantly elevated, and absolutely harmonious element, quite unconsciously and unintentionally exert an external magical pull upon matter. In this way, the natural law is not disrupted but rather fortified.
5. Accordingly, a peculiar urge comes to the matter, the urge to desert elementary states and to master higher levels. However, the Over-Sphere allows such an increase, usually referred to as the evolution of matter, only as an *imaginary* and *imitative* approximation. It is merely a coincidental occurrence of a singular kind when matter enters the phase of conscious life ...
6. Nothing changes concerning this state of facts even if a person elevates herself to a transcendental subject because the latter is nothing more than the product of her perpetual longing for the Over-Sphere, which remains eternally withdrawn. Thus, to the one who knows, existence appears as false and un-

true, and everything points to dissolution. For, while the beyond-godly nature becomes evident by the complete absence of all human qualities, human nature is, on the contrary, {13} a product of the lack of noble and pure qualities. The beyond-godly Sphere could have no relationship with a person without robbing her of her transcendental capacity; [the beyond-godly Sphere] is too unique to be communicable. Thus, paradoxically, it is through the unbridgeable distance that the subject partakes of this Sphere, albeit in an inverted form.

7. Even if we also think highly of the Over-Sphere, we can grasp it only speculatively. There is no human relationship with it.
8. The Over-Sphere is eternally silent. Its inner constituents are forever unrecognizable; it stands in direct opposition to common theistic representations.
9. Even speculatively, we are only able to get to the outer limit of the phenomenon and not to the nucleus of the miracle. Everything else is left to the illustration by imagination. Personally, for instance, I conceive of the Over-Sphere as a plurality of centres that, in a harmonious alternation and transformation of potential feelings and intuitions, experience bliss.
10. On the one hand, our knowledge rises above Comteism, *which is silent, where philosophy has to impress its most sublime seal.* On the other hand, it rises above common {14} materialism, which only applies to the phenomena of the world perceptible by the external senses and whose superficiality culminates in an exceedingly harmful and foolish optimism. By pointing to the opposition inherent in the world, matter becomes reduced to its true value.

Accordingly, the material world is *eo ipso* to be regarded as pessimistic and, as we shall see, most tragic. It is precisely at the point where it produces its masterpiece, consciousness, that its inability to immediately and firmly maintain a degree of reason becomes evident.

3 Matter

1. {15} Matter is the Other, the lower, the self-polluted, dissatisfied, divided, fragmented, fissured, and discordant; that which experiences itself as alienated and unhappy; the formless, the abandoned, conceptualized in perpetual fleeing from itself, something eternally joyless, mutable, the constantly evolving, and finally, in torment and with involuntary irony, striving upward to a wretched and discordant stage of consciousness.
2. Because the category of Being is connected with the Over-Sphere, it leaves its primordial states in order to escape its poverty; it feels as if it has been chased and carried away; it hastens forward from level to level and—naturally al-

ways with the most conspicuous and painful relapses—reaches a kind of level at which it initially ends in animal, later in human consciousness, and thus, as noted, approaches the Over-Sphere in a purely imaginary way, though in a form compelled to suspend itself.

3. As far as the primordial states of matter are concerned, in the most profound sense, they cannot be identified. For, like substance, matter is also eternal; therefore, the natural sciences are only capable of describing an earlier phase, but {16} never the so-called primordial state. What the naturalists apparently pass off as a foundation is, for the true thinker, more a product of dissolution from earlier epochs.

4. Regarding the original composition of matter in its *present* constitution, it seems to consist of living points. I can imagine the changing ensemble (which, in a certain sense, is prone to advancement and develops into higher organisms) as nothing but a composition of vital and virtual fundamental entities. I call them monads. All living things also originate from living *things— omne vivum ex vivo*. While the atmosphere moves itself in vibrations of light, the forces move in electric and magnetic currents, as if in free orchestric vibrations, or as if dangerous demons suddenly emerged from the darkness, assuming heavy and classical forms in solid substances. From a particular world era, various types of vital vibrating corpuscles must have existed, which, according to their respective missions, have associated themselves differently and advanced in representing the forces, substances, elements, and forms of light and colour in nature.

5. {17} Everywhere in the material world, the monad is silent in material or spiritual form. Through the monad, life receives its flowing and flooding character. Everywhere, in the most intimate and instinctive understanding with its comrades, it brings about change, formation, progress and relapse, and in the end, consciousness and self-knowledge, this most difficult of all spiritual exercises, which at the same time includes in itself the annulment of the value of existence.

6. The matter is to be regarded as a contradictory opposition to the Over-Sphere, deterministic in all consequent phenomena.

4 Man as a Logical and Moral Impossibility and as a Curse of the World
Abolition of Man
Significance of Woman

1. {18} The focus of pessimism lies in the view of man. The only true and correct illumination of the world culminates in the demeaning critique of man.
2. According to his constitution, man is unworthy of his female companion, an impediment to wedlock rather than a bonding member. He does not at all fit into the framework of the world endowed with reason. For he is too crude and mendacious, his thought too fragmentary and diffuse, his outward ugliness too blatant to enable him to control life with tact.
3. Man is a hero of vulgar work, a born proletarian and the most ordinary plebeian. He is the evil and foolish devil who continually disturbs the peace in nature and turns life, which is laid out for joy, ease, and brevity, into an endless satanic hell. With his {19} sexual lust, he turned the human race, which as the noblest of all should have been limited to few valleys, into a swarming and dissolute mob, sick in innermost soul.
4. Man is a link between human and beast, for he is an abomination and, as such, cynically and ridiculously equipped so that he can be neither one nor the other really and completely.
5. Nature has branded man with an unparalleled disgrace, an indelible stigma, through the excessively conspicuous development of his genitals.
6. The superiority of sexual form asserted by the male gender in the whole organic world has been lost in man in two respects: first, concerning the more beautiful part of the animal world, and second, concerning his female companion. Rather, the goat and the she-monkey would deserve to be called his natural associates. For he is horribly constituted and carries forward his mud-pump-like sexual symbol as a criminal. The flat chest, the ugly hirsuteness with rolls of flab and flying hair tuft—traits which, in contrast to the dandyish adornment of most animals, reveal a base character—and finally, the generally excessively abhorrent and vulgar vocal organ, full of ancient and offensive guttural tones, all in truth assign him a very low rank in the realm of living beings. He appears to be a sort of joke.
7. {20} As a result of a truly divine irony of fate, he has been successfully so placed that at the height of education, he regards himself as a monkey-sprout. What would previous generations have said about this realization? Now, the whole of life has become a tragic monkey show for man! ...

The irony goes so far that some researchers have retrospectively named one of the ugliest simian creatures "Anthropomorph" ...

8. The arrogance with which the descendant of the monkey has placed himself at the head of the world and has impressed upon the majority of things the stamp of his nature must fill one with disgust. This circumstance might give rise to the most immense imaginings of revenge, as the work bears witness to its miserable and criminal mediator.

   We are indeed living in a world full of sorrow and folly, full of negligence and humbug. Man wanted to make the world arable, but he had only proved that *he was a born fool and a monster incarnate.* He is indeed, as noted, a sort of a joke; however, he has disgracefully realized himself by fabulous luck and wickedness.

9. Women are not only worthier and more gracious beings but *are of a more perfect and noble* lineage, as is reconfirmed by numerous associations {21} of women with the sea in the mythologies (one need only recall the birth of Aphrodite, the Nordic mermaids, Lorelei, Horace's *beautiful woman ends in fish*[2], and the Californian legend that men come from the forest and women from the sea[3]).—Both genders have encountered one another later, i.e. the men have delighted in ravishing the women, misusing them, and destroying their instincts most dreadfully. One cannot even ascertain how big the original difference between the two parts was.

10. Man is to be described as a *hominis genus* only because of his dexterity and inventiveness. But unjustly, he has never been content with this role, whereas women are *rightly* striving for a higher order because of the misuse of the word "human".

11. While the capacity for love—that is, women's ability to adapt to men—does not constitute an original motive, but rather is an artificial product of the hyp-

---

2 [Druskowitz paraphrases, in Latin, Horace's verse from *Ars Poetica*. In original (v. 3–4), it reads: [...] ut turpiter atrum / desinat in piscem mulier formosa superne [...]. Druskowitz reverses the poet's intended meaning. *Cf.* the first five verses:
   Human— to a human head if a painter should wish
   to join a horse's neck, and make multi-colored feathers grow
   on limbs gathered from all over, so that horribly in a black
   fish-tail she ends, a beautiful woman up above,
   would you, friends, let in for a viewing, hold back your laughter? (Ferris Hill 2019, xii–xiii)]
3 [It is hard to locate the origin of this myth that Druskowitz mentions. Druskowitz's image aligns with broader Indigenous Californian narratives that associate women with the life-giving properties of water, whereas men are tied to terrestrial, forested realms. The forest–sea dichotomy may reflect ecological or social roles, with men often serving as hunters or guardians of wooded areas and women as nurturers connected to coastal or aquatic resources. (Judson 1912)]

nosis that the stronger and, even more so, the thoroughly mendacious gender exercises over the physically more delicate and refined one, man, by contrast, is in fact and by nature the most *enamoured* and *lustful creature on earth*. The enormous distance between the genders conditions sexual passion for women. Man feeds upon women's {22} beauty and honour, and at every cost, he seeks to make her a collaborator of his sexual disgrace. While animal nurtures love only in brief phases, man is perpetually subject to sexual frenzy. In the actual phase of love, he is ebullient to the utmost extreme. One recalls with amazement all the love poems and novels which the overheated imagination of more gifted men has produced. Whole masses of such chimaeras are piling up before the proud observatory of the beautiful world. This is how the "link" behaves in the love phase: after the successful appropriation, man is equally intolerable, impertinent to the utmost, and worse in mood than a starving beast. He is the only creature that beats his wife, tortures her in the most refined forms, pursues other women, and makes them slaves of his scandalous and ridiculous sexual constitution... His concupiscence is even transferred to the animal world, as evidenced by the activities in chicken coops and among household dogs, whereas in the wild, sexual life is much less developed, and animals desire one another only periodically and in moderation.

12. Man is inclined to *murder*. He is a born demon and petty devil. He is the most dangerous of all living beings; he is the Fury of the Furies, the Megaera of the Megaeras. One need only observe his *practices against animals*, which he kills or captures {23} partly out of his *blind drive for annihilation*, partly out of his *blind possessiveness*, and partly sacrifices out of his *gluttonous hunger*. (The effect of Christianity is here absolutely nil so that in this respect, the Christian faith must be declared the worst and most useless of all world religions.)
13. Cultural history has established the figure of a noble Roman and a dissolute Jew as main representations of man's *shameful* and *unrestrained gluttony*. Only the male subject, who makes use of every muck worse than the wildest animal, has also introduced the pleasure of vast quantities of heavy drinks.
14. Man is the most *avaricious* of all creatures. He has ransacked Mother Earth every which way worse than a wild beast and extracted from her all her treasures.
15. He is the *most venal subject*. He is through and through a mean merchant and a shameless huckster everywhere. He is the producer and impresario of the lowest things, whether it is a matter of satisfying animal desires or pandering to the most vulgar drives.
16. Man is the *most envious of all creatures*. His notorious envy of other people's food knows no boundaries. This is the essential obstacle to the intellectual de-

velopment of the entire female gender, {24} a fact that could not be brought to the consciousness of even the most brutish animal since, in the animal world, everything is equally preserved.

17. As insignificant as female disputes often appear, so disastrous for life is the impact of male disputes and the desire for turmoil. Here, womankind serves as an excuse because the quarrelling element occurs moderately among women, while in men, it is condensed, as among the crustaceans. Man is *the most addicted to tussling* and *the most quarrelsome subject* in nature. With him, everything pushes to the outside. His daily habits are sufficient to indicate his proletarian character, his amateurish nature, and his contentious demeanour. His customary mistakes can be counted as handkerchiefs by dozens. His inclination to whistle, to hum, to throw his hands into his chest, his plebeian shrugging the shoulders, his ugly gesticulation—all of it leaves a sad taste.

    ... It is enough to read the gruesome accounts of parliamentary debates in many countries to know with what kind of leftover scum we are dealing with as representatives of the people who are usually elected in a pub room... There comes a war, which is the most brutal manifestation of male rage, desire for scandals and bigotry. It is known or can be thought that simple arbitrations summoned at the next local court or {25} short contests of young men and women should yield the decision in favour of one or the other party with ease. Instead, in reality, broad masses are brought into conflict with each other without any prospect of spiritual success since otherwise, according to the pessimistic principle, all men should slaughter all men and prepare a quick end to the world.

    ... The summit reached by man's scandalous stupidity consists of the invocation of the Lord God from both sides, provided that the war, as in Europe, is usually conducted between practitioners of the same religion. This nonsense is reminiscent of the anecdote of the two boys who had to occupy two chairs in the Grand Opéra in Paris for an obese man. One day, by mistake, the reserved places were separated from each other, so when the patron appeared, the art boys gave signs from different sides.

18. Man, highly presumptuously, does a lot of talking everywhere and is *the most chattering* of all creatures. What women are perceived as doing in this respect is nothing but weak chirping and cooing. There is a very striking lack of participation of women in daily operations and in public affairs, which is why the world history and the present time make the well-known desolate impression, since it is mainly populated by men. {26} The entire history, with few exceptions, is simply "male history" and therefore raw to the utmost and a bad example.

19. Man's blasphemous and crazy arrogance is less evident in an election of a chief, which is circumstantially necessary, than in a choice of a numerous nobility of all ranks. Thanks to the divergent mentalities of different nations, this nonsense is not to be found everywhere. Unfortunately, however, the true and only plausible aspect of the matter has nowhere been considered: namely, that, strictly speaking, nobility should be conferred only upon women. For, in order to represent it worthily and as humanly as possible, it requires the purity of appearance and the non-animalistic nature, which is a decorum only of womankind... It has never been understood that nobility amounts to theosophy and not to the persecution of womankind, torture of animals, neglect of knowledge and skills, etc.[4]
20. Comparatively minor faults and peculiarities are also found in male species. It would happen then that the common male habitude would be used by women to send men themselves to the frontline and to embarrass them so much that the devil would laugh himself to death. In order to understand what I am saying, one must only bear in mind that men are the founders of daily newspapers, yellow press, {27} fashion magazines, and the common trash literature. One can also add a truly brutish pleasure of the male gender in sports, amusements, and games of all kinds... Accordingly, man's constitution is subject to philosophical criticism in such a way that the most stupid animal could be his moral guide.
21. With very few exceptions, he is born an adversary of reason and humanity, spoiling the higher species from the outset. What an animal accomplishes entirely by itself by the use of nature, man must first find with the help of his best mind and then elevate it to the guideline. Therefore, the whole culture, or however we may call the nonsense which unfolds before our eyes and that is established and governed by man, cannot be highly esteemed.
22. A philosophical spirit, which emerges only in isolated cases, sees everywhere devastations brought about by the lack of understanding and reprobacy. Everywhere there is the terrible affect of landowners and rulers, sometimes as ambition and rivalry, sometimes as hatred, envy, lust for sex, concupiscence, avarice, and pugnacity.
23. How much imagination is contained in man's individual production, yet everything appears as a pearl in the shell, "as a disease of the animal".

---

4 [It is unclear whether Druskowitz here refers to *theosophical movement*—a syncretic spiritual and philosophical amalgamate of esoteric traditions, Eastern religious concepts (e. g., Buddhism, Hinduism) with Western mysticism, occultism, and idealism—or to *divine wisdom* as an inner experience aiming to bridge gaps between science, religion, and philosophy in an era of rapid modernization.]

24. {28} By his unrestrained sexual desire, by his lack of real reason in every relationship and despite all the venality with which he has put forth countless gimmicks and amusements, as a counter-weight to the world, man turned life into an incomparable jeremiad, a terrible Procrustian bed full of cruel stretches, an agony without end. It is carried out in *two oscillations*, one of which degrades subjects to slaves of the rudest and most daring works, which properly speaking have been arbitrarily assigned and constructed, the other that labels them as polyps of the most luxuriant and immoral pleasures. Rather than restricting the number of marriages and the entire population growth, he keeps on adding more and more motives to make the labouring ball worse than hell and to bind the creature to an unhappy existence with millions of snares.

25. To what does the whole comedy of our stupid half-culture, often glittering in the most unclean colours, boil down? Everything revolves and turns first and foremost only around clothing, housing and means of transportation. Nature, on the other hand, voluntarily gave animals the most envied furs and the most beautiful plumage, which are not subject to fashion. Like a philosopher, an animal carries everything important to itself {29} (*omnia sua secum portans*), often makes up its home of only a few flowers and with its agility or even with its capacity to fly, presents an ideal for man, who for the time being cannot devise anything higher than flying machines, which are almost completely inadequate and serve as man's disgrace. This makes not only the bird but also the butterfly, even the May beetle, an unassailable master! Likewise, the "link" is always dissatisfied with his weaving and materials, alters and constantly changes fashion, sets his life according to the worst and most careless principles, and after that finds himself, *despite all quasi-culture, in most respects deeply below the level of animals*. Moreover, in most cases, animals live under philosophically more favourable conditions than human beings because *it is difficult for them to find nourishment*, and therefore appear only scattered or in small herds. In contrast, human beings have stored massive amounts of nutrients, allowing them to multiply and sustain themselves and their livestock indefinitely.

26. The same dissatisfaction prevails in all fields of science. The best-known sentences are questioned again, and thus, the whole structure may well collapse with ease. Personally, I take the liberty of declaring astronomy wrong. The heavenly miracles, for me, are only pictures of electromagnetism, warmth and cold, and the seasons are purely {30} meteorological processes and fluctuations. There can hardly be any discussion of progress in fundamental sciences. It would be going backwards, like crabs. The most painful fact is that,

for example, older philosophers have often already discovered and taught the truth, while later teachers darkened it and poured their murky waters over it.

27. Yet science is a kind of benefaction because it serves as the most important weapon against religion. Unfortunately, man has also instituted this, as well as every kind of superstition and nonsense, and must now invest a lot of effort in getting rid of the annoyance.

28. One can raise much stronger objections to the arts than to the sciences. They were overestimated even by the philosopher Schopenhauer. Hasn't the great Plato, this king among the thinkers, already given the arts their proper place, a subordinate one? According to Schopenhauer's opinion, it is not true that the arts are exercised without the participation of the will. This will, which is directed at other extrinsic things, is equally as good as the one which refers to one's own interests, which are often the most important, especially in an exceptional position in life. Moreover, our sympathy for certain epochs and {31} representations is marked in such a way that the subject is most excited precisely by the artistic perception. Finally, the enormous prices that are wasted on pictures, etc., prove that not only the pure intellect comes into play in artistic matters. Taste is subjective, in the field of the arts as everywhere else; only the simplest forms of liking are objective among the elements of art. After refuting Schopenhauer in short sentences, it suffices to point out that the arts are not to be considered only as instigators of affection, as servants of idols and superstition, and as mediators of every sort of false and frivolous appearance as life produces it, except for only a few works, which awaken almost only pure sensations, but also are *injurious*, and have to be regarded as *pitfalls* for the enhancement of the joy of existence. As emanations of an enormously increased capacity, the arts can only be regarded esoterically and not be disclosed to the crowd.

29. Nor should the mystical phenomena be massively accumulated, and the dead must be left in their sphere. Whoever has not yet understood the truth of mysticism remains a simple-minded fool lifelong!

30. All statements which I have pressed against the male gender, whose aspirations and works {32} are to be rejected, are based on truth. They can be subjected to the most severe criticism but will nevertheless prove to be valid.

31. Therefore, it is hard and rare to bury oneself in the theme of man because, firstly, it is difficult to master, and secondly, it is extraordinarily unappealing and unaesthetic. His mundanity and disingenuousness are abysmal so that the incriminated, who otherwise would have to turn himself in, recoiled before his own excrement, is eternally the highest bidder of himself, whereby the lie grows immensely.

32. Only seemingly is man a funny adventure of nature; in reality, he is the most poisonous and dangerous experiment in the entire world.
33. The male gender must be severely curtailed even in relation to its advantages, which nevertheless manifest with immense intrusiveness, for through its products, it confers an excessively prolonged duration upon existence. Consequently, male genius, too, ought to be admitted solely for scrutiny, lest it be relinquished to the public sphere. Only the philosopher is entitled to make himself heard before the world; for he is not merely a *rara avis* and thus a remarkable phenomenon, but even where he appears fragmentary, he acts as balm since he resides on the path toward truth. Therefore, he must also keep his word to bring about redemption in a just manner in due course.
34. {33} The excellent qualities which we find in exceptional male natures and the ordinary peasant rules of morality are neglected because goodness in man comes too late, and he only begins to reflect upon himself after having opened, with the greatest insouciance, the floodgate to the vices of the most absurd form, and the errors. Hence, the plethora of jails and madhouses in which stupidity, crime, and perfidiousness celebrate their most shameful orgies.
35. The blind will to power, as this impure fundamental trait in man has been called, is, in our opinion, the most *reprehensible* and *foolish* element in the entire natural order. Retribution is manifested as a diminution of intelligence in his descendants, for the monster that blindly pursued power often leaves behind nothing but fish spawn—a reality demonstrated by the mental constitution of our nobility. Among the most infamous follies by which Germandom has ever been enslaved is the veneration of a certain Nietzsche, who flattered this vile trait in the most condemnable and foolish manner. How Germanic intellect could have come to praise that absurd Swiss philologist—whom the renowned town clerk and novelist G. Keller so excellently parodied as Count Strapintzky in the story *Clothes Make the Man*[5]—{34} remains incomprehensible. Fortunately, people swiftly rebuked this stupid and utterly idiotic writer, and we hope never again to be forced into the embarrassing position of exposing such a figure, inflamed by the common nobility and clericalism,

---

5 [Druskowitz misspells the name of the main character, Strapinski. Gottfried Keller's novel *Kleider machen Leute* (1891) follows Wenzel Strapinski, a poor tailor's apprentice who is mistaken for a Polish count due to his elegant appearance. He falls in love with the daughter of a local magistrate and plays along with the mistaken identity despite never claiming to be a count. After being exposed as an imposter, Strapinski's fiancée defends him, and they marry with her inheritance, enabling him to become wealthy and successful, ultimately proving the truth of the saying "clothes make the man."]

along with their absurdities. For that fool was not only a mortal enemy of philosophy but also an adversary of simple Christianity, whose moral teachings, though lacking intellectual depth, can still be deemed good and are free from base arbitrariness.

36. The tasks arising from our cardinal principles are not difficult to deduce. According to them, the lion's share of existence would fall to women. *They are the true humanity. The honour* due to womankind lies in the recognition of female superiority in all essential respects. It suffices to know that women are physically more humanely and beautifully constituted, naturally chaster, purer, and holier in character, and finally, imbued with a natural philosophical instinct—which, as we have learned, is entirely lacking in the common man—insofar as women abhor the monstrous expansions of life's sphere, desire existence to rest on simple and rational foundations, and instinctively prefer non-being to being. Unfortunately {35}, female instincts have been horribly suppressed, yet all it takes is a sudden mustering of resolve to reclaim the ideal level. Since the foundations are inherently excellent and all misery ultimately stems from the wickedness and intellectual poverty of the other gender, womankind need only be purified, emboldened through free and bold education, an early career choice, and segregated by dividing cities according to gender, through restricting the number of marriages—which will ultimately lead to the elimination of matrimony. Then, women will be holy by nature and worthy of true veneration again. Feminism must be endowed with fire and brilliance. It is the most sacred ideal of the modern age. That the noble natural rights of women were discovered so late casts a ghastly light on so-called human developmental history. To the uninitiated, there may be something unsettling in feminism, yet once we reach this point, philosophy raises its noble head and proclaims: 'The new doctrine entails only the priesthood of women. It proves the truth of pessimism and the necessity of world misery under the current constellation, but not the endless continuation of existence.' Then women, in accordance with their higher mission, will recognize themselves as superior beings, {36} as priestesses of their gender, as natural nobility. Upon perceiving the higher law of life, their philosophical destiny will become fully clear: to appear as guides into death, preparing for the ultimate end. This shall then become the ideal, replacing an aimless and endless ideal!

5 Men's Table[6]
Standard Propositions for Male Gender

1. {37} You have to intensely think about yourselves and diminish your arrogance. I can not speak to you with lightning and thunder but from the most profound conviction and out of the most serious considerations.
2. You should live in a stubborn struggle for yourselves and your nature but not follow its course. If you listen to your inner voice, you know that you are continually harming yourself and undermining your main aspirations. That is why it is inconceivable that you are at the head of all the institutions and that you believe you can master the world.
3. Let a pessimistic assessment substitute your self-love and self-assertion; examine and scrutinize yourselves relentlessly, and you will overflow with hatred of yourselves and your existence.
4. Examine yourselves externally, and you see a subject which, strictly speaking, can no longer compete with the simple male animal body in general. You have lost the primacy {38} of the male figure. Your female companion is much more the crown of creation. You have inherited from the male animal only the strength and not the superiority of the beautiful form concealed by the natural arrangement of the genders. As with corporal punishments, you carry the sign in front and show just as little humanly worthy as a smooth face.
5. Inquire within yourselves, and you will find a subject full of fundamental errors, full of folly and foolishness, complete of the most arduous and laborious circuitousness, stumbling at every step, and full of lust, offering substitution for fundamental errors so that the crowd is constantly misguided towards new foolishness, which occurs until the world has become a madhouse, a place of general disgrace, a kaleidoscope of the crudest lies and absurdities, and an aviary for the most colourful caricatures... Have you not, among many, many other principal errors, also created religions with their jumble

---

6 [The terms "Männetafel" and, later, "Frauentafel" have multiple meanings. Similar to contemporary settings, these terms refer to discussion groups or roundtables specifically for men or women. These are organized spaces where participants discuss everyday topics such as family, health, and integration, guided by trained moderators.

Historically, especially in the context of courtly or ceremonial banquets, similar terms could refer to separate tables for men and women at large feasts or public meals. The seating arrangements at such events were strictly regulated according to rank and gender, and it was common for men and women to be assigned different tables or areas. Sometimes, in literary contexts, "Frauentafel" can also refer metaphorically to a set of rules or norms for women, as seen in 19th-century texts discussing gender roles and societal expectations.]

of nonsense, false morals and silly ceremonies, with their unfortunate consequences for progress, peace and order? You are now, however, concerned with declaring these false doctrines as void. However, first and foremost, this discovery comes much too late for millions of souls. Secondly, despite or because of the materialism that needs further refinements and the vague Comtism, there is a lack of {39} a coherent and satisfying teaching: it must be the pessimism with its fundamental elements of the rapture of a possible metaphysical instance and the nullification of the world, mainly because of the imperfectly constructed humanity that will lead to victory.

6. Look further into your inner being, and you will know, or you know it already, without betraying yourselves, that you are many times over the most violent among all beings. If the most savage beast is guilty of certain crimes, not through viciousness or ravening, as his classification into plants and carnivorous species proves, man, on the contrary, shows himself as a master in all evil and black things, so that he also makes womankind most guilty for the heaviest things, and even surrenders them to the executioner through the miserable conditions brought about by his lust for sex and reproduction.

7. In all higher and collective matters—which, rightly understood, are merely the consequences of overpopulation—you must not formulate and implement resolutions without including the other half of humanity, toward which you involuntarily strive and to which this misfortune has now come to pass. Otherwise, you become arbitrariness and tyranny, and this with double excess, for you subjugate the genuine and sympathetic part of humanity to your wicked despotism {40}. Know that your tyranny is intolerable and that no beast would tolerate it if it could conceive of it! It is utterly horrifying that in a world full of women, men—moreover marked by inferior traits—dictate the terms. Hence, I call it your duty and obligation to put an end to the scandalous despotism, which stands alone in the whole realm of beings. Your mendacity must not reach such a climax that you *exclude* women, who surpass you morally and sexually, from all affairs that they should manage and attend to *in the first* place. When a stone starts to roll, the entire weight comes crashing down, so too, a slight concession in nature has given you the right to establish the most gruesome autocracy. So powerful is the hypnosis you exert that the majority is hardly aware of which unbearable situation they occupy.

8. Give back to women all their rights, no longer live by their glory, and do not seek exculpation for your natural faults from them. If she does not desire marriage, free her from your immediate presence, be no more harmful to her health, let her be entirely to herself, let her dwell in her own city as a priestess of her race!

9. Let women fill out their own sphere entirely on their own! Women should be their own educators, teachers, doctors, economists and senior {41} officials. In some respects, you are the rudest thing that has ever been within the development of the state. For if, in the old mythologies, the highest allegories for the law and science and natural powers were female representations, and the Romans, moreover, attributed their entire wisdom to priestesses, you are utterly devoid of such ideals, and the pestilence of the odourless masculine kind is everywhere!
10. Exactly this must be different. Not only some fields but all areas are to be penetrated by women's power. Initially, there should be no committee that invites women or announces their participation. All meetings and representations of urban and rural areas must have a corresponding number of women. A reigning queen, since it is a rare appearance, has to be doubly and triply eulogized, and finally, the republics have to put women at the top.
11. You have an enormous amount to rebuild and must transform the world power that you have fundamentally established from its foundations. For you must prove yourselves ideally—that is, in all general institutions—and materially or physically through the renunciation of your company of and communion with women. Return all their domains to them and suspend the notion of the 'rejected' or 'injured pearl.' If none of this convinces you of the legitimacy {42} of such demands—though only a stomach that can digest iron, nails, and burning coals could remain indifferent here—then consider how intolerable it is for many of you when free principles are weakened by political fluctuations and the rise of individual demagogues who threaten every higher conviction. Therefore, begin with yourselves, scour the entire field on which you have so glaringly mismanaged affairs, and you will be compelled to embark on reforms of the grandest scale.
12. As your reward, you may anticipate the comforts of cultivating your own habits, a clear conscience, a cloudless sky, and the consciousness of having thought and acted—in the end—like philosophers of the most sterling breed: a renown you yourselves likely never dared to dream of!

6 Women's Table
Maxims for Women

1. {43} You must be true to yourselves!
2. You shall not strive to reach God! This is nothing but a flawed product of a masculine brain, full of errors and mistakes. Let it be sufficient for you to ennoble the inner values and to maintain a higher level of thinking and feeling.

Moreover, as philosophical thought proves, an Over-Sphere exists, which forms the purest opposition to matter, is connected with it only by the category of Being, and is confronted with it in an unassuming and indifferent manner. The Over-Sphere presents itself as both logical and poetic, embodying the ideal female form, and deserves to be repeatedly brought to vivid imagination, especially by womankind.

3. You should not be impressed by men, except for individual cases which, however, confirm the rule. Man is by no means an acceptable example. By his sexual appearance deeply beneath his own domestic animals and utterly unworthy of his wife, by his lack {44} of self-control and unity of the will, he is the most feared of all living creatures, by his immodest thinking and striving, which stands in an irrational relation to the natural disposition of his gender, he is a more questionable and doubtful spirit or a perfect fool—he is ill-suited to stand at the head of the world and generally to tyrannize women's gender.
4. You should feel surrounded by your immaculate beauty, your mild nature, and your clear mind as higher natural beings, as a nobler, more aristocratic race of natural priestly nimbus. Believe that you are traced back to other higher natural beings and connected to men only externally!
5. Hate men and wedlock! Feel as a collective power of high cultural value, which increases to the highest philosophical importance and, as such, decides over life and death.
6. Therefore, declare every new religion or alignment with such to be null and void ... for such a thing would again be optimistic, whereas the wisdom of woman is ethical and pessimistic with regard to the general course of things and profoundly delivers her own gender to extinction, after having liberated it from impure contact.
7. Conduct a sacred struggle against the male world in order to regain lost honour and freedom, {45} and to prove that the end of your race seems to be preferable to the continuation of life in sin and shame, in mental weakness, and total stupidity of the senses and taste.
8. Know that, for conscious and universal reasons, celibacy is the chief sign of the genial feminine constitution; indeed, it is the genius of the woman herself.
9. Vehemently urge your share of the jurisdiction in the state! Energetically demand the unilateral and eternally unfair male state to stop existing and to ensure that all governmental and administrative areas be attended to by women or on their orders.
10. Know that where women's affairs or cases are discussed, women should not only be advised but have the first voice, primacy, or decision.
11. Since you have to be alone, demand the division of the cities by genders and the concentration of the whole female activity in your own half of the city,

which self-evidently should contain specific gender *cemeteries*. Only when the disgusting promiscuity of men and women, which assumes such an intense character among the nobility, so that both genders are distinguished only by nicknames, ceases, only when you live and dwell {46} separately, will you have all the rights and exercise all the decent professions with ease. On the other hand, where the struggle is still raging, and the whole knot is entangled in one, the male envy and the challenging and hypnotic manner of the robber and murderer—man—is striving all over again to wrench the laurel from womankind.

12. Keep away from all the harmful worship of male works and creation. Choose all the best and most useful... For man, through his proletarian lust for labour and production, has immeasurably obtruded himself to consciousness. It is, therefore, necessary to defend oneself from his idle performances and lures. The apparently noblest types of poetry, such as tragedy, are based on an overestimation of affect. The mature mind, on the other hand, avoids the heavy commotions and disdains to indulge itself again in ugly or even nefarious things or events which the real world carries with itself, in a so-to-say pseudo-artistic mirror image. Except in the conquest and assertion of your rights, live in sympathy for your gender, as well as in the finest etiquette to it, for your taste has to become only purer, your self-feeling more steeled and the preference for your own gender, for its claims, and progress more condensed. Thus, the {47} chivalry of the women should be established, and they would join the priesthood of women, live in moderate emotions inspired by mild feelings and in the enjoyment of the inexhaustible beauty of nature![7]

Hymn to the Over-Sphere

Behold! Oh, behold! How your hopes deceive—
She stands wholly apart; she did not mould you!
Else she'd loathe herself, her essence grieve,
She knows you not! In vain, the rabble folds anew,
Prostrate before her knees, their pleas renewed!
Futile the prayers, the cries, the desperate din!
In tranquil, glorious majesty, she reigns!
Yet ever barred to you, who dwell within

---

[7] Special thanks are due to Andrew Gilligan, who suggested some nice solutions to the translation of the *Pessimistic Cardinal Propositions*.

The crude, base clod of matter—she sustains
Connection only through existence's chains.
Thus, though it writhes to break its own crude frame,
Despite all form's vain play, no aim secured,
At last, when consciousness grants empty fame,
It scorns itself—its core principle obscured:
To rise is rooted in disgrace, endured—
And hails Death as its crowned chieftain, revered.

Curse Upon Emperor Titus

{48} Though you've expertly sown the seeds of scorn,
Which surely strike those who provoke such spite,
Whether you've lent the poet themes well-born,
As sound as wheat, to fuel their venomous write;
Whether you've scattered to the winds with haste
A wretched horde, forever hate's dire prey,
Or freed a fertile land once sorely graced
By vile infestments, scrubbed of rot away;
Whether you've stripped them of their pride and soil—
Home, hearth, till even the last clod's denied—
A mob sustained by shame, through ceaseless toil,
Hounded by fate's decree, nowhere to hide!
Yet still you err, still falsify your deed:
You banished sinners, damned to starve and plead—
Thus, cursed be you! Let vengeance take its heed!
When you expelled this plague of blighted souls,
Did you not herd that barren, craven breed
To trade their lives in faith's degraded roles?
In dreary nooks, in pens of stifling air,
Condemned to slander, haggle, stink, and trifle,
A people steeped in baseness, foul despair,
Mocked, jeered at in each square, each stifling rifle.
Yet even they, in time, turned poison's fang,
To taint the world with their corrosive spite.
Blind, blinding others—philosophers they hang,
And stall the wise who seek to shed true light.
Does all hope not fly to the winds, unspooled?
Thus, curse you once more, emperor most fouled!

Bibliography

Ferris Hill, Jennifer, trans. 2019. *Horace's* Ars Poetica: *Family, Friendship, and the Art of Living.* Princeton and Oxford: Princeton University Press.

Judson, Katharine Berry. 1912. *Myths and Legends of California and the Old Southwest.* Chicago: A. C. McClurg & Co.

Keller, Gottfried. 1891. "Kleider machen Leute." In: *Gottfried Keller's Gesammelte Werke*, vol. 5, Berlin: Wilhelm Hertz, 11–62.

Index of Names

Alighieri, Dante   24, 78
Aphrodite   158

Baillie, Joanna   18, 19
Barrett Browning, Elizabeth   18, 19
Baumann, Julius   131, 150
Biber, Magdalena   4
Blavatsky, Helena   2
Borelius, Johan Jakob   130, 131
Breitinger, Heinrich   24, 25

Carneri, Bartholomäus   127
Cohen, Hermann   1
Comte, Auguste   19, 29, 40, 50, 74, 77–95, 103, 123, 134, 136

Darwin, Charles   29, 31, 43, 135, 140
Druschkovich, Lorenz   4
Duboc, Julius   29, 41, 95, 107–113, 123, 137
Dühring, Eugen   17, 29, 41, 43, 46, 76, 95, 107, 111–118, 123, 135, 137, 145
Dworkin, Andrea   36

Eaubonne, Françoise d'   37
Ebner-Eschenbach, Marie von   1, 5–7, 10, 11, 20, 23
Eliot, George   18, 19
Emerson, Ralph Waldo   122
Engels, Friedrich   41
Erasmus   54

Feuerbach, Ludwig   27, 29, 40, 53, 67–70, 74, 77, 80, 86, 91–94, 123, 136
François, Louise von   6–10, 17, 20, 23, 46

Gizycki, Georg   119, 145
Goethe, Johann Wolfgang von   18, 50, 56, 136, 138, 144
Guyau, Jean-Marie   127

Hermann, Ludimar   3
Herzl, Theodor   1

Horace   158
Husserl, Edmund   1

Kant, Immanuel   39, 40, 50, 51, 54, 55, 61, 62, 64–68, 92, 93, 101, 119
Kautsky, Karl   1
Keller, Gottfried   164
Kohut, Adolf   8, 9
Krafft-Ebing, Richard von   1, 35, 36
Kym, Andreas Ludwig   24, 25

Lange, Friedrich Albert   41, 43, 86, 95–98, 130, 131, 133
Lombroso, Cesare   1
Lorelei   158, 288
Luther, Martin   54
Luxemburg, Rosa   1

Mainländer, Philipp   43, 144
Mach, Ernst   1
Malten, Therese   6, 9, 12, 47
Meyer, Conrad Ferdinand   6–10, 14, 17, 20, 23, 25, 46
Mill, John Stuart   40, 50, 87–91
Möbius, Paul Julius   2, 36

Negri, Gaëtano   111
Nietzsche, Friedrich   13–18, 29, 33, 41, 42, 50, 99–104, 106, 137, 143, 153, 164
Nogarola, Isotta   37

Overbeck, Franz   13, 14

Paul the Apostle   117
Paul, Jean   144
Paoli, Betty   5, 6
Pappenheim, Bertha   2
Pizan, Christine de   37
Prel, Carl du   43, 140–142, 145

Rée, Paul   39, 40, 55, 57, 58, 61, 65, 62
Rehm, Hermann   3

Reich, Eduard   95
Ribot, Théodule   60

Salis-Marschlins, Meta von   2, 16
Salter, William Mackintire   9, 29, 41, 42, 46, 50, 104, 107, 118–123, 129, 135, 137, 144, 145
Savage, Minot Judson   135
Schiller, Friedrich   35, 98, 134
Schleiermacher, Friedrich   134
Schmeitzner, Ernst   14
Schopenhauer, Arthur   14, 16, 17, 28, 39, 40, 50, 54–58, 63, 64, 66–68, 92, 100, 101, 104, 163
Schwartz, Agatha   36
Shelley, Percy Bysshe   5, 14, 16, 18, 46, 56, 78, 119

Solanas, Valerie   36
Spencer, Herbert   43, 51, 59, 60, 86, 102, 134, 135
Steiner, Rudolf   2
Strauß, David Friedrich   94, 134
Suttner, Bertha von   2

Vaux, Clotilde de   78, 79

Wagner, Richard   14, 99
Weininger, Otto   2, 36
Windelband, Wilhelm   1
Wundt, Wilhelm   135

Zetkin, Clara   2

Index of Subjects

affect; affection   63, 65, 66, 78, 81, 91, 104, 138, 149, 161, 163, 170
altruism; altruist   69, 79, 80, 86, 89–92, 103, 153
art; artist; artwork   2, 4, 5, 10, 12, 19, 20, 32, 50, 74, 81, 82, 85, 87, 88, 95, 99, 116, 127, 130, 132, 133, 138, 146, 152, 160, 163
atheism; atheist; atheistic   30, 40, 51, 73, 75, 77, 111, 128, 130, 153, 154

Buddhism, Buddhist   53, 54, 76, 161

Catholicism; Catholic   77, 133
Christian; Christianity   17, 19, 26, 29, 31, 41, 52, 54, 73, 77, 86, 95, 98, 110, 111, 112, 116, 117, 126, 128, 159, 165
Comteism   155
conscience; conscientiousness   40, 66, 69, 92, 93, 104, 116, 121, 149, 168
consciousness; self- consciousness   1, 28, 29, 31, 32, 43, 54, 57, 57–60, 64, 65, 67, 69, 70, 92, 94, 97, 107, 108, 110, 123, 131, 138, 140, 142–145, 152, 153, 155, 156, 160, 168, 170, 171
culture; half-culture; quasi-culture   1, 14, 34, 42, 82, 103, 118, 119, 124, 145–147, 149, 161, 162

Darwinism   16, 29, 104, 140, 142, 145
drive; aesthetic drive; drive for happiness; drive for life; drive for self-preservation; poetic drive   24, 32, 35, 37, 40, 63, 65, 68, 69, 71, 79, 92, 109, 127, 130, 132, 147, 152, 159

Earth   30, 31, 37, 74, 76, 105, 109, 120, 122, 133, 140, 146, 147, 159
ecofeminism; ecofeminist   37, 38, 43, 44
ecology; ecological 37, 38, 44, 158
education   1–4, 6, 15, 22, 23, 25, 28, 39, 41, 72, 84, 98, 100, 108, 147, 157, 165
egoism; egoistic; self-love   27, 40, 68, 69, 103, 166
emancipation   3, 5, 20–23, 33, 34, 45, 46

emotion   59, 81, 87, 89, 102, 110, 111, 122, 130, 133, 145, 170
evil   24, 32, 38, 54, 65, 69–72, 102, 103, 105, 109, 110, 113, 133, 152, 153, 157, 167
evolution; evolutionary theory   29, 31, 32, 41, 43, 44, 78, 135, 140, 141, 144, 146–148, 154

female see woman; womankind
feminism   17–19, 21–23, 33–35, 43, 44, 165
– force; driving force; higher forces; natural force   27–30, 65, 70, 71, 74, 83, 85, 87, 90, 92, 104, 114, 115, 117, 123, 127, 139, 140, 143, 144, 145, 147, 149, 156
freedom   18, 24, 27, 39, 40, 53, 54, 56–58, 60, 63–68, 70, 75, 90, 92, 102, 109, 115, 116, 120, 127–129, 153, 169
freethinker   30, 73, 128, 130, 133

Gender   2, 12, 13, 19–21, 23, 34, 35, 37, 38, 44, 45, 51, 83, 152, 153, 157–161, 163–166, 169, 170
genius   8, 11, 16–19, 82, 88, 100, 101, 106, 143, 146, 164, 169
god   30–32, 34, 51, 52, 75, 82, 86, 91, 92, 96, 97, 105–108, 111, 113, 126, 132, 134, 135, 152–154, 160, 168

hatred   17, 24, 69, 71, 82, 161, 166
hallucination   10–12, 27, 35, 131
humanity   24, 29–31, 35, 37, 38, 41–43, 65, 66, 77–89, 91, 92, 94, 95, 102, 106, 109, 110, 112, 123, 127, 128, 131, 132, 134, 139, 140, 143, 144, 146–150, 161, 165, 167
hunger   35–37, 159
hypnosis   167, 170

identity   13, 68, 69, 92, 164
illusion   15, 30, 39, 53, 55, 57–66, 83, 127–133, 149, 153
immortality   30, 76, 83, 90, 107, 123, 126, 132, 148
instinct   27, 35, 80, 81, 83, 103, 114, 126, 158, 165

Index of Subjects

intellect   7, 15, 20, 32, 33, 51, 66, 80, 102, 103, 107, 114, 163, 164
intelligibility; intelligible   57, 67, 120

love   8, 14, 22, 27, 34, 35, 68, 71, 77–80, 83, 84, 87, 88, 91, 92, 105, 121, 149, 158, 159, 164

man; male; mankind   3, 8, 10, 14, 22, 31, 34–38, 40, 44, 51, 62, 63, 79, 80, 82–84, 86, 87, 90, 102, 105, 106, 108, 110, 118–122, 127, 129, 133, 135, 140–143, 152, 153, 157–167, 169, 170
matter   32, 34, 42, 154–156, 169, 171
misogyny; misogynistic; misogynist   1, 2, 17, 35, 36
monad   156
monism; monistic   32, 130, 153
mysticism; mystical   2, 12, 27, 161, 163

nature [except when synonymous with "essence" or "core", e.g. "human nature"]   28, 29, 31, 37, 38, 44, 54–56, 58, 68, 70–72, 74, 79, 80, 86, 88, 90, 93, 94, 98, 101, 112–115, 118, 123, 133, 135, 139, 141, 144, 149, 154, 156, 157, 160–162, 164, 167, 170
nobility   42, 161, 165
Neo-Kantianism   1

optimism   40, 109, 110, 155
overman   104–106
Over-Sphere 4, 32–34, 41, 51, 52, 154–156, 169, 170

Patriarchy; patriarchal   4, 12, 18, 19, 22, 23, 25, 34–38, 44
pessimism   4, 32, 34, 35, 40, 43, 76, 108, 110, 147, 157, 165, 167

Positivism   1, 77, 78, 81–85
principle; high, higher, highest   32, 79, 149, 152, 154
prophet; prophetic; prophecy   14, 43, 56, 140, 141, 147, 148
Protestantism, Protestant   119, 131, 133

reason [as a mental faculty]   15, 21, 31, 39, 42, 51, 67, 80, 81, 91, 94, 95, 105, 107, 131, 140, 155, 157, 161
representation   60, 74, 75, 95–99, 107, 111, 112, 116, 130, 131, 133, 135, 137, 139, 152, 154, 155, 159, 163, 168

science   1, 30, 31, 74, 77, 79, 81, 85, 87, 95, 99, 115, 119, 122, 126, 128, 131, 135–137, 139, 140, 145, 146, 156, 161–163, 168
self-consciousness   28, 29, 57, 58, 65, 69, 70
sex; sexual   4, 34, 36, 51, 157, 161, 162, 167, 169
spirit [as a mental faculty] 51, 56, 73, 81, 82, 88, 96, 97, 100, 119, 120, 127, 132, 133, 135, 138, 139, 144, 154, 161, 169
substance   154, 156
supernatural religion   75, 79, 88, 89
superstition   73, 77, 95, 117, 132, 133, 142, 163
Supreme Being   82

theology   54, 134
theosophy   2, 161
transcendental freedom   27, 53, 68

utilitarianism   145, 149

volition   58, 63

woman, womankind   2–5, 8–10, 12–14, 16, 18–23, 33–38, 44, 45, 47, 51, 83–85, 93, 153, 157, 158–161, 165–168, 169, 170

www.ingramcontent.com/pod-product-compliance
Lightning Source LLC
Chambersburg PA
CBHW030234170426
43201CB00006B/214